A
Lonely
Rage

A Lonely Rage

The Autobiography of
Bobby Seale

Foreword by
James Baldwin

Times
BOOKS

Library of Congress Cataloging in Publication Data

Seale, Bobby, 1936-
  A lonely rage.

  1. Seale, Bobby, 1936- 2. Afro-Americans—
Biography. 3. Black Panther Party. I. Title.
E185.97.S4A33 1977   322.4'2'0924 [B] 77-79046
ISBN 0-8129-0715-9

To my son,
Malik Nkrumah Stagolee Seale

CONTENTS

STAGOLEE

I WISH I'd kept my notes concerning Bobby Seale and Huey Newton and Eldridge Cleaver, so many years ago. It was, actually, only a little over ten years ago, but it seems much longer than that. Everyone was so young—except Eldridge, there was always something of the deacon about that one. Huey was the dedicated poet, and strategist. Bobby was the firebrand.

I first met Huey in San Francisco, but don't remember meeting either Bobby or Eldridge then. My first recollection of Eldridge is in Hollywood, at the Beverly Hills Hotel; he was part of the Black Panther escort for Betty Shabazz. As for Bobby Seale, I first met him, if memory serves, with Marlon Brando, in Marlon's hotel suite, in Atlanta, the day of Martin Luther King, Jr.'s funeral. He had been sleeping, was still groggy—was as tense and quiet as the air becomes when a storm is about to break. This was certainly due, in part, to the climate of that momentous day, but it was also due to a kind of intelligence of anguish living behind Bobby's smoky eyes.

This intelligence is unsparing—Bobby certainly does not spare Bobby—and informs this modest, restrained, and passionate book. I feel completely inept, almost presumptuous, in attempting to write a foreword to it. I did not go through what Bobby, and his generation, went through. The time of my youth was entirely different and the savage irony of hindsight allows me to suggest that the time of my youth was far less hopeful. I speak of this savage irony because the political and spiritual currents of my very early youth involved a return to Africa, or a rejection of it; either choice would lead to suicide, or madness, for, in fact, neither choice was possible. Though the American Communist Party, as it was then constituted, anyway, never made any very great impact on the bulk of the black population, its presence, strategies, and mercurial shifts in moral judgment disseminated, at the very least, confusion. Our most visible heroes were Father Divine and Joe Louis—we, in the ghetto then, knew very little about Paul Robeson. We knew very little about anything black, in fact, and this was not our fault. Those of us who found out more than the schools were willing to teach us did so at the price of becoming unmanageable, isolated, and, indeed, subversive.

The south was simply the hell which our parents had survived, and fled. Harlem was our rat and roach infested haven: *Nigger Heaven*, a vastly successful novel about Harlem, was published around the time that I was born.

I have suggested that Bobby's time was more hopeful than my own: but I do not wish to be misunderstood concerning the nature, the meaning, and the cruelty of that hope. I do not mean to suggest that the bulk of the American people had undergone a "change of heart" as concerns their relationship to their darker brothers by the time Bobby Seale came down the pike. They hadn't, and it is very much to be doubted that they ever will. Most people cling to their guilts and terrors and crimes, compounding them hour by hour and day by day, and are more likely to be changed from without than from within. No: the world in which we found ourselves at the end of World War II, and, more particularly, the brutal and gratuitous folly with which we ushered in the atomic age, brought into focus, as never before, the real meaning of the American social contract and exposed the self-serving nature of the American dream. And one of the results of this exposure was that the celebrated Negro problem became a global instead of a merely domestic matter.

It is in this sense that Seale's era is to be considered more hopeful: in spite of the horrors which he recounts, with such restraint, in these pages. The beacon lit, for his generation, in 1956, in Montgomery, Alabama, by an anonymous black woman, elicited an answering fire from all the wretched, all over the earth, signalled the beginning of the end of the racial nightmare—for it will end, no lie endures forever—and helped Stagolee, the black folk hero Bobby takes for his model, to achieve his manhood. For, it is that tremendous journey which Bobby's book is about: the act of assuming and becoming oneself.

James Baldwin
St. Paul de Vence
October 25, 1977

ACKNOWLEDGMENTS

For the assistance I have had on this book, I thank Cicely Nichols for her skillful final editing and Emily Granrud who most patiently saw the book through publication. I thank Roger Jellinek for his professional and personal encouragement, and for persuading me to develop my own skill to write, and not to tape-record for another writer. His faith in my ability to transfer my verbal stories to paper and his insight into my own experiences kept me going for three years. And I thank Adeline Sneider for her helpful concern when I needed many things done "my way."

I am grateful to my mother, Thelma Seale, and my sister Betty Williams and her husband Theodore for their continued loving support and financial aid in more than a few hard-time periods; to my brother John Seale who helped me to recall so vividly in many early morning hours of talk our common early experiences and adventures; to James Baldwin who shared his literary insights and gave me the title; to Elizabeth E. Johnson with the deepest appreciation for her caring support and practical help that enabled me and my family to complete this work; to Romaine and Malik, my sons, to whom I hope this book will give special inspiration for the future.

But most of all, I would like to pay tribute to Leslie M. Johnson herself, the guiding and devoted spirit who saw me through the painful process from the first handwritten draft of these stories to their final completion, and whose monumental patience and devotion through this longdrawn process was unswerving.

A
Lonely
Rage

PART I

Naaasty Niggers and Jesus Christ

THE FIRST TIME I saw the fat man was out in front of the house my Daddy was building. The fat man was sitting in the cab of his old black panel truck, with a shiny knife in his hand, peeling an apple, talking to my Daddy. The long red apple peeling got longer as the fat man turned the apple against the knife. My Daddy went into the house. I stood there amazed at how the fat man cut the apple peeling with the knife.

"Can I play with that?"

"This knife?" He looked at me. "No!" he said.

"How come?" I asked.

"You cut yourself. Too sharp, boy."

He had a hefty growly voice. The way he looked at me had almost made me scared, but I asked again.

"Let me cut with it?" I whined.

He stepped down out of his truck. His fat sweaty face scared me now—would he whip me? I took a few steps backwards.

"I'm going to cut them ears off!"

My ears? I stood there.

I'd seen a knife stuck in the throat of a goat once, and I ran when that goat bled out. I remembered the gush of blood. Then the fat man jumped at me, holding the knife out in his hands.

"I'm going to cut them ears off!" he growled at me. "Come here!"

I cut out running around the side of the house. I stayed near Mama the rest of that day.

3

*

When we first came to Port Arthur, Texas, my Daddy worked on a job in the daytime and built our first house on the weekends and in the evenings after work. He would work on our house into the night aided by an electric light with a long black cord attached to it. He'd take a handful of nails and his hammer and hit nail after nail square on the head, powerful hammering blows driving them into the wood. He'd never miss a nail, and all of a sudden, some loose piece of wood would be structurally tight and in place.

Our house was just about finished one evening and Daddy had been painting the front till he'd painted his way to the porch. He gave me a paintbrush. I tried to imitate his snappy but smooth moves, slapping and brushing as I helped smooth the paint over the fresh-smelling pine wood, now dominated by the smell of paint. I thought the bright pink paint really looked good. The next day when I saw it I could have cried. Mosquitoes were stuck all over our fresh pink paint.

Mama told me we were going to move to San Antonio.

"When?"

"As soon as your Daddy gets back."

"When is he coming back?"

"Next week."

"How far is San Antonio, Mama?"

"It's a long ways away."

"Is Daddy gone to Jasper?"

"Nope. He went to San Antonio."

"Why?"

"He got a job working for the Government."

"What kind of a job is that?"

"A wartime job."

"Is Daddy building houses with the war job?"

"I don't know, Bobby. He'll be back and then you ask your Daddy."

"Is we gonna move when Daddy get back?"

"Yes Bobby," she laughed. "Now go on and play and stop asking so many questions." I was glad at first—I had seen the fat man in his old black truck pass by the front of our house a number of times. But now that we were moving, I really didn't want to leave that house and my Mama didn't either.

I watched the trees pass by as we sped down the long road in my Daddy's new car. I watched all the green grass and fields of things growing. The world seemed to get bigger and bigger as we drove. I missed our house already. Mama and Daddy had decided to rent our house instead of selling it. Daddy wanted to sell it, but Mama had argued, and won.

I told Mama that I didn't want to leave our house. Mama picked me up and sat me on her lap. Sort of talking to herself and me, she cried so it made me cry. Then she said to me: "Bobby, you always remember this is our house. Our home. Someday you going to grow up and be a carpenter like your Daddy, and you going to build a house."

"I can build one, Mama," I spouted with confidence.

"Bobby, you can't build one *now*," she laughed, with delight and tears on her face, "but when you grow up you can. Your Daddy helped his Daddy build houses when he was just thirteen."

"Is that long?" I wished I was bigger.

In San Antonio I sat at the table eating, looking and listening to Mama and Daddy arguing while I stuffed my mouth and chewed my food.

"George," Mama said, "when we going to get a house?"

"We'll get one," Daddy answered irritably.

"Well I sure hope you don't throw away the little money we got," Mama shot out.

"We'll build a house, Thelma! Shit, every time I sit down to eat, Thelma, you start that damn shit!"

"Now George, that ain't no way to act."

"I'll act the way I want to act."

"Here we is rooming," Mama said, "just like we did before we built our house in Port Arthur, Texas."

"If I build another house we got to sell that one, like I've said before."

"You're making enough money. We can build another house without selling the one we got. When this war is over we can go back and live there—we ought to keep that there house." Mama shook her head disgustedly. "I hope you don't throw our money away, running with them Wilcoxes."

"Now God damn it, Thelma," Daddy shouted, halting in his eating motion. "Shit! I don't want to talk about it no more!" Then he scared me as he glanced at me.

"George, we got to get some place other than this room," Mama emphasized. "We all just bunched up in it." Mama moved her arms out and up into the air. "I needs my own kitchen. Ain't you tired of rooming, George?"

Daddy sat at the table in his undershirt. He didn't say anything. His arms were big, and his arm muscle would get bigger as he moved his forkful of food back and forth from his plate to his mouth. I was six years old, a skinny, barefoot kid. I watched him, stuffing food into my mouth then chewing, chewing——

"Bobby!" Daddy yelled out. "Stop that smacking!"

I was startled and frightened. I stopped eating—what is it I'm doing? What was smacking?

"Lord," Mama said, and she sighed in her words, "I sure wish we was back in Jasper, so I could be nearer my Mama."

"God damn it, Thelma," Daddy shouted loudly, "I'll get a house. Now I don't want to talk about it no more!"

"Now, George, you ain't got no reason to be acting like that in front of these chilluns, cussing me and carrying on. The other people in this rooming place be wondering what kind of father you is."

"These damn folks ain't going to tell me what to do, Thelma! I got my own money, and I'll do things the way I want to, shit!"

"I just wish we'd get some place to stay."

I gulped my food. The argument made me forget about——

"Cut out that damn smacking, Bobby!" my Daddy bellowed. Smacking must have something to do with eating, but what?

The next day we moved into a big house, an old one, next to an old creepy white-painted church. The house creaked and cracked at night. There was no toilet; Mama had to take the slop jar over to the church's toilet and empty it. The paint was peeling off the house, and you had to go outside with a pail to get water from the faucet, out in the back. Betty, John, and I believed there was a boogie man in the church at night; the creaking house made me believe he was walking around looking for me to cut off my ears, like the fat man. I'd put my head under the covers in fright.

We saw less and less of my Daddy. He surprised me one evening as I sat at the table, gulping my food down. "Bobby!" he hollered. "Stop that God damn smacking! Stop eating like a damn hog!"

I was shocked and scared, scared to chew the food already in my mouth. I would not eat now, as my Daddy sat down at the table.

I began to forget about helping to build another house. Daddy would be gone two and three days at a time. When he did come home, he would shock Betty, John, and me. We would be playing loudly sometimes, not knowing he had entered the house.

"Cut out all that chin music!" he would bellow.

Just that one phrase and you could hear a pin drop.

At other times, one of us might spot Daddy coming. We would run to tell the others. "Ooooh," we seriously, fearfully, and quietly warned, "here come Daddy."

We liked it when our Daddy wasn't around. Whippings grew few and far between. I approached seven years of age during the first summer at the house next to the old church.

I liked summer. I played freely in the weeds and grass of an empty lot by the big old church, intently watching, time after time, how the big red ants moved back and forth carrying bits of bread that I dropped along their trail near their anthill. One day red ants got all over me, making me shiver and jump. I was so shook up—jumping around trying to get the ants off, imagining them biting me—I unknowingly stumbled into the anthill itself, falling over it, right into the ants. I jumped around spastically knocking ants off me. I got a bucket of water and tried to drown the ants. I saw ants swim in small puddles of water as the water slowly seeped, disappearing into the anthill.

Going to Sunday School, that bored me. Then I had to go to church, where I was vague about understanding hell, the real meaning of fire and brimstone burning forever and ever. The boogie man, though, I associated with the Devil. The preacher shouted and bellowed "Repent!" and the people sat in the hot church, fanned themselves and patted their feet and moaned and amen'd, and I would all but go to sleep. I would be awakened by the choir singing "Amazing Grace" when the church service was just about over.

I would run down to the corner store and buy penny candy. I stopped giving the pennies and nickels that I would find to Mama so she could save them for us. I would beg Mama, when I wanted one of the pennies. When she wouldn't give me one I would get one out of her purse, until one day she whipped me with a switch. I didn't understand why I couldn't have a penny or nickel she was saving—and why was it stealing? I began to beg and beg the man at the store for a piece of candy until he would give me some. The man finally told Mama and she stopped me.

One night I was awakened by loud cussing. My Daddy was threatening Mama.

"And the next time you bring that shit up to me, God damn it!"—then a rustling noise—"I'll knock your brains out!"

"George!" Mama screamed out in fear, and I shivered all over. Then I got up out of the bed and went to the bedroom door and opened it. I saw Daddy holding a chair up high in the air, standing over the bed, as Mama lay in the bed, crying.

"So you go any God damn way you want to!" he said. "Up, down"—and he pointed at the ceiling then to the floor—"out"—he pointed toward the door—"or back, I don't care!" Then he slammed the chair to the floor and turned around and spotted me standing in the open door.

"What the—get your ass back in bed," he shouted, "and don't you ever—*get the hell to bed*!" I left the door and fearfully got into bed. And then the door slammed shut, making the room completely dark. They quieted down, but that picture of Daddy about to hit Mama stayed in my mind. I had a dream of everything being out of shape, either extremely, bulgingly fat, or tall and extremely skinny—the smooth shapes of people with no features, like blank store-window mannequins that got bulging fat and then tall and skinny, then fat——

There was a two-by-four railing at the top of the fence in our backyard, up almost three times as high as I was. I would climb to the top, then stand up, shakily balancing myself, and slowly walk it, pausing every nine or ten steps, all the way over to the back of the church. Whenever my Mama told me to get down, I would, but I just had to walk it. I'd seen a cat run across that two-by-four.

I was walking and balancing myself on the top of the fence one evening when my Daddy called out, "Bobby! Come here."

"Yes, sir," I answered, and I scrambled down into the dirt. He was taking off his shirt at the wash bench in back of the house. The first thing to jump in my mind was I was going to get a whipping—what had I done? He got out the white wash basin, ran some water in it, set it back on the wash bench, and put his shirt into the water.

"I want you to wash my shirt," he said. He picked up the bar of soap. "Wash it, and hang it on the line."

"Yes, sir," I said. He dropped the soap into the basin and went up the back steps to the kitchen.

I began trying to rub soap on the shirt, splashing water, dropping the slippery soap. I then tried to rub the shirt between my hands, my knuckles gripping the shirt, like I'd seen my Mama do. I could hear Mama and Daddy begin to argue. Mama was talking about "them Wilcoxes" and someone named "Frankie May Wilcox." I was used to their arguing but Daddy's cursing was more loud and angry this time, it seemed.

My mind drifted, though, as I tried to rub and scrub the shirt with my hands. I saw a bird light on the fence. I got a rock and threw it, missing the bird as it flew away. I scrubbed at the shirt some more, a couple of minutes, then decided to climb the fence to finish walking it over as far as the garage.

"Bobby!" my Daddy shouted out. "I thought I told you to wash that shirt, damn it!"

I almost lost my balance squatting and grabbing hold of the two-by-four and scrambling down off the fence, hitting the dirt ground with my bare feet. My Daddy was up on me, whipping me. I tried to scramble out of reach of his belt. "Yes, sir, Daddy, I'm going to do it!" I cried, hollering and yelling while the licks of his belt stung and hurt me. I had no shirt on, and short pants. Then he grabbed me by the arm, beating the hell out of me.

"George, you whipping that boy too much!" Mama hollered out at Daddy, as I kicked around under the whipping. Dust and dirt were flying.

"I told you,"—*whap, whap, whap, whap*, I was about to pee on myself, the licks kept burning as I jumped, yelled, and hollered—"to wash that shirt, damn it!"

"Yes sir, Daddy." And pleading, "Oh please Daddy, yes, sir, Daddy, I'm going to do it," I jumped and screamed. Daddy slung me and I stumbled to the ground by the wash bench. I got up out of the dirt, crying.

"George!" Mama hollered at Daddy. I saw her out in the yard with us now. "You whip Bobby too much."

"Now, wash that shirt like I told you!" he ordered. Daddy walked up the back-door stairs.

Mama followed him: "George, I wash your shirts. Why you got Bobby doing that?"

Daddy was cursing Mama loudly in the kitchen while I scrubbed at the shirt. I stood there crying and scared, hearing the harsh cursing and the angry words. Time passed; I sulked, rubbing at the shirt, paying little heed, tears running down my face. I was hurting all over.

The screen door flew open. I looked up quickly at my Daddy saying, "You ain't finished?" He hollered angrily, "Damn it!" and came down the stairs in two leaps and was on me, whipping. "I told you"—*whap, whap, whap*—"to wash that God damn shirt!"

I yelled, cried. He beat me as I jerked and jumped, telling him, "I'm going to wash it, I'm going to wash it!"

The next thing I knew Mama had the belt in her hand, saying, "You don't need to whip that boy like that!"

"Thelma, I'll break your God damn neck!"

Daddy grabbed at the belt and Mama jerked away. Daddy followed her, cursing, and Mama said, "You just whipping that boy for nothing, and you know it!"

I had to hurry up and wash this shirt. I started scrubbing, crying, hurting and paining, fearful of another whipping. How do I finish? I remembered Mama saying when she washed, "Bobby, run me some more water in that bucket," and I wanted to play so I'd ask, "Why do you need

so much water?" She'd say, "So I can rinse the clothes three times." I had
to rinse the shirt three times to get through washing it.

Mama and Daddy were hollering, accusing, arguing, and Daddy cursing. I hurriedly put the basin under the faucet again, filling the basin, and
put it back on the bench. Clumsily, I went through the same motions,
trying to rinse and squeeze, going as fast as I could. Twice, then a third
time, I filled the basin and dipped the shirt up and down. I folded both
ends together, as I'd seen Mama do. Feeling weak from the whipping, I
wrung, twisted, and squeezed the shirt. There was my Daddy, now,
standing at the top step. I wanted to run, but I was scared to; I just stood
there, with the dripping shirt in my hands.

"You finished washing that shirt?" he bellowed.

"Yes, sir," I said, quickly but nervously. I handed it toward him with
both hands, and I noticed the belt in his hands.

"Hold it out, shake it out, so I can see it."

Would he whip me because I hadn't hung it on the line?

"I told you to *wash* that damn shirt!" he shouted, coming off the stairs.

"George, you just whipping that——" Mama was shouting.

Whap, whap. I yelled and cried. *Whap, whap, whap.* Mama snatched
Daddy's belt. I was lying in the dirt crying as Mama tussled and struggled
with Daddy. Daddy snatched the belt away and came at me again, wallop-
ing me, rapidly, all over my body.

"George!" Mama was shouting, "George! George, you done whipped
that boy too much!"

"God damn it, Thelma! I'm skinning this cat, you hold his tail!"

"You just don't want me to see what's on your shirt—just whipping that
boy for nothing." They were in the kitchen; their arguing continued.
"You treat that boy like he ain't your son."

I got up off the ground, crying, in dreadful pain. I sucked air in spurts
and tried to catch my breath, not understanding why I'd got whipped so
bad. The shirt was lying on the ground in the dirt. I went and picked it up
and hurriedly rinsed, wrung, and squeezed it out twice. I felt weak and
scared. I took it over to the clothesline, got some clothespins; standing on
the tips of my toes, I pinned it up as best I could.

I wanted to leave—I didn't want him to be my Daddy. I slowly walked
away. He ain't my real Daddy—Mama said he treated me like I ain't his
son.

I could hear Mama, "George, you going straight to hell, you and them
Wilcoxes."

"I'll break your God damn neck, Thelma, shit! Now shut up, damn it!"
A quiet pause, then, "Shit!"

I walked over to the church steps, hurting all over me from the whipping. I sat there imagining and wishing I was someone else who did not get whippings. It was getting dark—I'll break your God damn neck, he'd said to Mama. I shivered all over. I got scared, driving the thought away. I felt lonely; it was getting darker.

"Bobby!" Mama called out, "come on in this house so you can eat."

I got up and walked slowly to the house, wishing and hoping Daddy had finished eating.

My Mama said, "Homer and Doritha is going to come stay with us awhile." Mama stood over the dishpan, washing and picking over some greens, putting them into a pot. "Homer's your cousin."

"I thought Alvin is my cousin."

"You-all got *so* many cousins. First cousins, second cousins, third cousins, just a whole heap of them. You got more than a hundred cousins."

That was amazing—a hundred cousins. "Isn't Alvin my first cousin more than the rest of them all?"

"What, Bobby?"

"Because I saw Alvin first, and Alvin's Mama look like you, Mama."

"That's because Aunt Zelma, Alvin's Mama, she's my twin sister, Bobby," Mama laughed.

First Homer's wife, Doritha, arrived, and two days later Homer. Betty came outside: "Bobby, Homer here."

I burst through the kitchen door as Homer walked into the kitchen with Doritha. Boy, was he big.

"How you-all doing, Aunt Thelma," Homer said, smiling.

"Ooooh, Homer!" Mama exclaimed, a joyous, smiling greeting. She stepped back, looking at Homer. "In your Army suit and all! Homer, you sure look good. Lord, you just done growed on up."

I had played being a soldier, but Homer was real. Betty, John, and I stood there, amazed, admiring Homer. Doritha was hugging close, hanging onto him with her arm around his waist, and he had his arm around her shoulders. I looked him up and down. His boots shone like glass.

"I see you ready to go over there and fight that old low-down Hitler," Mama said. "Homer, I sure hate to see you go."

Homer looked at Betty, John, and I—we were staring at him, full of awe.

"Yes, Lord, them's my three chilluns, Homer. You and Doritha be having them of your own soon."

"Yeah, she about ready now," Homer looked at Doritha and patted her on her belly, and smiled and reached down to give her a quick kiss.

She shut her eyes and said, softly, "Come on, honey."

"Homer," Mama said, "you-all just make yourself at home, hear? I'm cooking some dinner—we can eat after awhile. You and Doritha can have mine and George's room in there, so you two just make yourselves at home and stay as long as you want, go where you want, and do what you want." Mama laughed.

Betty, John, and I went into the pantry closet so we could see Homer some more. We played in there a lot, and there was a hole in the wall. We could see just about all over Mama and Daddy's room.

I stood looking through the hole and saw Homer and his wife kissing and hugging. All of a sudden, Doritha stepped back, saying, "Come on, honey," pulling up her dress and quickly taking off her bloomers. Homer was taking off his clothes as Doritha got on the bed, lying on her back, her dress pulled way up with her legs wide open. There were black hairs between her legs—that was surprising. Homer took off his shorts. Boy, his peter was big! And he had hair too.

Betty, John, and I had always called our penises and even where Betty peed our "candy"—when we took a bath together, Mama would tell us to "wash your candy." At school, I had learned to say "peter." The older boys would say, "My peter's bigger than yours," or we would have contests to see who could pee the highest and the farthest.

I was looking straight at the bed, looking at the bottoms of their feet, as I saw Homer, with his hand, put his big peter into a reddish spot in the middle of the hairs between Doritha's legs. He took his hand away and began to move his butt up and down and back and around—I watched intently, as his big long peter went in and out of the red spot.

They moved and moved, then: "Oh, baby! Honey! I love you, Homer, baby! Oh, baby! Oh, it's *so* good!" Doritha was saying softly. The bed was beginning to make noise. "Oh, Homer baby!"

"I love you, Doe!" Homer was saying. "I love you!"

Doritha got a little louder: "Oh, oh, oh, oh! I love you, honey, oh!" She was even louder now: "It feel so good, Homer baby."

"Let me look, Bobby," Betty said, "I want to peep too."

They were quieted down. "Girl," Homer said softly, "I'm sure crazy about you." He lay there on top of her with her arms now wrapped loosely around his back. Both of them were saying, "I love you."

I understood they were happy. Then I wondered, was that something I wasn't supposed to see? They loved each other, I thought with my childish understanding; they said they did, over and over again. Did Mama and Daddy do that? But Mama and Daddy argued, they didn't do that. I had looked through the hole at Mama and Daddy, but they didn't do that. When I get big, I'm going to be a soldier with a big peter, just like Homer. And I'll get a wife, and I'm going to love her just like that.

When Homer came back again about three weeks later, Betty, John, and I went to the pantry closet as soon as we saw them shut the door to the room. When one of us saw them going into the room, we'd go and get the others and say, "Let's go peep." We began to call the act that we saw over and over through the hole in the wall, "peeping."

My Aunt Zelma and Alvin, my cousin, came to stay with us later—they would stay for two or three months this time, while on their way to California. Aunt Zelma looked just like my Mama, her twin. When Aunt Zelma arrived, there was always conversation going on between them. Off and on I would overhear them talk about things that struck my interest—

"How is Doritha and Homer getting along, Thelma?" Aunt Zelma asked, picking her teeth, as I stood at the entrance of the bedroom, looking and listening.

"Child, every time I turned around, Doritha was hanging all over Homer, talking about how much she loved Homer and pulling him back off in that bedroom. And sometimes I'd hear them with the door closed."

"Is that right?"

"Girl, it's only going to be a few short months before that baby'll be turning and kicking."

"She's going to have a baby?" Aunt Zelma paused, and she gazed off into space. "I sure hope he treats her right. I hope he don't do her like Alvin's Daddy, Tome Turner, did me. Just low-down! Thelma, you know, some men want to stick they old peter up you, and put babies in you, and leave. You have a whole lot of babies and they go on off and leave you."

Stick they peter up you and put babies in you? That's what Homer did.

"Bobby," Mama had spotted me. "Go on out of here, this is grown folks' talk. Go on outside."

I wanted to make a baby. One day, I was by myself when a neighbor girl came to our backyard. I asked her, did she want to peep?

"What's that?"

I thought she knew. "That's how you make babies. Come on." I took her into the garage—it had no front door, it was just an old empty rundown garage with a dirt floor.

"First, take your bloomers all the way off, then pull up your dress and lay down on the ground and open your legs," I said, matter of factly.

She lay flat on the dirt ground. I got down on top of her and tried to put my peter in her. It didn't seem to go anywhere, but just lay there. I got back up and looked to try and find a pink spot, which I found by pulling the lips back.

"You have to say 'I love you,'" I said.

: you," she said.

we can make a baby."

d again, but there was no real hole like Doritha's. As I pressed and , my little peter got erect and hard. I liked that, so I pressed my little peter, moving and saying, "I love you, oh, baby, I love you. Now you say the same thing."

The neighbor girl and I did that off and on for some time, way after Aunt Zelma and Alvin left for California. I would look almost every day to see if her stomach got big, but it never did. Then I concluded that I had to be big like Homer, with a big long peter like his. I periodically dreamed of being big, a soldier, kind and married and smiling and I would go and fight Hitler and come home, peep, and make a baby.

Aunt Zelma and Mama talked about men and what they do, about babies and having them, about menstrual periods and 'filthy' women, preachers who may, or may not, have done something wrong. If we were caught piddling around in the kitchen, trying to overhear them, they would tell us, "Get on out of here, this is grown folks' talk."

But Betty, Alvin, John, and especially I would sneak around and come back, hiding behind some door, or listening from below an open window. Subjects, facts, and stories were mentioned two, three, and four times in different ways as they talked and gossiped, scorned and denounced, prayed and praised.

"Chil'," Mama would draw out the word. "The Lord knows it ain't right. It just ain't *right*. All this killing in the world—that low-down Hitler, he's going straight to hell——"

"Thelma, Hitler ain't nothing, but a low-down nasty white man," Aunt Zelma would utter, matter of factly. "Kill up us Negroes worse than he'd kill up them white folks over in they own place. Just like these old low-down nasty white folks killing us and lynching us right here. Them old Ku Klux Klanners, they ain't got nothing but the devil in them."

"I wonders why white folks wants to treat us so bad?" Mama would ask in conversation.

I had not heard of Ku Klux Klanners. I had seen white folks from a distance all my seven years, but I had never been close to one. I listened on.

"Like Limbrick's boy back in Jasper, was taken out in the woods and just killed for nothing. They found him all shot up and ain't nobody done it but them old nasty white folks."

"Oh, ain't nobody did it but them," Mama confirmed.

"Just did it 'cause they felt like it."

Mama would bitterly exclaim, other times, talking to Aunt Zelma, "Girl,

George won't come home. Just every now and then. He be running with them Wilcoxes and that Frankie May Wilcox."

"And Thelma, he got a good job, ain't he?"

"Zelma, George ain't never been without a job. Now he got a good government job. Out there working at the Randolph Field."

"Honey, that's the best kind of job you can get."

"All through the Depression when there weren't no jobs, George Seale kept himself a job and a new car."

"Just building houses like his papa, Arch Seale, huh, Thelma?"

"His Daddy, Arch Seale, taught George and all them chilluns to be carpenters," Mama put in. "But Arch Seale would beat them and cuss them so bad——"

"He was just mean and no good, huh, Thelma?"

"—Had the devil in him—and if he don't ask the Lord for forgiveness, he going straight to hell. Lord, Zelma, they made the money—here I am begging George to leave money at this house. They just won't do right. I bet George there right now spending money on that Frankie May Wilcox. They won't do right."

"Tome Turner, too—won't give me and Alvin nothing. Running women! Just went off and left me and cuss me out and be talking about killing me. Just low-down naaasty niggers, want to ram that old peter up you and leave you with a baby in your belly, and Tome Turner would be out running women, whoremongering."

"George told me quite a while ago how his Daddy, Arch Seale, would beat him so. Then Arch Seale, you know, he hired all them boys to build that whole town called Wiergate, it's almost over to Louisiana. Well, there was some white folks who didn't like it, the way Arch Seale was building the whole town."

"Well, how did he do it, Thelma, them white folks must of wanted to hurt him about that."

"I think it was old man Seale, the white man who owned the bank in Jasper. He seen to it that Arch Seale built everything. Arch Seale had his brother, Ed Seale, and Ed's boys and even Cubbard and George and Tome and Zelus and Edel, and just a host of 'em that Arch Seale had hired to build them houses."

"Well, didn't Arch Seale build a big old house for old man Seale?"

"Arch Seale built so many houses for white folks. But there's something George told me and I don't understand. Arch Seale built old man Seale's house in downtown Jasper. Then Arch bought the land next door and built his own house right next door to old man Seale."

"Is that right? Arch Seale sure had his ways."

"And you know, Arch Seale wouldn't pay George. George went and asked the white man, old man Seale, how come he couldn't get paid like everybody else. Arch found out about it and took a tree limb and beat George. George finally ran off because Arch Seale would beat him and cuss him so bad and still wouldn't pay him half the time."

"Arch just drove them chilluns of his way from 'round him."

Aunt Zelma was always saying that her husband, Tome Turner, was a naaasty nigger. I asked Alvin, "What Aunt Zelma mean when she say your Daddy is a low-down nasty nigger?"

"All I know is she say he going to hell and burn forever and ever."

"Well, ain't there no way he can get out of going to hell?"

"He got to be saved."

I'd heard Mama say that a lot but never really paid much attention to it. "Is you saved, Alvin?"

"Yeah."

"Well, how you get saved?"

"The Lord have to talk to you. When my Mama gets on her knees and prays and cries to the Lord, she says a whole lot of things so nothing will happen to her and nothing will happen to me. She ask for forgiveness so all her sins will be washed away. Then she starts singing and crying and praying and she be reading the Bible and shouting in the church where she can't help herself. That's when you saved and you ain't going to go to hell."

"And you saved and you ain't going to go to hell?"

"Yeah, Mama told me I would be saved when the Lord was talking to me one night. I woke up and I was shouting, saying 'I don't want to go to hell, save me'—so I'm saved."

"Well, what if you do something wrong again?"

"I'll go to hell if I don't ask for forgiveness."

"No you won't!" Betty exclaimed. She'd come in on the scene.

"How come?" I asked Betty.

" 'Cause we ain't twelve years old yet."

We all had heard Mama say we ain't accountable for our sins until we got to be twelve years of age. "That's right!" I exclaimed to Alvin. "Mama said."

One night Alvin's mother put him down on his knees even though he wasn't twelve yet and had him say the whole Lord's Prayer with the Bible open in front of him. When he finished saying the Lord's Prayer, she told him to pray for forgiveness for all the sins he had done or might have thought of doing. And she told Alvin to pray that he won't go to hell like his Daddy, Tome Turner, and had him say: "Lord, please forgive me for all the times I've sinned. And help me to obey my mother. And let me be saved so I won't go to hell and burn in fire and brimstone forever and ever like my Daddy. Please help me, God——"

Alvin would go on and on being directed by his mother until he cried and shook on his knees with his head bowed.

In the second grade I learned to write—not print, but write—my name and address. I'd also write other things, but one day I wrote over and over on a clean piece of paper, about five times, "Bobby George Seale, 508 South Olive Street, San Antonio, Texas."

Mama had taken a wartime job at the Kelly Field. I brought my writing exercise home and showed it to her when she got back from work. I was carrying on about what I'd written—and Daddy came into the kitchen. Mama told him to look at it. Then she talked about how she had taught us our ABCs, that it was good, and said to Daddy that he should be teaching us how to become carpenters.

Daddy took me into the big open room and started asking me to add. "What's two and two?"

"Four," I said.

"What's four and four?"

"Eight."

All the even-number addition problems I could do. Somehow, too, I could figure out an even number added with an odd number. But I couldn't add two odd numbers, even counting on my fingers.

"What's twelve plus twelve?" my Daddy asked.

"Twenty-four."

"That's good," my Daddy said.

I felt fine standing there running off the answers.

"What's nine and seven?"

Two odd numbers. I didn't know. I tried to count. Then I said, guessing it was another odd number, "Fifteen."

"Nope. That ain't right."

How was I going to do this? "Nineteen," I said.

"Now, Bobby, you ought to know that. Thelma, where's that blackboard?"

He had me write the figures on the blackboard, with a plus sign. "Now figure out the answer—what's nine plus seven equal to?" His voice was changing.

I didn't know. I tried counting on my fingers. He told me not to count on my fingers, sounding angry. I wished he would tell me. I was scared now. Would I get a whipping? "Thirteen?" I whimpered out.

"Bobby, you ought to know what nine plus seven is. Now figure it out. What is it?"

I was scared. I had to pee. I said to my Daddy, "I got to pee, Daddy."

"You ain't got to pee. You just trying to get out of it." Then he took off his belt. Tears rolled down my face as I stood there, fighting with the idea of getting a whipping. I didn't know. I had said thirteen, fifteen, nineteen—then I said, real slow, "Seventeen?"

Whap, the belt caught me, and I yelled out, "I don't know, Daddy. Please! I don't know!"

"Yes, you do!" *Whap*. The belt stung me as I jumped away from the blackboard. "Get back up there."

"George," Mama said, "that ain't no way to teach these chilluns."

"I'm skinning this cat, Thelma, you hold his tail. Now, what's nine plus seven?"

I just stood, then *whap, whap*. I couldn't think any more for fear of the belt.

"Get back up there." *Whap*.

The whipping and the standing at the blackboard got rough—not only for me, but Betty and John, too. Sometimes, though, Betty and John learned from my answers.

One night, eating at the table, my Daddy bellowed, "God damn it, Bobby, stop that smacking!" I sulked. Then he said, "Can't you eat with your mouth closed?"

Was that what it was? "Yes, sir," I said.

My Aunt Annie May, my Daddy's sister, came to stay with us for a few days. She told me she had a boy named Johnny, our first cousin, and he was staying with our Grandpa Arch, back in Beaumont, Texas, and she was going to California. It seemed like everybody was going to California. What was in California? I'd asked Mama were we ever going to go. She said, "Yes, when we saved enough money." In time, Daddy left for California—and the whippings stopped.

PART II

The Self-Righteous Sinner

THE FLOORS WERE SMOOTH, slick cement and had thin cracks running across them. This was where we were going to live—an apartment, not a house, in California. There were four rooms on the ground floor, and a bathroom with a flushing toilet and face basin.

After a short while, Mama sighed and said how she was "glad we're not rooming no more." She and Daddy went into the bedroom and closed the door. Betty and John went outside.

I looked out the narrow window, out into the courtyard. In a month I would be nine years old. Black children were playing noisily near a red brick wall, and beyond, by a giant leafy tree. Betty and John were standing looking at some girl swing real high on a rope swing. I turned the faucet of the face basin. Rusted water jettisoned out. I let it run until the water ran clear. I fiddled around the apartment. I liked it okay, but it was smaller than a house. We had not built a house in San Antonio, but maybe we could build a big house here in California like some I saw when we were driving to this apartment.

The front door flew open and I turned around to see Betty crying and John behind her.

"They pushed me!" Betty whined, "Bobby, they—they won't let me swing!" With tears on her face and dirt on her dress and in her hair.

"Who won't let you swing?" I asked, looking at her close and believing she had definitely been hurt.

19

"Bobby, you going to beat them up?" John asked. His eyes were wide and excited, looking up to me. "Huh? You going to beat them up?"

"Beat who up? What happened?" I asked. Did I have to fight?

"They won't let us swing," Betty said. "That boy, they pushed me off the swing," Betty whined, pointing toward the courtyard. "He pushed me on the ground."

"You going to beat them up, huh, Bobby? Huh?" John spouted. "You going to beat them up?"

I looked out the window at the rope swing, at a whole lot of black children, and at the curly-headed boy Betty pointed out. Eight or nine children stood looking. The barefoot curly-headed boy slightly hung and swung, holding and gripping one of the large knots tied into the rope, as another girl with "good" hair tried to grab hold of the swing.

"You going to beat them up, huh, Bobby?" John persisted.

"Come on," I ordered. I opened our kitchen door. "You-all can swing."

I walked straight out, up to the boy. He had seen me coming, but he turned his head away, holding onto the swing.

"Who said they can't swing?" I shot out, trying to sound tough—pointing at Betty and John, who had stopped midway under the branches of the tree. Share and share alike my Mama had said many times.

I stepped toward the swing, stopped, then flung myself to grab it and missed as the boy slung himself around and around with his bare feet dragging in the dust and dirt. His eyes caught mine one time passing, then again, and he was smiling—with a smirk on his face. He looked like he was laughing at me. That irritated me.

"Bobby, you going to beat them up?" John called.

The boy slung himself again. I grabbed the rope swing, jerking it.

"This is our swing!" the boy shouted. Then he swung out some.

A big-headed little boy with close-cropped hair said, "Ooooh, he going to take the swing!" A little girl who sucked her fingers jumped up and down, still holding her two fingers in her mouth.

The curly-headed boy, pushing with his feet, sort of slung himself again; but before he could get up too much high swinging motion, I jumped and grabbed the rope with him on it, trying with all my strength to bring him and the swing to a stop. "My sister and brother can swing on it too!" I was angry now. I felt I was right, and I tried to look real mean and mad in the face, as I'd seen in the movies. I felt a raging anger toward the selfish boy, and I balled up my fist, stepping close to him.

"You best not hit Robert Jr.!" the good-haired girl shouted. "If you hit Robert Jr., I'll tell my Mama!"

In all the confusion, it flashed in my mind to hit the girl, then I angrily remembered that this curly-headed boy had pushed my sister. With all my might and moving strength, I hit his chest with both hands, and Robert Jr., went sprawling to the ground—*wham*—hitting dirt hard and surprised. I grabbed the dangling rope swing as all the other children became excited and overjoyed.

"Ooow!" and "Yaaa!" The big-headed little boy jumped up and down, hollering with wide-eyed glee. "He took it! He took it!"

"Now Bobby going to *really* beat them up!" John bragged.

Robert Jr. quickly scrambled up. He stepped back and balled his fist.

"We can share the swing!" I yelled, looking him dead in the eye. "So we can swing too!" I balled up both my fists.

"I'm going to tell my Mama on you," the good-haired girl whined.

Robert Jr. said, "You motherfucker!"

He had called me out of my name—but what was it he had called me?

"Don't call me out of my name!" I shouted angrily.

"You ain't nothing but an old stupid God damn fool, motherfucking asshole!" Robert Jr. was acting confident that he had really insulted me.

"Same to you!" I shouted in rage; I didn't know how else to say something better or badder or more insulting to him. "I'll break your neck!"

"Yeah? I'm going to tell my Mama and Daddy, 'cause that's our swing."

Then I remembered and smartly spouted, "Tell it! Smell it! Go down and sell it! Bring it back and I'll make pork chops out of it!" I was shouting out, waving my hands in a dare-you gesture.

"Ooooow!" a few of the children exclaimed. "Say it! Say it!" A bald-headed boy hopped around, saying, "Say it!"

All of that made me feel good. Whatever he had called me, I had told him a thing or two.

Robert Jr. walked off toward their apartment. I grabbed the swing, and gestured to Betty to take the swing. The little girl with her fingers in her mouth quickly jerked her hand out and asked could she swing too, and jammed her fingers right back in.

"Everybody can swing, take turns," I said. There was a joyous outburst from the crowd of children. I really felt liked by them now.

Robert Jr. came back down the stairs, and a woman's head stuck out the window—I figured it was his Mama, and I was a little worried. Then she said, "Robert Jr., you and Sis, you just *share* that swing with everybody else!"

Good! I was right. They had to share it, too. I walked over to the door of our apartment, then stopped and stood looking at the curly-headed boy before I went inside.

*

Robert Jr. and I got to be tight friends—by chucking rocks at a tin can, the next day in the courtyard. I grew to know Robert Jr.'s words—he could cuss with a true creative sense. And he and his sister could dance up a storm. I admired their father—he wore zoot-suit pants and a long chain dropped down from his waist and disappeared into his pocket; he wore pretty striped shirts and he wore a hat. His style, mannerisms, and dress were just totally different. I was impressed.

But my Mama and the other religious women would tell each other, "Child, they always having them old sinful parties, drinking and carrying on." The things most talked-about were the blues and boogie that blared out of Robert Jr.'s parents' place. "That old blues!" Mama'd say. "Playing cards and that old blues and boogie. Just a whole lot of sinning mess." I was of two minds about Robert Jr.'s cussing: I admired it, but I deemed it wrong.

Mama had taught us to actually write letters back in San Antonio. She had taught us to write Alvin, Herman, and Lewis—our cousins back in Jasper. I had even written a letter to Homer. We wrote letters to Santa Claus. I wanted a bicycle. Robert Jr. said he was going to get a bicycle. John wanted another wagon and a scooter like the ones we'd had back in San Antonio. We both wanted BB guns. Betty wanted two dolls and a play house with play furniture, play dishes, and a play stove with play pots and forks and knives.

Betty wanted us to have a Christmas tree. But Mama said we didn't need a tree, and she didn't know if we would have the money.

"But Santa Claus got to put our toys under a Christmas tree, Mama," Betty, John, and I all whined, pouting and yammering on with our mouths poked out.

"You-all just write the letters, and I'll see if your Daddy'll give me some money to get a Christmas tree," Mama told us in her disgusted and worried manner, signing it off with "Lord, Lord, what am I going to do. Lord, please help me."

We stayed up late Christmas Eve until we got sleepy, watching Mama bake cakes and sweet potato pies, and called ourselves helping Mama here and there while we played and dreamed and licked the cake and icing bowls clean. Mama made a pineapple cake and a coconut cake and put the turkey in the oven just before we went to sleep that night.

When Christmas day came, we woke up that morning and found our three stockings—Daddy's socks—we had hung on the wall. They were filled with fruit, nuts, and candy. There were two pairs of pants and two shirts for John and me, and Betty had two dresses and a coat. These things were on the floor under the stockings. That was it for Christmas.

"That's all Santa Claus could bring you-all. Now, you-all—oh, me——"
Mama sighed with a worrying tone. Then she said, "Now just go on and play."

"Shoots, this is the same clothes we found in the closet two weeks ago. But I wanted a doll, and a play house," Betty whined, crying. "And all we got was nothing."

Mama looked around at us. Tears were rolling down her face. I wanted to cry when I saw the tears, confused between not getting anything, and Mama crying about it now!

We looked out our back window, when we heard other children playing. I saw a boy with a scooter. Then I saw some smaller children with toy cars and wagons. Betty cried when she spotted a girl with a doll. There were children with tricycles and even girls with bicycles.

Betty had made eight years old that December twenty-first, three days before Christmas. She said, "I didn't even get nothing for my birthday. I don't want to go outside."

"Me neither," John said.

We fiddled around in our room, looking out the window, and wishing we had some or just one of the array of different toys we saw. Then we would go to the front bathroom window, and then to Mama's window. We ate our fruit and candy and nuts.

"Maybe next Christmas, Daddy will give Mama some money and Santa Claus will bring us something," John said. "I want a wagon and a scooter."

"I want a doll, even without the dollhouse."

"I wish Daddy would come home right now," John said. "With a whole lot of toys for us," he added, with a smile on his face. "And then——"

"Then we could go outside," Betty said, cutting John off. "We'd all have what we wrote in the letters."

"I'd go over to Gloria's," Betty said, starting to smile. "And I'd have jacks and everything, and——"

I didn't feel so bad as before—it had settled, realizing that we had not got anything for Christmas, along with clinging to the wish that my Daddy would come home any moment with the things.

But it was still too embarrassing to go outside. I spotted Robert Jr. riding on his new bicycle, wearing his new cowboy suit with two guns strapped to his hips.

Later that day Mama set the table with turkey, dressing, English peas, yams, greens, spinach, rice, cornbread, rolls, coconut cake, pineapple cake, and sweet-potato pie. I stuffed myself. I wished my Daddy would come with all the toys, as my full stomach made me dream once again.

Mama tried to get us to go outside and play. "But we ain't got nothing for Christmas," we said, and Mama didn't say anything else.

Betty and I finally got up the courage to want to go outside when John went on out. "It won't be so bad," I said. "Maybe Robert Jr. will let me ride his bike, and we can just say our Daddy's going to bring us something later."

"Yeah," Betty agreed, "but we still might not get nothing."

Outside, we stood still, looking around. Robert Jr. rode past me fast on his bicycle, and Sis—Robert Jr.'s sister—came over to Betty and me, who were standing there sadly. "What did you get for Christmas?" she asked Betty.

"Our Daddy ain't brought it yet," I said, walking away toward the rope swing. Not wanting to talk about it.

Robert Jr. rode up to me as I hung slightly on the swing. I admired and wanted to ride his bike. "What did you get? Did you get a BB gun? I did," Robert Jr. asked and stated.

"When my Daddy bring it," I replied, and looked away. I wanted to cry.

"What else you get?" he asked. I wished he wouldn't ask.

I was sad. He was my friend, so I said, "Nothing."

"You didn't get nothing?" he asked loudly, with a surprised look on his face.

"Naw." I really tried to act like I didn't care. The whole thought of my Daddy coming home with our Christmas things fell apart inside me.

I saw that Sis had walked away from Betty. I climbed down from the rope and I went over to my sister. She was crying again. "Did Sis ask you what you got?" I asked her quietly.

"Yeah," Betty said sadly.

"What did you say you got?"

"Nothing."

On green spring Monday mornings I'd wake early following the slow church days and early-to-bed Sunday nights. I developed a desire and a wish to know and do everything—against the "stay 'round this house, Bobby" and "come straight home" instructions of Mama's.

Some days we played hooky from school, leaving at lunch time, with all the other older boys that John, Robert Jr., and I tagged along with.

One Sunday kind of hooky developed into a profitable business. I talked Betty and John into going to a picture show—I think it was *Gone with the Wind*, which we talked about wanting to see because Clark Gable said "damn" right in the movie. We began in business because coming home late after that long movie, we knew we hadn't been to church like Mama told us. Walking through the white section, where there were flowers growing in the yards, Betty told some woman that our Mama was home sick in bed, and could we have some flowers for our sick Mama? She was no way sick, of course, but we thought flowers might help our case. We got the flowers, and a few blocks later another white lady asked if she could buy some of them for fifteen cents. We sold all we had, then went back to some other houses and lied some more, sold some more, and still had some to take to Mama. We began flower-selling on a regular basis. Sometimes we'd just take them, instead of going through the stories, and sell them to people in the government projects near where we lived. We'd have a few nickels, and we'd have an excuse to come home late Sunday afternoons: "We been selling flowers, Mama. Here's some for you, Mama."

There were big houses, with beautiful lawns and big peach trees, where we got the flowers. The kind of houses we'd thought we were going to be living in when we came to California on the train, the kind that we could see from the train—not like the government project building we lived in; that wasn't a home as I thought of homes.

Life became a free comedy. I was so happy with our new life in California, for the homes we saw in the Berkeley Hills would yield many flowers. In the closer districts, we began to get caught red-handed and neighbors would run us off. Later, we found the police knew about us: one day a cop warned, with his growly, mean, red face, that if he caught us stealing flowers, he would "put your little asses in the clink."

I saw—awed—wished, and wondered, how did the white folks get such big houses, as we wound farther and farther up into the Berkeley Hills. And to watch the wild profane cussing of Robert Jr.! Cussing out grown white people and seeing their mouths hang open, amazed shock on their faces as they were trying to believe all that was coming out of his mouth: "Motherfucking bitches, eat shit bastard, kiss my motherfucking ass and fuck your God damn chicken shit butt." A few of the older white people called us "little filthy black bastards" as they chased us. But it was a feeling of defying power, when that unbelieving shock appeared on their faces and they would mostly walk away exclaiming to themselves, "Oh! My God! What are these people coming to be!"

"Kiss toy, bring me first," Babe said.

Six of us were playing marbles, "fishes." Everybody but Babe had lagged to the twenty-foot line. If Babe's "toy"—the marble you shoot with—would kiss or hit the toy closest to the line, Babe would automatically have first shot at the fish shape full of marbles. We had declared that no steelies could be used as toys.

When Babe lagged, he kissed the closest toy, and Babe got first shot. He missed. Then his brother, Billy Rogers, shot, also missing. When John shot, he cleaned up some twenty marbles. Then John missed, as his toy went far away, and the rest of us took our shots. When it got around to Billy's turn again, he hit two marbles at once. With his next shot, he leaned his body over the whole form of the fish, shot again, kept shooting, and then I hollered out:

"Billy you cheating! He got a steelie, you-all, that ain't right!"

Billy shot again, hitting the marbles, his toy sticking and spinning. He kept putting marbles in his pocket.

"Billy!" Babe hollered, "you can't cheat with a steelie!"

"Aw, Billy, you ain't playing fair," I yelled.

"I'll shoot with what I want to," Billy said, looking up at me with his mean face. "Fuck you!"

I wanted to jump on him, but he was too big, I thought.

"Aw shoots, I don't want to play." Willie Lee said disgustedly. "Billy always cheating all the time."

"Billy," I yelled, walking up to him, "give me my marbles back!" I patted with my hand at his pocket with marbles in it. Billy pushed me hard. My butt and back hit the dusty dirt ground.

"I ain't giving you shit!" Billy was standing over me with his fist balled up and his mouth poked out looking mean and fighting mad.

I scrambled up off the ground now. "You old cheating motherfucker!" I hollered, backing away from him with my own fist balled up. I looked around for something, anything—I was not going to let him beat me. I'd go in the house and get a knife. I saw a stick, I broke and ran and picked it up; I'd beat him with the stick. I whirled in a mad rage and ran at Billy holding the stick in a ready position to strike him.

Billy tried to duck as I struck him hard, *whap*, across his back, and again he ducked away hiding his head. I swung and hit him again and again as he scrambled away—with me hollering, "You give me my marbles back!" I swung at him again, now missing. "Billy you give me my marbles! You cheating all the time!" Crying and yelling, I swung and kept missing Billy in my uncontrolled raging anger, scared deep down inside. Billy was charging me and rammed his head into my stomach, knocking the wind out of me, and knocking me to the ground. Billy grabbed the stick with one hand and hit me in the face with his fist—*whap, bam*. The paining slap-thudding licks of his fist hurt as I saw flashes of light.

When Billy got up off of me I was raging and distraught, now not caring about his size or anything, with the single thought that I had been done wrong.

"You old stupid cheating motherfucker!" I yelled, and ran at the stick, crying and mad, and picked it up—then ran at Billy again, wildly swinging the stick at him, trying to hit him and missing as he dodged. Billy snatched the swinging stick out of my hand and easily pushed my skinny body to the ground.

"I'm going to bust your head open," Billy said angrily, "if you don't stop, Bobby." Billy walked away and threw the stick hard and high up, and it disappeared in the air above and over the roof of our long apartment building. "Sucker!"

"Ooooow, Billy beat up Bobby!" the children were saying. "Bobby got beat up! Ooooow!" That made me feel bad.

I wanted to cuss Billy out, but Mama was standing in the door now telling me to get inside. I heaved in my breath, sucking in air, quick uncontrollable spurts of air, feeling beat up.

"I'm going to cut him up next time, just wait and see," I said.

"Bobby, now you-all don't need to be fighting out there. You hear me?" Mama angrily said. "And don't you be running around here talking about cutting nobody, Bobby! That ain't right. Now go on in there and wash your face."

I looked in the mirror. I touched the slightly swollen places that hurt. My head and face were gritty and dusty.

Billy was too big for me to beat up. That was the first real fight I'd had— I should have hit him harder. Why don't he play fair? Me and Betty and John played fair. And Robert Jr. and Babe both played fair. I wished I was bigger. My body ached and hurt here and there—if I was big like Homer and Alvin, like my cousins, I'd really beat up Billy. I raised my skinny arm, looking into the mirror, and made a skinny muscle. I was too little.

If Billy mess with me more, I'm going to get a knife and that'll scare him. That's what I should have did—I should have come in the house and got Mama's butcher knife. I know he'd run if I'd have had a knife.

That night I dreamed that Billy Rogers was chasing me with Mama's long butcher knife. I ran and ran and then he caught me, pushed me down on the ground. He was almost about to cut me, putting it at my throat, and I scrambled out from under him and ran. He chased me, swiping at my ears with the knife. I must fly, fly, fly—I ran and leaped up into the air. I was rising up off the ground, I was flying! I was getting away, higher and higher. I was flying and now Billy was down on the ground. I flew all around the big tree in our courtyard. Everybody was looking at me. I flew up to Albany Hill and looked out at our school. I flew higher up over to the Berkeley Hills and saw the whole bay and the bridges and water——

Betty came into the kitchen crying and wailing about Billy Rogers having chased her home. "And he threw rocks at me, and"—Betty paused, and sniffed and pointed aimlessly, whining her frightened story—"he, he started chasing me, when I ran, to keep him from pulling on my hair, and he always bothering me at school, Mama," Betty yammered, sucking in her breath.

"Lord," Mama sighingly interrupted her, "these chilluns, these chilluns, that young'un of Ethel's is so mean."

"And, and, I don't want to go to school no more," Betty went on.

"I'm going to beat him up," I said. "With a knife. I'm going to cut him up, Betty."

"Now, Bobby, you ain't going to do no such a thing," Mama said.

"Mama, I don't want to go to school no more," Betty repeated.

"Now, Betty Jean." Mama paused. "Lord, Betty Jean, just—just go on in there and stop crying. I'm going to talk to Billy's mother. Lord, that child Billy!"

Later that night my Daddy came home, and Mama called Betty into the kitchen to tell Daddy what happened. Mama was saying to Daddy, "And George, you need to take more interest in your chilluns here at home." Betty stood in the kitchen. John and I sat down in chairs, putting on the serious, attentive air we always did when our Daddy was around. Betty timidly began and told Daddy the whole story, about this time and three other times.

"Well you ought to fight him back," Daddy angrily said. He stood up and took off his shirt. His arms were big and muscular.

"But he's too big," Betty said. "And he threw rocks at me and——"

"So you ran," Daddy said, looking at Betty.

"Yes, sir," Betty said.

"You should have knocked shit out of him with something."

"Well a good run," Mama broke in, "is better than a dead hero." She walked over to the table with a full plate of food and set it in front of Daddy, saying, "These chilluns, George, ought not to be——"

"Naw!" Daddy shouted. "What she should have did is picked up something and knocked the *shit* out of him, Thelma! That's what she ought have did!" Eating his food, he said, "Shit!" He looked up and pushed his face forward. "They better fight."

"George," Mama said, shaking her head. "Lord, Lord. I just hope nothing don't happen to them, getting cut and scarred all up."

"Now George, if we spend the rest of that money we won't have nothing left. We need to build another house with what we got," Mama stressed and sighed her point.

I stood in the bathroom listening, dreading; they hadn't started arguing and cussing yet.

"I could be done made enough money to outright pay for a house so we don't owe nothing on it. Shit. Thelma, I could have five, eight, or ten thousand dollars saved in two to five years with my *own* business. Then we can get out of these damn projects."

"Well George, now I'll tell you. If we spend that money on buying you a shop, and if you just bring the money *home* and let *me* see to it that it's put in the bank in *both* our names, then I don't see nothing wrong with that. But other than that I'm against it if you ain't going to bring the money home."

"Shit!" Daddy's voice got suddenly louder, as their door opened. "You can save the money, it don't make no difference. But I just got to go into business." Daddy was coming into the dark bathroom. "Bobby? Let me use the bathroom."

"Yes, sir."

"Bobby," Mama said from her open door, "I thought you-all was asleep."

"We going to get another house, Mama?" I asked, in a low tone.

"I don't know, Bobby. Me and your Daddy trying to work it out."

"Did we sell our house in Port Arthur?"

"Lord, we sold that house back in Port Arthur just before we came to California. Lord, I sure hate we sold it."

"Is we going to have more money, Mama?"

"I hope so," Mama said. "If your Daddy just do right." Mama sat on the edge of the bed with her palm under her chin, resting on her elbow.

Now we don't have no house. That night I dreamed we were in a house built just like the house in Port Arthur, and I helped Daddy build it. But it was in California, up in the Berkeley Hills.

In West Oakland a large sign soon read, "Seale's Cabinet Shop. Refinishing. Furniture. Repair." I was proud of the sign and my Daddy's new business. Other black men hung around, and John and I didn't miss a day to be there at the shop.

Daddy seemed always to have money now. He bought himself clothes, and he would go fishing and hunting with his friends. He lent his friends money. When he came home with bags of new things, we wished, hoped, and wondered if they would be for us. Each time, though, we would be disappointed. We would not ask Daddy for money; we either begged Mama, hunted bottles, or sold flowers for money and whenever we didn't sell a bouquet of flowers, we would bring them home to Mama. She would cry, and with tears in her eyes express her loving feeling toward us for thinking about her.

At other times Betty would be crying, off to herself. I found out it was gossip about us, about our Daddy. "Sure treat his family bad" and "He being a carpenter, ought to have good furniture in they house, with a shop to do it and all." The money problem got worse each month. We were really raggedy-looking now. We weren't truly short of food at home, but we were ashamed. Mama worked in some catering center and she'd bring home sacksful of breadloaf ends—it became an embarrassment that the other kids at school had sandwiches where the bread pieces matched, and our sandwiches didn't match.

Mama begged Daddy to buy us some new shoes; that he was supposed to take care of his family. The argument got worse and went into a lot of cussing and Mama making references to "them Wilcoxes." Mama was hollering and pleading with Daddy that we needed shoes, that our feet were on the ground, telling Daddy he was going "straight to hell, treating your family like you do." Daddy stormed out of the house, slamming the door.

The very next evening Daddy came home with shoes for Betty, John, and me—three pairs of black, sturdy, strong, steel-toed brogans. The shoestrings were rawhide. The brogans were all right, I thought: we had been embarrassed with the flapping soles of our present overworn ragged shoes. John and I put the brogans on.

Betty sat looking at hers; they were "boys' shoes," not for girls. Mama made comment about that to Daddy, saying she would take them back to the store and get some girls' shoes.

"Look, God damn it!" Daddy ordered, "put them shoes on!" Daddy threatened whippings. Betty put the shoes on with sulking, sad, tear-filled eyes and face. Daddy told Mama she had better not take the shoes back to the store.

Every day and time for a few weeks after when Daddy came home, he would make reference to the shoes and Betty. It was awful and even got worse. When it rained one time, I saw Betty crying about how the rain got in the high tops of the shoes, as they would not fit her skinny ankles no matter how tight she pulled the strings.

Daddy showed John and me the step-by-step furniture-refinishing process, first stripping it completely with paint remover, then sanding, then cleaning each and every groove, corner, crack, and crevice. If any small repairs were needed, we'd saw, fit, glue, nail, plane, sand, and reinforce, making sturdy, stronger pieces of furniture. Then the color with stain was applied and we'd make it shine and glow from a hand-rubbing process to the final four-coat wax job.

At noon, Daddy would go in his wallet for a five-dollar bill and tell me to go to the store, get a loaf of bread, some sandwich spread, a pound of chopped ham, a pound of cheese, lettuce, tomatoes, two large bottles of carbonated soda pop or chocolate milk and a large package of cookies.

Daddy would get paid and he'd say to John and me, "Now don't you-all tell your Mama about the job today."

"Yes, Sir," we said. "All right."

"I got to do a few things with some of this money and your Mama got money."

"Yes, Sir."

"You-all want to go fishing with me tonight?"

"Yes, sir," John and I happily answered in unison.

When Mama was told we were getting ready to go fishing, she protested, and asked Daddy did he make any money.

"I ain't got no money, Thelma."

"Now, George, we got to pay this rent." Mama really tried to plead calmly. "George, you told me you'd have some money tonight."

"Well, I ain't got none."

"Well, what you going to use to be *fishing* with?" Mama sat in the chair at the kitchen table saying, "Lord, Lord, George, you know it ain't right for you to leave this house tonight going fishing and we got to pay the rent Monday. And taking these boys fishing on a Sunday is a sin! Going out *fishing* on a Sunday!"

But we went fishing.

It was always an ordeal going to the store for Mama. The over-and-over instructions to get anything, especially something on sale, had always frustrated Betty, John, and me when we had to go. But lately Betty had not minded having to go to the store. She even had been asking Mama did she need anything from the store.

Betty having some money after she went to the store struck me funny. One day Betty bought some of the little one-cent packs of sweet-tart grains we licked from our hands; she had just returned from doing Mama's shopping. I knew she hadn't hunted bottles that day, she hadn't been to sell flowers either.

"Ooow, Betty," I exclaimed. "You always got money." She gave me a nickel. "How do you get money after you go to the store?"

"Well, I ain't going to tell you, Bobby, 'cause you'll tell everybody."

"Naw, I won't, tell me."

"When we get to go to the store for Mama, I'll show you then." Betty stopped walking and looked at me seriously, then warned, "But you best not tell nobody."

Just two days later Mama wanted Betty and me to go to the Gilman Market to get a five-pound sack of corn meal.

"Bobby, you got to swear," Betty said, "you ain't going to tell nobody. You got to swear and cross your heart."

In the store, she looked around, I looked around. "You get a big bag, it's better," she said, and got one. No one was looking at us; I was nervous as hell. A lady rolled a cart into the aisle, looking at items on the shelf. Betty feigned looking at items, holding the bag and turning her body away from the woman. I wanted to leave right then and there. When the lady went out of the aisle, Betty picked up a sack of corn meal and slipped it into the bag. We took off walking.

Betty acted just like she had bought the corn meal in the bag, and she walked out the front door. She made it! I quickened my pace when Betty was out the front door and caught up with her. "Oooow! Betty!" I exclaimed.

"Now all you got to do is keep the money," Betty said calmly, smiling at me as we walked. Betty was *smiling*. She hadn't smiled in a long time.

I always wanted to go to the store after that, as the new stealing tactic became a breeze for me. Betty and I later showed John, Robert Jr., his sister, and Gloria Brown how to do it. This was now our new, and favorite, ingenious hustle. By the time that the third California Christmas was approaching, we were expert child shoplifters, with a righteous shoplifting ring.

As it grew closer to Christmas Day, our spirit was high. We bought a Christmas tree on Betty's birthday with the flower-and-bottle savings Mama gave us. The next day we went out and stole, in professional style, three sets of electric lights for our Christmas tree. We swiped extension cords, icicles, snowflakes, round colored bulbs, a star with a special light in it. We stole wrapping paper and ribbons, and bought two wreaths for our door and window. We cleaned up our house real good, preparing for Christmas. This Christmas tree, the first I ever remember having in our house, stood taller than me by a foot. Mama joined with us and stood and looked happy, with tears in her eyes, that we were having a real Christmas.

The next day, Christmas Eve, we caught the bus to downtown Oakland. We each had a shopping bag. We put our old coats on, with the usual rips in the top inside portion of the linings, ready and open to fill.

We roamed in and out of the stores from twelve noon that day, shoplifting and stealing among the great hordes of people—games, junk, cap pistols and caps, marbles, small dolls, candy and cookies, slinkies, pick-up sticks, and Old Maid cards, five decks each; everything from more wrapping paper and ribbons to apples and oranges when we got hungry.

We told Mama, that night, we had spent all our money, and said we had other money that she did not save, that we had saved on our own from the bottles and flowers. We still had the money she'd given us in our pockets as we lied glibly to Mama with the pleasurable excitement of Christmas in our house. At one point Mama sang "Silent Night" to herself as she cooked, and in our bedroom, we wrapped presents.

We were up the next morning before the sun rose. We didn't have BB guns, wagons, bicycles, or scooters. Betty didn't have a dollhouse and all. But we had all our presents that we had wrapped and given to ourselves, and we had presents we gave Mama and Daddy. We went outside early; no one had to ask us, "What did you get for Christmas?" Some did brag about bigger and larger toys, but we surprised our friends when we handed out wrapped presents from all of us.

Through our rear bedroom window, after school one day, I saw a lot of people and some government project men and their cars. I opened the window and jumped out onto the ground, and ran down the short sloping hill. People were clapping their hands and singing, standing out in front of one of the project buildings, and other people's heads were sticking out their windows. "We shall not be, we shall not be moved." Everyone was singing but two government project men, standing out, looking toward the crowd of people.

"Just like a tree that's planted by the water, we shall not be moved." A man was saying, "We can't let them move us out like this——"

"You-all children get back away," someone said. But I didn't want to get back.

"So, we staying right here!" a man standing at the top of the stairs shouted. "We going to *fight back!*"

" 'Cause we 'ain't got no place to go, but down to a poorer life."

"Amen, you tell it" and "Uh *huh!*"

"Mrs. Seale!" Mrs. Freeman, our neighbor, called out distressfully. "Oh, Mrs. Seale?"—in a worrying tone of voice—"Oh, Mrs. Seale. Honey, Lord these chilluns done gone to *stealing!* Oh, Mrs. Seale!" Her loud sorrowful tone of voice sounded out as she walked closer and closer.

Our front door flew open. "What is it?" Mama was looking with a worrying and questioning face at Betty and me standing there in our overcoats in the summer heat.

"Stealing?!" Mama exclaimed. Then she stood looking at the Chinese storeowner who had chased us and who had stopped there in front of the door.

"Lord, honey, I just don't know," Mrs. Freeman said.

The Chinese storeowner said to Mama, "You parent? They steal out my store. They rob all time." He held the cookies in his hand, gesturing. "I see them before."

"Betty Jean, Bobby, John Henry? You-all get on in this house," Mama said to us with an angry but disgusted realization. Then she quickly mauled my head as I tried to step by her fast, ducking her oncoming balled-up fist, but Mama mauled and knuckled me hard, and then Betty.

"They steal. I catch your boy. He your boy, huh?"

"Yes," Mama said. "Ah, step inside please."

The Chinese man stepped past Mama inside the open door a couple of steps. "No like to—no want your boy to steal. They all steal. See, see, let me show." The man walked over to me then, pulling my coat and showing the shape of something in the lining of the coat.

"Get them coats on off, you hear me, Betty, Bobby?" Mama went through the coats, putting all the items on the table.

The evidence spoke for itself.

"You not let kid steal at my store. I not tell police."

Our shoplifting thieving ring was broken up. Mama had Daddy whip each of us that night with a short whiplike belt that Mrs. Freeman gave her. We really got it, buck naked. At one point I jumped out the open window, running from the terrible licks of the whip he lashed me with. Daddy came outside in the night and took me back inside and finished the whipping.

Babe, John, Robert Jr. and I were in the yard under the tree shooting marbles. Louise had wanted to play. Babe and Robert Jr. flatly rejected the idea.

"I ain't playing with no silly girl," Babe said.

"I can shoot better than you-all," she argued.

I stood ground with Babe and the boys my age.

"Old stupid girl," Babe said.

"You a old stupid boy."

"Aw, Louise, go away and leave us alone," I said to her. "You don't know nothing about playing with nobody."

"I can do anything you-all can do."

"Aw, you can't do nothing," Babe put in.

"I can climb that tree and jump any place down at the creek. And I bet I can shoot marbles better than all of you-all put together," she angrily retorted, then stuck out her tongue. She went and sat up on the red brick wall.

"Aw, girl, you can't do nothing."

"I bet you-all can't *fuck* like I do," Louise said. " 'Cause I got a real pussy!"

"Nasty!" Babe said. "Old nasty girl."

"Old nasty girl," we all said in some unison.

THE SELF-RIGHTEOUS SINNER

"And you-all's dicks can't even fuck!"

"Your mouth's nasty, Louise," Babe said.

"See, see? I got a pussy."

I looked around, astonished and surprised. Louise had raised up her dress sitting there on the brick wall, and was pulling the crotch of her drawers to one side and spreading the lips of her pussy open, showing a pinkish red spot.

"Girl, you nasty; look, Babe!"

Babe looked, then Robert Jr., and we stopped looking, turning our heads away.

"*Awkk*!" Babe gestured. "She nasty!" Then he spat. "Let's go. *Ugh*!"

Babe picked up a rock and threw it at her, and Robert Jr., John, and I followed suit; we threw rocks at her, driving her away. "Old nasty ugly girl!" We finally got her to run away, dodging the rocks, ducking behind the clothesline fences.

Over the next days, I kept up the talk scorning her as nasty. Inside I felt I wanted to try and do it and see if she could make a baby, but I couldn't let Robert Jr. and Babe know.

One day everybody was outside playing and I saw Louise go into her house. I snuck off from the playing and followed her. She was in the bedroom. I didn't know what to say, but as I came in the room I asked, trying to be friendly, "Say, Louise?"

"Huh?"

"Do you really know how to do it? I know how to do it!" I said.

"Aw, you probably ain't never done it." She cut her eyes at me, then smiled.

"Yeah, I did. A long time ago."

Louise raised up her dress and took her drawers off and stood up against the wall, saying, "Come on," with her dress raised up with one hand. I walked up to her and she grabbed at my dick while it was still inside my pants. "Come on—take it out and stick it in."

I took out my erect penis and got up to her placing it up to the hairy lips of her vagina, as she stood against the wall, bracing herself and opening her legs wider; then she took my penis with one hand and guided it in her as I felt it slip into her pussy, and she then put her hands around my back pulling me closer to her.

"Now come on. Move like me," she said, as she began to move her butt around and pull me tight, close to her moving butt, back and forth.

"Louise," I said, "I love you more than you know." I said that believing I'd have to say it to make a baby. As she continued, she seemed to get stronger—panting, pushing her pussy all over my dick. Then we heard the front door open, and I split out the window.

I wondered would Louise now have a baby? I hoped she would. I could not let anyone know about it, especially Babe and Robert Jr. They would say it was nasty and scorn me and probably wouldn't want to be friends or play games with me anymore.

*

Emptying the garbage, I took the glass objects out and threw them against the knee-high red brick wall, shattering the glass into bits. I had been told not to "break that glass like that, 'cause somebody will get hurt."

"I ain't going to hurt nobody."

I reared back, taking aim, and threw the jar. As it left my hand sailing through the air toward the bricks, I saw seven-year-old Willie Lee jump, hopping toward the jar with a stick in his hand, his right arm stretched out trying to stop the jar. The jar caught him on the naked portion of his forearm: "Ooooow, ooooooow!" made me know he was really hurt.

Then I saw the blood. Blood was gushing from his arm, so much blood. I grabbed onto him—I actually thought in that moment his arm might fall off. I was scared and shocked at all that blood, as Willie Lee whooped and hollered, and I held onto him.

"You ain't had no business breaking that glass," Mrs. Freeman said. Suddenly she was there. "I told you, Bobby, I told you." Mrs. Freeman took Willie Lee by the arm, slapping my tight grip off. "This child's going to bleed to death if we don't get him to a hospital right away!" she cried in a frightful and terrifying rushing voice. "Oh, my God, he's going to bleed to death!"

I stayed in the house, worried and scared and ashamed, the rest of the day. I could hear talk about a big hospital bill Mama and Daddy would have to pay, and how I shouldn't have been throwing that glass and breaking it. It wasn't until late that night I found out that Willie Lee wouldn't die.

A rubber-gun war was on, down at the creek. We would cut a strip off an old inner tube and stretch it over a gun-shaped piece of wood, put rocks into it for ammunition, or even bent-up nails. We had this kind of rubber rifles we'd made and rubber machine guns, and I made a couple of rubber cannons on platforms it took four of us to pull. We, the Harrison Street kids, were wearing the Wilson Street kids out. I was almost twelve years old, wearing patched and starched khaki britches, tennis shoes, and a summer short-sleeved shirt. We had fought this particular rubber-gun war for quite a while. Most of us wouldn't stay dead long, unless we had run out of ammunition, become injured, or had to go home because our mothers had called us. My street's kids decided that I should go back to our treehouse store of ammunition and get the reserve supplies. The ammunition was left there in case we had to retreat to the courtyard.

So I sped up Fifth Street, to go for more ammunition from our treehouse. I climbed the tree, got the supplies, climbed down and headed for the creek. Then I heard a woman screaming.

I looked up. She was maybe a block away. She was screaming, hollering, and running on the grass, coming in my direction. She was fat. She was almost stumbling, and waving her arms in the air.

"Help! Help! He's going to kill me, help!"

A man came after her. *Boooom!* A loud startling shot rang out! Quickly again—*booooom!* The woman kept running, and then she did fall. The man caught up and he was whipping the woman with his gun while she scrambled on the ground waving her hands and trying to dodge and kick. Blood was gushing from her face and head. Then he kicked her and kicked her, then paused, cussing her as she lay on the ground.

People started shouting: "Lord, Lord, somebody call the police. That man's out there killing her!"

Somebody hollered, "Bobby, get away from there."

The woman tried to scramble away onto the grass and the man with the pistol kicked her again. Then he stomped her again and again in the head. Blood was everywhere—on the man's shirt, on the gun, on the sidewalk, and on the green grass. The woman was bloody all over.

An old black car came up the street and squealed to a halt. A black soldier jumped out, came running, hollering out, "Nigger, you need killing, doing my sister like that!"

Boooom, boooom, boooom. Three rapid shots.

The soldier's arms flew up in the air, he stopped and stumbled back somewhat, then he slammed to the ground, face down, his arms stretched out in front of him.

"Lord, Lord, he done killed somebody. Lord, Lord, call the police," a woman's voice was hollering. "Why, why did that man have to do something like that?"

Then the man who was beating his wife walked off at a fast pace, swinging his arms with the pistol in his hand.

People from everywhere came around once the man was gone. Mothers and children came out of their houses. All the rubber-gun gang kids, both Wilson and Harrison streets, had come up. I wanted to cry but I held back the tears.

Then I heard sirens, and the police cars and the ambulance drove up. The policemen got out of their cars, pushing and telling everybody: "All right, let's get back. All right, let's everybody go home. Come on, let's go home." Then they said, "All right, you people, who saw what happened?"

"I ain't saw nothing," a few people were mumbling to themselves.

And I hollered out, "I saw it. I saw what happened."

"Who saw it?" the policeman asked out.

"I saw—" Mrs. Freeman grabbed me and put her head down to me, looking directly in my eyes, and said firmly to me in a low voice while she squeezed my arm till it hurt, "Shut your mouth, Bobby boy, you ain't saw nothing, and you ain't got no business saying nothing to no policeman." She grabbed me by the ear with her other hand and began twisting, hurting me, and walking me toward our house. "You hear me? That man'll come back here and kill you. Now you get on in this house, boy, till your Mama comes home from working!"

"Repent now, from thieving!"

"Amen! Yes, Lord!"

"Repent now, from lying and cheating on thy neighbor!"

"Help me, Jesus!"

"Repent now from gambling and fighting and whoremongering—and you youngsters, some of you-all trying to lay up with each other, living in *sin*!"

"Amen. Yes, Lord."

"Tell them about it! Yes! Yes! Yes!" one lone woman's voice responded. I was half awake. It registered in my mind that the service in that hot church was getting closer to an end.

The shouting at one point had been too much. Ushers and others had carried uncontrollable women out into the air. It scared me when they shouted, jumping up and down, some even spitting and slobbering at the mouth. Pleading, crying, and praising the Lord in nondeliberate but apparent violence, slinging, slamming, and striking and seemingly hurting themselves, with a few people getting out of their way. I always wondered and feared that my Mama would all of a sudden jump up and shout, too.

Mama was all dressed up in her Sunday hat. There was a churchy smell of face powder and women's sachet perfume and the large church was redolent with cleanliness, with five hundred people from the top balcony to the main-floor pews. The Reverend Watson beckoned and preached and near the end of service made his weekly call for those who "have been born in sin—come forth now! Don't be lost in a world of sin, bound for hell, fire, and brimstone!"

"Bobby," Mama sadly and softly said to me, "you ought to go on and join church. You don't want to be lost in hell. Bobby, the Lord is calling for all sinners. You ought to join now and be in the house of God." Mama went on with this now familiar plea: "And you accountable for your sins now. You twelve years old." I didn't move; I sat there, then I looked at

Mama with tears running down her face. "I don't want to see you going to hell, Bobby."

But I wanted freedom from church and the threat of the devil and death. I wanted freedom from the *fear* of hell.

"They fighting!" I hollered out to Babe, George, Robert Jr., and the others. "They—they fighting! Hey, look!" I tore out running under the warm midday sun, down the short hill across the long lawn in back of our apartment building.

Two black men were literally beating up four government project men, and some women were helping them. Others were trying to break it all up and finally did, shouting that they didn't want to "lose the issue!"

But the raging mad crowd of people, black and some white, taunted the government project men, making them get into their car. When they started up the engine of the car, a furious cussing crowd surrounded it. Some strong big black men picked up the rear of the old 1947 Ford, lifting its rear end up off the ground, then the car's rear wheels were spinning as the driver was gunning the motor loudly.

"Turn it over! Flip they asses over!" somebody coached.

The men held the car for what seemed like a short while. The people cussed the four government project men out. A wild low-rating conversation went on at the front car window as I ran around the other side out into the street. Men working at the pipe factory had stopped work and were looking on.

The men dropped the rear wheels to the ground, peeling and burning rubber as the car jumped forward, speeding, then slowed, made a U-turn, and came speeding back down the street as people got out of the way. I hopped to the sidewalk along with everybody else as the driver headed the fast-speeding car toward the curb, and more people jumped back, hollering and telling everybody to get back. Someone grabbed hold of me, jerking me back as the car's left wheels jumped up on the sidewalk with its right wheels in the street, whizzing by barely missing the seething, cussing crowd of protesting people.

"The sons of bitches! Trying to kill us now!" I remember some man excitedly exclaiming.

After that the people milled and rallied with a speaker; they talked, raved, shouted and made statements of standing and fighting. A half hour later, three government cars and five Berkeley police cars pulled up and another cussing raging protest had started.

The police got out of their cars, arresting a few people, and——

"We ain't moving, God damn it!"

"Now these police ain't shit, you-all!" a woman hollered out.

"Let me go, motherfuckers," a black man said, and then knocked one policeman down, making him sprawl on the ground.

That day people fought. Taking policemen's clubs, fist-fighting, turning cars over in the street, and one government car being set afire and the fire department coming to put it out. I do not know why the police did not draw their guns and shoot people, but policemen were beaten that day and were run off, leaving with a few people already handcuffed and locked in the back of cars. More than a hundred people, the great majority being black men and women, and a few white ones, all fought to save our houses, our apartments. They stayed there in vigil for days. The police and government people did not come back.

"Is we still going down to the tracks?" Duffy asked hopefully. He was talking about the railroad tracks, so we could try to make five dollars walking a racehorse over to the racetrack stables at Golden Gate Fields.

I went over to him. I had a sort of hip, bopping walk now, trying to reject being a child. "Aw, man, I don't know if I can go." But I wanted to go bad. "My Daddy's going to pick me up at twelve."

"Aw, man!" Duffy sighed. There was a pause. "You think they down there now?"

"They might be." I stood there wondering, figuring and thinking. Daddy wanted to pick me up at noon and take me to help him in the shop, and my Mama told me to wait for him, but I wanted to walk horses. The horses won out, and we left, walking down the spur track. I kept looking back, just in case I saw my Daddy's green pickup truck.

We got there too late. Shit! I thought to myself.

"They gone, man," Duffy said, sort of sad.

"I sure wish I hadn't waited."

"Yeah," Duffy sighed.

"Say, Duffy, let's go on over to the stables. We can hop a fence, man. We might still get a chance to feed a horse some hay and walk him around."

"Okay! Let's go." Duffy was excited again.

I led the way, running across the giant empty lot with the piles of dumped dirt, weeds, and bushes. We turned up the street.

In the instant when I heard the squealing of tires, the motor seemed behind me, then the car's horn blared out. I hopped into a fast run, but it all happened too fast. The horn of the car blared out again, then I was hit, right in the behind, and I was sailing through the air! I landed on my stomach, my feet stretched out wide apart in back of me. When I hit the ground thousands of small pebbles and sand grains dug into my knees and hands. Suddenly I was being dragged, in a sitting position, by my left foot, caught under the sliding tire of the car to the left of my face. I'm being pulled along, I'm being destroyed, mutilated, my butt dragging the ground. The car stopped.

"Take it off! Oooowaaaa! Take it off! Take it off!" I yelled at the top of my lungs, in panic. Dust was in my mouth and clouded up all around me as I hollered and screamed.

"You hurt, kid?" a voice says, and repeats, "you hurt, huh, kid?"

"Take it off! Take it off! Take if off!" I begged and yelled as my vision cleared. It was a white man. He stepped closer.

"Where does it hurt, kid?" He looked me in the face.

"Take it off—take it off!"

"Oh, God damn!" Now he saw it. He disappeared around the front of the car. The motor roared up, and the car rolled back off my foot.

The white man and Duffy shifted me around, eased me to where my feet and legs normally stretched out in front of me. My eyes were on my left foot now. Blood, pouring out! Meat-cutting men in white aprons came around.

"Oh, I'm going to die!" I whined frantically. "I'm going to die!"

"Take it easy, kid," some white man's voice said.

"Where does this kid live, hey, you know?" a voice asked.

I couldn't stop the blood. I squeezed my hands around my leg harder.

"Take it easy, kid. Take it easy."

The blood wouldn't stop. I would die and go to hell. "Mama, I don't want to go," I now pleaded. "Mama, I don't want to go! I don't want to go to hell!" I yammered and whined and cried, holding onto my foot until an ambulance came. I was put on a gurney by a Berkeley policeman, who tied something around my leg. A medic gently wrapped my foot. All during this procedure I kept asking and saying: "I'm going to bleed to death—am I going to die?"

And they kept saying, "You going to be all right, kid. We're taking you to the hospital and you're going to be okay, kid."

I was quiet. They convinced me I wasn't dying, but I knew my foot was mutilated. Destroyed. I'd never run again. I had won first- and second-place ribbons in school track meets——

"He's right in here, Mrs. Seale," said a white nurse's voice.

"You feel bad? You hurt real bad?" Mama asked me, tears in her eyes.

"It's pretty bad," the doctor said. "We'll have to amputate."

The doctor threw the sheet back, showing my foot. Mama looked and gasped, "Oh, Lord! Lord, please——"

"We'll have to amputate," the doctor said again.

I knew exactly what "amputate" meant. I imagined an axe being used to cut off my foot. I was being punished by God for not having asked forgiveness for my sins, for not joining church. I was scared; I looked at Mama——

"We'll have to take it off," the doctor said.

"Take it off?" Mama's voice changed. She had a loud tone now; she was mad. "No, sir! No sirree! You ain't cutting off his foot. No!"—vigorously shaking her head—"no!"

"Well, I don't know if we can save it."

"Well, I don't care. You ain't cutting my boy's foot off," Mama argued in determination. I had happy tears in my eyes, looking and listening to Mama. "Somebody can save it," Mama was saying. "And whatever doctor I can get, the best one around, that's who I *want*! You ain't chopping off my boy's foot!" Mama wasn't crying. She staunchly rejected any talk from the doctors about amputating my foot. Mama hadn't picked up on the word at first, but she sure had it now! "So long as it ain't nothing about taking off my boy's foot," Mama said, "I just want to know the best doctor around. Well, whoever, I'll pay them!" Mama sounded mad. "Who is he? I got the money!" she shot out.

"You want a——"

"I want to get the best!"

I had not seen my mother like this before; she was in such a rage.

After some two days and two nights on the road, late in the summer, we arrived at the farm in Jasper, Texas. I acutely remembered the farm; fresh country air and cow- and horse-manure odor blended with the happy welcoming voices of uncles and aunts and cousins. I became the center of attraction with my crippled foot, with everyone having believed it had been cut off down to a nub. We were all finally put to bed. Tucked under the thick homemade quilt, I fell asleep to the night sound of crickets outside.

For the first three or four days, we shucked corn, fed the livestock, and went from farm to farm, visiting.

My cousins Alvin and Lewis, who were my age, and Herman—a year older—and I had taken off barefooted, with our drop lines, to go fishing in that summer heat, walking down the sandy dirt country roads. Herman spotted a cottonmouth moccasin and killed it with a stick. Looking at the dead snake's white wide-open mouth, I shivered all over when Herman told me how dangerous the snake was and how one would be sure to die if bitten by such a snake. I wished we had worn shoes.

"It's hot," Herman said. "Let's swim, and then go fishing." I looked the swimming hole over as I waited for all of them to go in first. I wanted to be sure there were no cottonmouths there. John waited too, then he took off

his clothes and jumped in buck naked. My fear of snakes eased as everyone swam and frolicked in the cool water. When the playful swimming
noise would suddenly become quiet for a quick moment, I could faintly
hear a car or two pass periodically, in the far distance of the woods,
speeding by to somewhere.

"Come on, Bobby," Lewis kept saying to me, and finally I decided. I
jumped in stark naked and came up out of the water and began to do a
smooth-stroking American crawl, sort of showing off.

"Boy, old Bobby can really swim."

"Sure swim proper," another one said.

Then I turned and swam back across the wide long deep water up to
Lewis and we threw water into each other's faces with the heels of our
palms. It must have been a little while, we were still in the water swimming
and playing, when a gun sounded. I whirled around, floating in the water.
Just off the bank of the waterhole was a white man aiming a gun. There
was another white man and a woman smiling and laughing.

"*Boom!*" The pistol went off again. He was shooting at us! I looked
around to see which of us had been shot, as fear ran through me. We were
shocked and quiet as a pin, floating, looking at them. Then Herman
turned and swam. The man aimed again.

"Little black niggers are scared to death, Joe."

The white man with the gun laughed. "Yeah."

"Let me see if I can just shoot off a few arms and legs."

Boom! Boom! Boom! The pistol went off and I shivered. The water
ripples indicated he was shooting at us—maybe to kill us.

The man was beginning to reload the gun. The white woman was
laughing: "Look at them go. Ha, ha, ha."

"Bobby, Bobby, let's go, come on!"

Right! I've got to get out of here, my mind told me. Fear was all over me.
I turned and stroked away fast, pulling and separating the water. He
would shoot me. The white folks would kill me. I swam harder and
faster—it was taking so long. I swam on the surface, then ducked under
the water to swim, thinking, I'll keep him from shooting me. I couldn't see
much of anything under the water—*Blam!*—I ran into something—
the roots of a tree—I turned around under the water, still holding my
breath. Which way should I go? I kicked out, swimming under the water.
Then I decided to surface. I looked around and saw the three white
people laughing, and the one white man aiming the pistol at me—
Boom!

The sound of the shot made my flesh crawl, as I found myself scrambling up on the bank of the swimming hole. I was last out, everybody else
was gone! I could see John, naked, dashing off through the woods. I cut

out hopping and running in his direction, then looking back at the laughing white people.

Boom! Another shot rang out! I hopped away.

After that episode, I really believed that white folks down South would kill us Negroes. White people down South were mean.

I could see across the courtyard at first dark, as I turned the corner. Our apartment building was in front of me, the door was wide open. A loud cursing commotion was going on at our house. My Daddy was yelling angrily.

"George Seale!" I heard Mama saying in a scorning, sharp, hating manner. "Your black ass is going straight to hell! 'Cause you ain't nothing but a—" Aunt Zelma was shouting and Alvin was begging my Daddy, then I could see in the doorway Mama, Aunt Zelma, and Alvin all tussling with Daddy. All in one moment Daddy hollered: "God damn it, Thelma!" and raised up an ice pick over Mama. "I'll kill——" He was coming down with the ice pick. I ran like lightning for the door, six-seven yards away. The door suddenly slammed shut, and I was still outside it.

A scream shrieked out amidst tumbling sounds. It was Mama, and I jumped at the door trying to open it, but it was locked—Daddy was stabbing Mama to death with the ice pick!

Alvin was pleading, "Uncle George, don't hurt Aunt Thelma," and "You going straight to hell, George!" Aunt Zelma hollered.

I couldn't get into the house. I kicked the door and pushed and beat it with my body and head and hands. Panic—my mind reeled—my Daddy was killing my Mama——

I was shaking all over, I was crying, as the rumbling, cussing commotion went on behind the door and I began to yell, drowning it out, then screaming to the top of my lungs. Mama was being killed by my Daddy. I ran out into the courtyard, screaming and yelling, and I went into hysterics, falling to the ground kicking and beating my arms and legs all over, and rolling in the dusty dirt: "Oh, God! God, God, God!"

My body tumbled to a nothingness, a blob of nonexistence.

The next thing I remember, I was being held by someone, beginning to come to my senses. "Bobby, Bobby!" someone said, and I was shivering. "Bobby, is you all right now. Bobby. Bobbeee!" And I clung to and grabbed her heavy body, holding tight, and submerged my head under her chin; her bosom was soft and comforting.

"Bobby, it's all right," and she pulled me up off the ground and walked me. She held and hugged me as I clung to her and smelled her familiar odor. My mind was dazed and frightened, and then I began to realize that this was my Mama. We were in the kitchen, then. Mama held me tight, saying everything was all right.

Mama wasn't dead. Daddy had not killed her.

Daddy walked into the living room and calmly asked me, "Bobby, what was the matter? Is you all right?" But I just shook my head up and down timidly, gesturing "Yes sir."

"Bobby, what was the matter. Is you saved?" Aunt Zelma asked.

"Bobby, what was wrong?" Mama asked.

"I thought you was dead, Mama," I quietly said, in a quivering tone of voice. "But you ain't, Mama, and I'm going to do right, Mama."

"The Lord done spoke to him." Aunt Zelma said.

"Why you think that, Bobby?" Mama asked.

"Daddy, he, he, he was——"

"Aw, Bobby, we was just arguing," Mama reassured me, and told me to go and wash my face and take off my clothes and lie down——

I decided that night lying in bed that I did believe in God.

The blues and boogie music that played was all a sin to me now. The cussing and dancing that Robert Jr.'s parents and other grown folks did was now wrong, in my view. I did not run around with Robert Jr. much any more because he cussed. If I could only get him to stop doing wrong, since I knew him, that would be a good thing. I'd told him so, and he didn't like it, telling me I was a Christian fool.

Our friendship lessened as I stuck my nose up at him, walking off with my sense of being saved—even though I knew I had not been baptized or anything. But I would not sin.

When I came into the courtyard, who did I see but Aunt Zelma, fighting with what she called sinning neighbors, whom she believed had done something to Betty and Alvin. I knew Aunt Zelma disliked them because they were Catholics—but I saw her now violating her own Christian code of believing that fighting was a sin. She and Mrs. Brown, Gloria's mother, were really striking some blows, and it was over in a minute or two with Aunt Zelma's harsh cuss words and her threats to knock Mrs. Brown's brains out.

"I'll put your nasty ass in hell, bitch," Aunt Zelma said.

Wow! I really had to think on that. I was now in my fifth month of not sinning.

One night Alvin scared the hell out of everybody. He was shouting to the Lord and talking to God in "tongues." He ran all through the house waking everybody. Then he went out into the night with only his shorts and T-shirt on. After waking practically everybody, Alvin was told by his mother to get on his knees and pray—right outside in front of our apartment building. He did; with Aunt Zelma standing there, Alvin kneeled by a garbage can, he prayed and cried and begged the Lord to save him. I felt sorry for him because I knew he had really awakened from a nightmare.

Just before the beginning of summer, my father came home with a forty-four passenger army-surplus bus. That summer, the farm-labor contracting business gave us a new task, going to the fields every day. At 4:30 A.M., Betty, John, Mama, Daddy, and I would drive off to Eighth and Clay. Daddy would charge people one dollar apiece for a ride out to the fields in his Army bus. At the fields, the farmer would pay Daddy a dollar a head for bringing out the laborers. It was a real hustle on our part, and on the contractors' part.

"We got strawberries!" Daddy answered somebody getting ready to step into the bus.

"Is they any good?" the man asked.

"They better than any other I ever picked," Daddy would say.

All that summer we worked in the fields. We picked peas early, strawberries all season, beans in August. We picked apricots and plums—we'd shake the plums off the tree with a long pole, and pick them up off the ground, put them in boxes, identify the boxes with chalk marks. Daddy acted like some kind of foreman, and he'd have me doing the bookkeeping for him.

After a while, we took out two seats from the bus and put in a hot grill, where Mama made and sold sandwiches. We sold soda pop, too, there and in the fields. Daddy tried to tell Mama to charge a high price, since we could get away with it, but she wouldn't.

If you were caught outside your own particular territory—if you lived in the Village and you were caught being in North Oakland, say—then you were likely to get a good ass-kicking. But one night, thinking it would be cool to go to a party in North Oakland, we set out for a good time.

We'd been dancing an hour or so when a crash-the-party fight broke out. We were scared as hell. I pulled out my knife and backed off in a corner, holding my open knife down to my side, hoping and looking for a way out of there.

My friend Jerry grabbed my arm saying, "Let's go out the window." We jumped down into a flowerbed. There were fights out in the middle of the street and people coming out the window behind us and people trying to get away and the screaming and painful moans of people being hit with sticks and boards. We ran halfway down the block. We stopped a couple of minutes and watched, then decided somebody might get shot or killed, so we might as well go home.

We continued to look behind us as we walked—then we heard, "There they are!" Some dudes were running a block behind us, coming our way.

"Let's go!" Jerry hollered out. "Let's step, Bobby." And we took off running. I just knew someone was going to shoot at us now.

After many blocks, we looked back and noticed no one was coming behind us now. Panting hard, we walked on—if we could make ten more blocks, we would be past Ashby Avenue, in a place where we would be ok.

We were at the corner in front of a drugstore when we heard some cussing noise a block behind us: a carload of hollering young dudes drove by speeding down the street. Then some more people came running around the corner past us. About eight dudes came around the corner. Jerry and I were backed into the drugstore entrance as they stopped, looking at us, saying: "Yeah, these the motherfuckers."

I already had my knife out, open, holding it down in back of my leg.

A few more dudes walked up to us, one with a brick in his hand and the other looking six feet and husky with blood pouring down his light-brown face; he had a heavy piece of wood in his hand. "I'm busting some head open, motherfucker," he said, raising up the piece of wood. I stepped back and raised my knife, scared as hell.

A car drove up, squeaking to a halt right in front of us. Some seven or eight more dudes jumped out this car, saying, "Let's bust some head!" My hands were sweating, holding the knife. We would get killed.

"Wait a minute. Hold it," somebody said. I caught his face—it was Robert Jr.; he walked through the crowd of mad crazy niggers that surrounded us. "Naw, man, this is my cousin. No! You motherfuckers can't fuck him up!"

"But——"

"You heard me. Nobody jumps on my cousin. You heard me, mother fucker—move!" Robert Jr. ordered. "You got the wrong cat."

Damn! They moved back. He seemed in charge of them all. I hadn't seen him for a year since he had gone to Juvenile Home and his family moved.

The worst talked-about gang was the San Francisco Earring Gang. I had heard they killed dudes, cut them up, and shot them. I wanted no part of those notorious people, no run-in with them, as I heard they were now on this side of the bay, in Oakland. I carried my pocketknife everywhere in case someone wanted to fuck with me. I was running with the Village

Gang, a half-dozen boys from the project houses. We didn't have any special jackets or anything—we were individually trying to dress sharp and cool, keeping starched shirts on, wearing pegged pants or unwashed Levis with the waist worn across our asses, hair conked. I was fifteen years old at the time.

It was all over Berkeley High that some bad dudes from North Oakland were coming to Berkeley and beat everybody's asses. The previous Friday evening some Berkeley and North Oakland dudes had got into a fight at the skating rink. Rumors spread that on Tuesday, everybody would have it out.

I made seven clubs in school Monday, together with one other kid from the Village Gang—Tuesday, everybody was walking up to me asking me to make them clubs too. I made fifteen more foot-long clubs. As fast as I turned one out on the wood lathe and drilled a hole, a half-inch wide, six inches deep, Bill would take it and sneak it over to the plumbing section of general shop and get some friends to pour molten lead down the hole.

Berkeley High was ready. We all headed down Grove Street, and I mean the sidewalks were packed for three long blocks. There were more than three hundred of us, including the Village Gang. It was righteously a sight, everybody talking about kicking some ass, gripping and swinging clubs, testing and gesturing with bicycle chains and knives. Big shit was being talked when suddenly somebody hollered, "Here they come! They coming, man, that's they car."

"Come on, motherfuckers!" We started yelling out and daring everybody.

Dude after dude got out of the car with clubs, chains, and knives, and it seemed like twenty dudes piled out of that car. Two even got out of the trunk. That sort of blew my mind as I also realized they didn't seem scared at all.

Then from their side, someone hollered, "Let's kill these motherfuckers!" *Bang! Bang! Bang!* Adrenalin shot through me. Three rapid gunshots from their side and they came running across the street.

Berkeley High scattered in all directions. All the hundreds of us were moving, getting away from there. The Village Gang and I were stepping, humping down the street. I ran among the panic-stricken crowd, crippled as I was, ducking, sprinting, hopping hedges and across lawns, and even through some white folks' backyards.

The Village Gang, including Pogie and me, had made it to the South Berkeley YMCA dance. This was three weeks or more after the Berkeley and North Oakland mess.

After a few dances, I wanted to wipe the sweat off my brow. I walked over to Pogie and some dude he was talking with, to ask Pogie to let me use the handkerchief he had in his hand.

"Say, Pogie, man, let me use your snotrag," I said, bopping up to him, believing I was sounding righteously cool, making up a slang that quick.

"This ain't mine," Pogie started to say.

"Motherfucker! My handkerchief ain't no snotrag!" the dude said angrily.

"Oh, hey, I'm sorry, man. I was just saying it like——" I stopped, looking him in the face as he was acting like he was tough. At this time of life, Betty's boyfriends were telling her I looked like I was mean. "I'm not mean," I'd tell her; but if I look that way, I thought, maybe I can use it—it's as good as talking bad. I said to this angry dude, "Fuck it, man," and turned away.

"Say, look!" the dude said. "I don't like this motherfucker calling my handkerchief a snotrag."—then, to me—"Who you think you is anyway?"

I got that initial scared feeling and slid my hand in my pocket, taking a step back, putting my hand on my knife.

"Oh, you think you bad," he said, bracing a little. "This dude thinks he's cool. But fucking with me, he's a God damn fool."

I turned to my right a little, my thumbnail in the groove of the blade, ready to pull my knife out and whip it open without him seeing it. I was nervous inside, telling myself if he makes one wrong move toward me, I'm going to cut him. I'm going to cut this dude wide open.

"Look you," he said, "you better be gone when the dance is over, 'cause I'm going to kick your ass."

"Naw, motherfucker!" I got angrier. "If you fuck with me, I'll cut your ass wide open. And Pogie'll let you know that I cuts!"

The dude looked at me. "Just be gone, motherfucker."

"Come on, man," Pogie was saying, pulling at my shoulder. I stepped off with him. "Look, Bobby, that dude is bad, man. I mean, I knew him from jail. Stay out of his way. I mean, he got partners and they rough, man."

I was determined not to let this dude scare me off from the dance. I felt if I could just get the rest of the Village Gang to make sure none of the rest of the dude's gang jump in, I could beat him or at least let him know where I was at.

But: "Say, Bobby, man, I can't help you man." And: "I might fuck up some of my action in that part of town, man." And: "Man, look, why don't you just leave, man. It ain't no big thing."

That really made me mad! I knew if it came down to it, I would stick with any of them in a crisis. But they were running out on me.

Shit! I knew I couldn't handle those dudes alone. The dance was almost over. I went outside; I picked up a board I saw lying on the ground, ready to surprise him, knock the shit out of him. Then I thought about them dudes running out on me like that. I felt nervous, embarrassed, ashamed. After a few minutes I decided that I wasn't going to get my ass kicked over this shit, or even possibly killed.

If I only had a gun, I'd blow every last one of those motherfuckers' brains out! I left, wishing that; went on home.

PART III

Nigger Tarzan

IN THE SPRING when I was fifteen, death was on my mind, off and on, very seriously. Death was something that I would struggle to prevent from happening. I would just be cool, I planned, carry my knife, stop running around with that jive Village Gang, and stay out of the way of other fools who would want to jump on me for nothing.

If I could only fix the gun John found, I'd have a good pistol. A real gun of my own. I could shoot anyone who might try to hurt, beat, or kill me.

Lying on the grass, I suddenly saw a jet fighter streaking faster than the speed of sound. I sat up, trying to imagine death caused by an atomic blast. I'd read and heard that if an atomic bomb was dropped, everyone within a three-mile radius would die. San Francisco, right next door, was a city everybody said the Russians wanted to destroy. If a blast came, I then planned, in five minutes I could hot-wire and steal a car, and get Mama, Betty, and John together with whatever food we could carry. If there was a thirty-minute warning period, in twenty minutes we would be far out of range of an atomic blast——

I lay there on the grass where the woman had been beaten to a bloody pulp, and her husband had shot and killed the soldier. It seemed like trying to avoid a violent death was hopeless.

I looked toward Howard's Corner Store, resting back on my elbows, and saw Steve Brumfield walking up the street. He stepped sure-footed, in clean white tennis shoes. He had a dirk knife in a sheath on his belt. His muscles bulged. His brown face seemed very serious and stern.

I had never talked to Steve before. I wondered about him. I stood up, admiring how strong he looked, then thought—I'll ask him how he got all his muscles. Steve came closer, looking straight ahead. He was a little taller than my five-foot-eight.

He stepped past me. I walked quickly behind him, then walked alongside of him on his right, looking at his "guns," as we called biceps, looking at the handle of the dirk strapped to his belt.

"Hey, Steve—say, man. Ah, you and Alvin used to, ah, lift weights to get big like that, huh?"

"Yes." He kept looking straight ahead, peering out between tight eyelids.

"I sure wish I could get some muscles like that, man."

"Not good for you."

"Yeah? But you *strong*, man!" I exclaimed in admiration.

Steve walked very straight and erect, each step was calculated. I thought how slick it would be to have muscles like that, almost three times the size of mine. I bet *no one* would mess with him.

"Say, Steve, ah, where you going man?" I asked.

"To the hills."

"How long you going to be up there?"

"All day." He still didn't turn his head to look at me when he said something.

"Why you going?"

"It keeps me healthy and strong." He took a quick glance at me. "You want muscles, but bulkiness is no good. A slim, strong man, with a body like yours, can be healthier."

"How about if I come with you, and you hip me?"

"You probably won't be able to keep up with me."

"Yes I can. I been——"

Steve took off running in a steady, not too fast, striding pace. He's gone—I stood looking—Shit, I can probably keep up with him, if that's all the fast he is going to run. I took off running, telling myself I'd try to keep up with him, maybe become friends, and then I could get with him and lift his weights.

Steve got farther and farther away from me, as he headed out across streets and disappeared through buildings. I could see him, still running, two blocks ahead of me. Shit! Maybe I'm too skinny. I knew I only weighed about 120 pounds. But I kept running, watching here and there where I was placing my running steps, making sure I didn't hurt my injured foot. When I got to Tenth Street, I couldn't see Steve. When I got to Marin, I could see him striding and pacing, like a long-distance runner, four short blocks ahead of me. Damn! He could run! I could feel myself getting a second wind, based on a determination to fight against my feeling of being exhausted.

At the base of the Berkeley Hills, I stopped running and walked; I huffed and panted my way to the top. I walked, then stopped a minute, then walked another block and tore out running. I had to show Steve I could keep up, and in several more blocks, I caught up.

I talked and went on about getting some muscles. Steve stopped, took out his knife, cut a piece of branch from a young tree, peeled the bark, and walked, not saying anything to me, not even answering. All of a sudden, he tore out at another running pace, through a dirt trail that wound through trees and growth. I took off also, determined to keep up with him. Now and then, I'd spot him resting a quarter of a mile away, then going over or around those rolling hills, all that day.

It was three or four hours before we got back to Marin Street. When I finally caught up, I said nothing as we walked, tired and hungry.

"You are good," Steve said to me.

Monday in machine-shop class I did all the measuring with micrometers and telescope gauges, and in drafting class I did the drawings for repairing the thirty-two John had found. When school was out, I went hopping down the stairs to the ground floor. When I got near the bottom steps, I tripped and stumbled, sprawled out on the floor. The gun in my belt jumped out, sliding across the floor. I quickly hopped up, scrambled across the hall, and grabbed the gun.

"Hey, Bobby, man, that's a gun! Let me see it." Bill Sanders excitedly reached for it.

I put the gun in my inside suit-coat pocket. "Naw, man, be cool!"

I came out of the building, past the auto shop and over to the corner intersection.

"Say, Bobby." I heard Lee's voice. "Let me see your gun."

"Who told you, man?"

"Benny said he saw you with a gun. What kind is it?" I opened my coat and took the gun out. "Bobby, man, don't get in trouble, man." Lee looked big-eyed at the gun as I held it. "What kind is it?"

I caught someone out of the corner of my eye, walking, then he stopped. I glanced up. It was the dude who had threatened to get all his boys to jump on me at the South Berkeley YMCA dance. Fear was suddenly with me. He was looking at the gun, then at me eyeing him down.

I told Lee I had to go and took the gun. The dude turned quickly and walked fast across the street onto the curb, and stepped on the sidewalk and stood looking back at me.

"I'm not—I'm not fucking with you, man," he said nervously but with a stern face, as though he were ready to fight. I realized there was fear in his voice, and I saw it in his eyes.

When I walked on, after some tough remarks to him, the flashing thought of a dead body was in my mind as I imagined myself having shot him dead. Then I shivered all over, knowing I had surely developed the ability to kill in order to live; at the same time, struggling inside with my anger, in a strange dilemma—not wanting really to kill anyone.

"Say, Bobby," Earl said, "didn't Pogie get busted with a gun that was yours?"

"Who told you that?" I asked.

They all broke in asking at the same time. I denied I ever had a gun. I denied that I gave Pogie the gun. They didn't believe me, though.

Then Earl said I was jiving, and in an angry manner he asked, "Why you don't run with us no more, man?"

"I run with Steve, here. I run with who I want to, man."

When Steve and I walked off, Earl shot out, "Bobby and the Snake Man," making fun of Steve.

"They trying to be funny, Steve," I said, "but they won't fuck with you."

"I know, because they've seen me with snakes. They're afraid of snakes and me. So I don't have to prove anything."

I decided I would never run with them again. Steve and I began to talk about them, and dudes like them. Steve said they always fight each other, that Negroes are stupid. In the days of slavery, Negroes did not fight the white man as the Indians did; the American Indians were strong-minded and healthy.

I was determined to get stronger. We kept going to the hills quite often: during that time Steve pointed out that strength of the body, without strength of the mind, was no good. I asked him what did he mean.

"How many pushups can you do?" Steve asked.

"I don't know, about ten I guess."

"Ok, do ten correct pushups."

I got down on the sidewalk and did the first five correctly. I began to get tired and humped my butt up in the air, straining, on the sixth.

"Naw," Steve said, "correct! Keep your back and legs straight and rigid. In your *mind*, force yourself to do them correct."

I straightened my back. My mind was on that point. I said, "Eight, nine, te—te—ten." I squeezed it out pushing up the tenth.

"Now wait!" Steve quickly said. "Hold your exercise position right there."

"But I'm tired, Steve," I panted.

"Hold it! Hold it! Tell yourself to hold your exercise position."

I held it, struggling with the thought.

"Now, force yourself," Steve instructed, "to do just *one more pushup*. A complete, correct pushup. One more! And don't let yourself fall flat on the ground. Say in your mind, I'll do one more correct pushup. One more!"

To endure and develop a strong body and mind was the basic purpose of personal discipline, Steve emphasized over and over, explaining how Indians could run long distances.

We wondered about how, or whether, the Indians believe in a hell. We stopped at the library one day, looking for books on Indian religion, and the health ways and outdoor living of American Indians. After reading and discussing, we bought moccasins to wear in the hills. We found out that the god of the American Indians was called Wakantanka, and that one died and went to the happy hunting grounds. Hell was not mentioned.

We made our hair straight with conk, and made ourselves look like Indians, but with a shorter haircut.

I told Steve of my hunting ventures with my father, and we wanted to hunt, but on our own. Then we wanted to be good archers with the eighty-pound bows.

Steve and I saw *The Wild Ones*, starring Marlon Brando, three times. We walked out elated with the idea of having motorcycles and riding all over the place, being rebelliously cool. We discussed the term "wild" in relation to free animals, people, and American Indians, and we resolved that we were the wild ones. We kept our short Indian hair styles, but wearing Levis, black motorcycle jackets, and motorcycle boots.

Steve and I developed a righteous rugged outdoor life, testing our bodies and our wills, studying and working to live up to the Indians. That next summer, working on the harvest took me away from that new life. I wrestled with my beliefs and my need to break away from home. On the one hand, not being paid by my father, I felt cheated. On the other, I worked hard to please him.

When harvest season was over and fall was creeping into winter, we had done extremely well, and had about two thousand dollars saved in the bank. I suspected that as soon as my Daddy could find a house we would be moving, finally, into our own home again. But I was glad that season was over, so I could get back to the vigorous outdoor life and running with Steve.

One day while sitting on the Sixth Street lawn, where we had many lance fights, Steve and I took sewing needles and scratched our arms from the inner area of our elbows to the area of our wrists. The nearly two-inch high letters, as thick as a pencil, spelled a blood-seeping word *Sioux* ten inches long. We sat there, letting the blood dry. A few days later I picked at my scabs and the lighter-colored scars spelled the word clearly and stood out in contrast to my brown pigmentation.

Steve and I walked proudly, believing in our conspicuous roles. We wore leather vests, Steve with the yellow-painted drawing of a buffalo bull and the sun, and on my vest the drawings of the sun and trees representative of our names—Watanka and Hanpi.

We pierced our left ears and put in small round earrings. From time to time we would go on twenty-four-hour fasts, not eating anything in an attempt to have visions. We endured sticking hot needles into a quarter-inch of flesh without flinching, lighting matches and letting the hot tips fall on the back of our hands. We felt that if we could inflict pain upon ourselves, then no pain of battle or torture from others would make us yield.

There was a deep seriousness in Steve's manner. We would stand on the corner for hours, not saying a word to anyone as they passed by. People would walk past the corner, staring at us.

Our wrestling matches on the long green lawns became a real show. We would wrestle for the sheer sport of it, throwing and flipping each other everywhere, making wild Indian screams when the feeling got good. We were taking no mercy, knowing that each painful rabbit punch or blow to the body or slam to the ground was all part of developing our bodies and minds.

We began to have lance fights on a long lawn facing Sixth Street. At first we put tennis balls on the lances, not wanting to draw blood. But one particular Monday, we took the balls off. We fought without mercy on each other, knocking each other around. It became mixed with wrestling and flying kicks, and after an hour and a half, there were numerous spectators as we—two strong, bloody, black Indian gladiators—were slamming, striking, blocking, and knocking the natural hell out of each other. We dodged, ducked, and charged, yelling Indian yells, hopping into the air with our swinging lances.

Lee passed by, his joking self, loudly calling, "Nigger Tarzan."

Two Berkeley policemen drove up, standing and looking at us for a while. We ignored them and continued our fight.

When we did stop, still ignoring the police, I noticed there were more than two hundred people standing around. We turned our backs to the cops, walking away. Then we sprayed each other with a cool hose. We got our boots, jackets, and T-shirts, and walked off toward a big tree. The police followed us, along with about thirty or forty people.

"Why the, ah, fighting like that?" We said nothing, not even looking at them. We had no desire to talk to the *Skies*, white soldiers who took the land from our Indian brothers.

"You know, you can be arrested for that."

Steve turned. "Then arrest us. You know there's no law against a sport."

"What are those marks on your arm there?" one *Sky* asked Steve, looking at his arm. "I think he's been shooting dope."

"You are a simple-minded cuss." Steve raised his voice somewhat. "No man could fight in a lance battle like we just did if he shot dope. Both of you are a couple of foolish *Skies*, out of your minds."

The crowd roared, which embarrassed the *Skies*.

"Ok, ok, what's your name?" one irritated *Sky* asked Steve, taking out his pad and pencil.

We answered, "Watanka" and "Hanpi"—and defined the names for them, "Lone Bull" and "Climbs the Tree."

"What do you guys do, study Indian lore or something?"

We looked at each other, then back at them. "We study your ways, of you having enslaved Negroes and robbed our people of their land—but we'll fight your kind any time."

The *Sky* burst out laughing.

"Grown *Skies* with the minds of foolish children," Steve continued. "But who cares, since your ways are the mire of stupidity against nature and life."

The two *Skies* didn't even arrest us. They just left, laughing and joking to each other about us. But to the children standing around, we were heroes. "Nigger Tarzan, they bad! I bet Steve and Bobby would have really whipped them cops if they wanted to fight."

Every Monday had always felt like a new world to me—Mondays I was Nigger Tarzan, a nickname that came to be used admiringly by the younger children. Sunday would always be a dead day, for going to church or for being a sinner when you weren't praying and singing; then Monday I was free to be alive again. Monday I could start again.

We saw the movies *Iron Mistress* and *Saskatchewan*. We identified with the lifelike scenes of Indians riding horses. We now wanted horses, rifles, tomahawks, and an "Iron Mistress"—a Jim Bowie knife. I made the tomahawks in shop class; I also made us each a Bowie knife.

I shined and polished the knives with fine emory and crocus cloth, then, making sure there were no oil spots on the knives, I took the welding torch and carefully heated the thick portion of the backbone of the blade to a light blue, now making the back softer, doing it in a very delicate way. I could see the heat and color changes travel down toward the beveled cutting edge of the bright steel, until the thicker portion of the upper beveled area along the center of the blade began to turn a golden brown. With the tongs, I quickly doused the blade in water. I was elated—I had mastered it! Wow! "The Iron Mistress," I said aloud to myself as Benny and Lee watched and laughed.

Steve and I went down to the leather factory six blocks from my house, broke in, and stole leather: thick and thin leather, half-processed untinted leather, and some other leather that had been colored black.

We put our tomahawks together with wet rawhide. We made sheaths for the knives out of the stiffer, thicker leather, stitching the edges tight with wet rawhide strips, leaving the tomahawks and sheaths in the sun to dry. We each made a pair of moccasins out of some of the leather. Then we made ourselves saddlebags. We made mouth bits—for the horses we rode at night—out of coat-hanger wire and completed the bridle by using leather strips.

We would take off walking on a bright starry night for the hills. It was five or six miles to the ranches. We would quietly open the corral gate and approach the horses, being friendly with them, rubbing and patting them on the neck. We quickly put the homemade bridles on, then walked the horses out the corral gate and closed it. Then, using the horses' manes, we grabbed and pulled, hopping up on to the horses' bare backs in one leaping lunge. Two or three times a month, we would ride. When daylight was coming, we'd ride to the hill crest within a mile from home, and we would let the horses go wild and free in the dawn.

When the harvest started with English peas the next season in May, I was frustrated with the whole idea of working to help get a house, simply because Mama had told me that the nearly two thousand dollars that had been saved had been spent over the winter months, and that Daddy wasted a lot of the money. It seemed we would never get a house. I resolved not to work for my father any more, knowing he wouldn't even pay me.

During those past winter months Steve and I became more the *macho*-Indian, Nigger Tarzan pair, who stood against the norms of society and upheld an ideal of Indian life, at one with nature, someday to rebel and fight for the land. We even spoke our English in a broken idiom, some-times using sign languages like the Indians.

All those months we toughened our bodies and our minds. We prac-ticed throwing our Bowie knives, we did balled-fist pushups on our knuckles to toughen them; we beat our knuckled fists against a tree. We planned and talked of leaving home as soon as we turned eighteen. Many a night we dreamed and talked of taking back everything the white man had stolen. We walked in the night talking of going to South Dakota, to Pine Ridge Reservation, and working on a cattle ranch and maybe getting married to some Indian girls, living under the open skies in an outdoor life that couldn't be matched.

I talked about getting a job and beginning to save money to go to South Dakota. There was a man who wanted someone to do some small carpentry repairs and landscaping at his house, and he would pay a dollar an hour. I checked on the job and got it.

I did a few small house repairs, did gardening, and when school was out, built a form to pour a concrete patio in the backyard. Mama agreed in my behalf when I told my father I had my own job, and that I didn't want to work for him because he wouldn't pay me. He was mad, in a rage, telling me I couldn't work for the man and arguing that he needed me to help him with the harvest.

Two days later, when I got to the man's house ready to do my work, I learned my father had called, told him I could not work for him. That burned me! I resolved that I would never work for George again, believing he had no right to do that. Steve and I planned and schemed—we stole bicycles and left home.

On the highway I felt free, in a speeding moving bliss, covering ground, covering highway—we were gone! Pumping and coasting, riding away from my Village home, headed for Wyoming and the Black Hills of South Dakota.

We got to Sacramento, and beyond it, too, before we knew that this was going to take too long and we weren't up to crossing the High Sierra Mountains. We went back after four days—and we felt good, telling ourselves about the venture, and how our strength and endurance was at a peak. We compared our ability with other young Negroes our age—how they would have never been able to keep up with us on such a trip, an over-two-hundred-mile ride on bicycles, and if some did, their minds would not have let them ride such long distances. I arrived home late at night. Everyone was asleep. I took a shower and oiled my body down and went to sleep in the nude.

My father kept after me, telling me I had to work for him.

One evening I listened to him while I ate, deliberately smacking my food in front of him. He argued that if I was going to stay in the house, I would have to work for him. I stood listening to him, then walked off into our room, his cussing making me angry. As Mama was trying to cool him down, I hopped out the back window.

Most of the time I would stay out until one, two and three o'clock in the morning, then crawl in the back window, sleep with my clothes on, and either awake before my father or hear his voice or movements in the house and get up and leave the house early in the morning—coming back later when he was gone—or meet Steve and go into the hills and camp out. I even started going down to the tracks and sleeping in an empty boxcar.

With our saddlebags over our shoulders, our knives, the twenty-two single shot rifle broken down in the pouch, and our tomahawks, we walked the Union Pacific tracks four miles to the Oakland freight yard at first daylight. We figured on hopping a freight train.

We stepped out across the tracks, ran until we got near a slow-moving train, then slowed, running, matching its speed. We walked the top of the moving, rumbling, high boxcars, jumping from car to car until we climbed down a ladder into the wagon car with its numerous high rolls of steel. We lay down between the rolls of steel and I fell half asleep, aware only of the train's blaring horn at its head engine and the noisy *clickety-clack*.

We were finally on our way to the vast midwestern plains of Wyoming and South Dakota. We would meet Indians at Pine Ridge Reservation and maybe I'd get married someday and have Indian children with a pretty Indian girl. I imagined and dreamed of big thick braids hanging over her shoulders. I made a pillow of my jacket, half dreamed and half slept.

"Hanpi," Steve said.

I sat straight up, then stood up.

"Got any idea where we are?" Steve asked. The train wasn't moving.

"I don't know." It seemed we were in some kind of freight yard. I saw other long trains farther ahead across a wide and long, vast freight yard. Cars up ahead, far away on other tracks, were cut loose one by one and two by two. Groups of cars were coasting by themselves onto different tracks and slamming and locking onto the rear of other trains, making up new trains. I saw the High Sierras in the background.

"We're still in California," I said to Steve.

"Yeah, the mountains," he replied.

"This looks like it's going to take awhile."

We ate our beans and corn nuts, talked for a while, wondered how long it would be, as the train periodically moved a very short distance, then stopped, then moved again, then stopped. I lay back down. The sun was hot, beating down on my face, so I closed my eyes, turned away from the sun, and half dozed off to sleep again.

A voice on a loudspeaker pervaded the area. "Two of them." It was loud.

"Hanpi," Steve said. I raised up, looking at Steve getting his gear together.

"You two! Out of the car!" the loudspeaker blared. "Let's go! Off the freight!" I stood up quickly.

"They're kicking us off." Steve jerked his head toward a high tower with tinted green glass all around at the top. I could make out a white man standing inside the glass, looking straight down at us, binoculars hung around his neck.

I was already snatching up my gear and jacket, putting my tomahawk in through my belt and pants. I followed Steve, climbed over the side of the car, the side away from the tower.

"Hold it. Right there!" A southern drawling voice hollered. "Hands up! In the air, or I'll blow your brains out!" A short white man in khaki dress with sweat soaking his shirt held a pistol on us. "Put them up, you black bastards!"

Steve and I looked at each other, then slowly raised our hands and turned and looked directly at the man. He seemed to be some kind of guard.

He stepped toward us. He was shaking. The inclination toward fear left me. He was scared of us, and *he* had the gun.

"Drop everything in your—in your hands there and put them back up!" We stood there now keeping our eyes on him. "I'm going to shoot you— drop it! Drop everything, right there on the ground," he nervously stuttered, pointing. "Them axes too!"

We let our arms down, dropping our jackets, then letting the saddlebags slide off our shoulders, and Steve let down the leather pouch with the twenty-two rifle. We started taking our tomahawks out from our belts.

"Easy boys, real easy now," the nervous railroad guard said, still holding and pointing his thirty-eight at us. "Don't try nothing. Just lay them axes on the ground nice and easy." Steve and I looked at each other again. Steve smiled, and suddenly this shit reminded me of the movies as we laid the "axes" on the ground.

"I was hoping you boys wouldn't try to throw them things. Would have had to shoot you."

We were the Indians and he was the white cowboy, the *Sky*. We took our big Bowie knives out of their sheaths and laid them on the ground. His being scared of us—a white man, *Sky*—was all part of this greater confidence we had. Steve and I both knew if we had the drop on him, he could be dead. We still had the small dirks in our swimsuits.

We walked and stepped across the tracks, both of us here and there glancing back at him, still holding the gun on us under the heat with the noise of the huge freight yard in the background.

Another guard opened the office door.

"I got them, Hank. Boy, they got axes!" the gun-pointer spouted. "And big old Bowie knives." He looked at us. "They dangerous, I tell you. Look at them clothes. Like a couple of wild Injuns, and I just——"

"Joe! Joe! Just hold down," the new one demanded, firmly holding his hands up at Joe, then looking at us. "Don't pay Joe no mind. He gets nervous and excited sometimes." The new guard sat us down and asked us all kinds of questions. He told us the thing about riding freights is to not get caught—and he seemed like a good guy, even though he was a *Sky*. The one named Joe went back outside.

"Say, look," he said. "I can't let you fellows go on. I mean, I got to send you back home. I know how it is when you are on the move and you just want to be free, go, move—and I wish I could let you fellows just go, but, well, you're seventeen—if you were eighteen——"

Joe burst through the door. "Hey, look Hank, look at this. Look at these *axes*! And these Bowie knives!"

Hank picked up one of the tomahawks and looked at it a moment and laid it back down. "You boys are some real outdoor fellows."

"I tell you, they dangerous, Hank!" Joe rested his right hand on the butt handle of his holstered thirty-eight pistol.

"Naw, Joe. They just moving—ah, don't pay no attention to Joe. This is the most exciting thing that's happened 'round here." Hank shook his head.

We were taken to a police station. Our parents would probably pick us up soon, we were told; in the meantime, the policeman pointed to an open-door cell down the hall and said we could wait there. We ate some of our corn nuts and talked about being underage and having to go back home; then we lay down on the benches against the cell walls. I was really tired and began to doze off——

"Hey!" I heard the voice of the policeman. "Hey, you! Come out here for a minute!"

Steve and I sat up on the benches, looking across the cell at each other, coming fully awake. "Well, I guess somebody's here, you think?" We got up and walked out the cell, down the short hall and across the large open room. I could see the *Sky* had Steve's diary out, open, lying on the counter.

"What is this writing you do?" he asked Steve in an angry manner. "Why you want to say crap here that—why you hate white people? It says——" The guard began to read from the diary. I listened intently, as I had never read Steve's diary:

The white eyes, the *Skies*, have plundered the earth. They are ruth-
less against nature. They have stolen this land, this great continent

from all my Indian brothers, the Lakota, the Cheyenne, the Comanche, the Iroquois, the Navajo, and all the great tribes who once lived, one with the naturalness of life and of the earth. White men are the barbarians of all times and I must someday kill some of them and then die from their hands in the future uprisings of all who suffer the cruelness of the white man. He must be wiped out. His soul and conscience must be cleansed, and I will probably hate him and all his ignorance against nature and life until he changes and develops a respect for humanity.

"You write this crap, boy? You want to hate *me*. You know I could have locked your ass up, but I——"
"Don't be so insulting." Steve cut him off. "You frighten no one," he calmly said, looking directly at him.
"Well, just wait a minute——"
"I'm sorry you feel insulted by my true feelings and knowledge of your people's present and past. You will be hated for a long time for your ignorance."
"Now, just, hey look. I could have locked you up, but I left the damn door open. Do you like being locked?"
"No. Open skies are the——"
"But you want to kill me. You young punks never learn."
"I don't care to argue with your angry ignorance except to say, don't become angry in my presence and do something you will regret." Steve turned to walk back to the cell and I followed him. Steve shook his head and looked at me and smiled.
Then we both heard the police noisily walking, with keys jingling. He came closer.
"You ready?" Steve said to me. I knew Steve meant we may have to fight.
Then the door to the cell was slammed shut and the keys clanked in the lock. We lay back on the benches and went to sleep.

My father came to get us and all the way back, he talked about "I need somebody to help me with the business," and "I could make some money if Bobby would stop running off and work."
My father was always going into a business of some kind, making money, but Mama would never get another house, and that was a fact, to my thinking. I wasn't ever going to take care of him. He never half took care of us. He wouldn't pay me. Wouldn't let me work for myself. He cheated me and would sit up and demand that I work for him, telling me that I have to help him. Shit, I thought, as we rode on into the night.

We dropped Steve off and then we went straight to the bean field. When we got there, the people were working already. I got out of the car, ready to leave that scene.

"George, you won't pay me. I'd rather work for myself," I said nervously, but firmly.

"Well, God damn it, go on! Shit! Get one of them hampers and pick beans! 'Cause you going to work. Shit! Go on, get out there and pick the beans."

I walked off toward the scales.

I picked a half-bushel and decided to stop. I felt tired and hungry and very sleepy. I lay down on the ground and went off to sleep.

Suddenly, I was being struck with something heavy. I thought I was dreaming as I jumped and was hit again and again by the thudding blows that registered and vibrated throughout my entire body. I came to myself, scrambling up to my feet and looking around. Then I saw the long branch in my father's hands coming at me again. I was hot as a firecracker. I was boiling.

"I told you to pick them beans, God damn it! Now get back over there and work, God damn it!" he roared at me.

I thought how I could let him swing that branch one more time, take the blow, then take the branch from him; and my thoughts reeled toward defending myself to the death. "Wait a God damn minute!" I bellowed out looking straight at him, looking him directly in the eyes. "If you ever hit me again, so help me, I'll kill you! I'll kill your no good nigger ass!"

I walked off across to the end of the field away from him and did not look back. My insides raged. I walked over to the fence next to the road, hopped it, walked out to the edge of the road and walked on down it. I must have walked near five miles until I got to the highway. I hitchhiked home.

"Who is it?" Ann's voice said. "Bobby?" The door opened and she looked through the screen. "Bobby?"

"Yeah, it's me, Ann."

"Well what is you doing here?" Ann asked, unlatching the screen door and pushing it open for Steve and me to come inside. This was my Aunt Ann, in Los Angeles. "Come on in. This is a surprise. What you doing here?"

"Ah, Steve and I, we came this way to try and find a job."

"A job! You-all come on in here." I could remember that familiar clean old-house smell of Ann's home. "You-all sit down. You hungry?"

"Oh, yeah. We could eat."

"What's wrong?" Ann asked in her concerned manner as she started getting food out for us. "You having problems at home?"

"George—Daddy, you know—he wants me to work for him, but he won't pay me. He say I work for him or I get out. Then him and Mama always arguing. Daddy cussing her out." And I introduced Steve—Watanka.

I went into the swanky den, TV room upstairs, turned the lamp on and looked around, remembering. We had made it to L.A., hitchhiking. I felt I could do anything or go anywhere in the world I wanted to.

For the next few days we looked for jobs—in carwashes, in bowling alleys, loading trucks—walking and riding the streetcars across the city. Ann had called Mama and George and told them I was there; she became very concerned about me not finishing school, constantly telling me that I ought to go back to Oakland and graduate or enroll here in L.A. and stay with her. I felt her concern, but stuck to my objective of going to South Dakota. Steve was my righteous friend and we would stick it out and make it to South Dakota.

At the end of one week we cut out from the house one morning, headed to check out a carwash. The proprietor couldn't use us. We walked the streets that morning for a long while and decided maybe we should go back home, join the Army, and get away. Then when we got out of the Army, we would go to South Dakota, get married to some Indian girls, and live with our American Indian brothers. It would just take awhile.

Steve felt sure he had better try and get in the Army. He talked about how his dreams had shown death to him if he stayed at home and in cities. "Visions of death are approaching me." He asked me had I had any visions of my death. I told him no.

"Then if not, Hanpi, you should live to be a great warrior of these times. You are the only and closest friend I've ever had, the only real brother I know. I have no one else that I know and believe in. You make me believe in myself."

We stopped for a moment as Steve looked around at the environment, the big stinky smelly city. I looked at him closely. I thought to myself and realized and sensed that he wanted to die.

We started walking again. I wondered now about myself—and what we would do—there were no jobs. I worried, as we walked, about what Steve would do. I had been lonely for such a good friend, and I had let my friendship be his, while admiring his strength as a person, a wise friend—sometimes happy, other times sad and quiet. Now I thought he needed something: he needed to get out of this filthy city he hated, into the valley.

"Hey, Watanka, let's make it to Highway 99 and make it home, man. We'll join the Army, be ourselves."

"Yeah," Steve said. "We'll join the Army, I'll learn to fight, and then, I know, I'll die."

"Come on,"—I put my arm up around Steve's shoulders—"let's get a map from that service station.

"Steve, man, some day we'll make it to Wyoming and South Dakota, the land of our great Sioux brothers. Sitting Bull lived to be a great leader of his people. He kicked Custer's ass!" We hopped across the street. "And man, we might not do the same thing, but we can *live*. I don't care if they do call us Nigger Tarzan."

We found our way to the highway and began to hitchhike and walk. At two o'clock in the day we came upon an orange orchard. We picked and ate juicy ripe oranges. Steve was happy again. We were free once more on the outskirts of the great Los Angeles metropolis, hitchhiking, eating and living, walking in the fresh air. I was wanting my close brother, Steve, to be free from the idea of death as I felt I was. I realized he was more Indian than I was. He identified in a stronger way. Oh, I believed, but he was much stronger, I felt, like a free but lone bull.

Steve made it into the Army; I didn't. They didn't want somebody with a crippled foot. I tried two different times, saying I could run, I was strong—no way. So Steve was gone, now.

I sulked, feeling a great inner loss. I was still in "rest gym" in school, because of my foot, and I refused to go to rest gym. I had cut the classes for a week, showing up, then leaving. Mama had begged me to finish school and graduate—that's all she hoped for me to do when I told her the Army had rejected me.

I had the Iron Mistress—my Bowie knife, the twin of the one I'd made for Steve—under my jacket, stuck down in its sheath inside my pants. I walked in to rest gym and was accounted present, then I started to leave. The teacher called to me that I better not cut class, I'd better go and get into my gym shorts and stay in class.

"This ain't no gym class. It's for cripples, and I can do any game from football to—you name it. If I stay, I ain't going to do this baby shit!"

"Look, Bobby!" He raised his voice: "You are a cripple!"

I turned to walk out, mad, wanting to really show him, fight him, let him know I was a strong warrior and not a cripple.

I walked down a long hall, then stopped when I got to the stairs to go down. I pulled my knife out, thinking that if I put this knife to that teacher's gut, he'd shit! I imagined the ignorant Army recruiter and the gym teacher, both rejecting me, telling me I'm a cripple. A mad rage overwhelmed me.

Whack! The sound echoed in the stairwell. I struck at an angle the corner of the thick varnished banister with the Bowie knife, sinking the blade two inches deep into the wood.

I can fight. I could kill them, I thought.

I snatched the blade out of the wood, took one step, and with another devastating surge, I raised and came down with a raging blow, swinging the knife back at the same deep chop. I took another step and *whack!* Step, *whack!* Step, *whack!* Down the stairs with a rhythmic step, *whack!* Down to the bottom step.

I felt good, relieved. I felt my anger ease a little. I walked off the campus, deciding to cut my afternoon classes, walked up and roamed in the hills.

Inside, lonely rage gnawed within my total being. The only thing that soothed me was memories of my righteous friend, Steve. I was remembering all the places—nature, life, cool water in a lone stream, standing on a high hill looking over the vastness. I was wanting to cry, feeling sorry for myself, but holding back any tears, as they would reflect not being a brave warrior.

A November morning, I was at school. I had decided I would finish school for Mama, because I saw she wanted me to graduate real bad. I was standing alone against the building looking at the students sitting on the slope, especially one girl. I was acutely aware of my dress: T-shirt, rawhide necklace hung with animal bones, soft-leather vest with sun and trees on it, Levis with Indian designs running up and down the seams, moccasins. I had tied two feathers to the shoulder part of my vest. They hung down lazily across my slim, oiled, muscular arms, which were folded. I saw the girl glance at me out the corner of her eyes as she went into the building. I wished she could like me the way I was, but just maybe——

I took off and walked to the end of the building, going to take my sister's advice and say something to that girl. I spotted her and hurriedly stepped right there in front of her, trying to make a pleasant face, hoping I did not look mean, and said, "Hi, Carol."

She looked at me quickly, as though she were startled, then looked back down at her open book, not saying a word.

Five minutes later I came on Lupe and a couple of his Mexican friends standing in front of the print-shop door. I noticed they were dressed in peg pants with pistol pockets, wearing DAs, like everybody except me. A few people walked up and down the halls. I took about three steps from the corner of the hall, walking away from Lupe and his two friends.

"Da-da-da-da, da-da-da-da!" The TV Dragnet theme was being imitated.

I stopped cold in my tracks, turned around, and started back. Lupe kept on with his TV Dragnet music. This motherfucker thought he was cool and I was getting mad. I stopped, looked at them with a stern face, mean and angry.

"What's the matter, Nigger Tarzan baby?!"

"Say, man, Nigger Tarzan's going to get upset, baby," one of Lupe's friends said, and they all laughed. "What's the matter, Nigger Tarzan? Don't like it?" They laughed, taunting me, and I thought, They're fucking with me because I'm different. Some other people stopped, looking at the scene, laughing too.

I'll cut this motherfucker, I said to myself. I thought about how Steve would say, Ignore them; but, *no!* These motherfuckers would think I'm scared of them. I quickly reached inside the vest and snatched the Iron Mistress out and jumped into a fighting stance.

Lupe's friends scrambled back away from him as I angrily said, "That's right, motherfucker. I'm Nigger Tarzan! *Yeeiaiyieee!*" I leaped into the air toward him, swinging the big blade, with all its shiny sharp glitter and threat of death.

Lupe jumped, scrambling out of my way as I darted toward him. He dodged and jumped, backing up. I kept my eyes on his every move, going toward him slowly. I was going to kill him.

He was scared. Fear engulfed his body.

I gave another loud Indian yell, and by this time Lupe was already barreling down the hall. I took off running after him with the knife in my hand. Lupe looked back at me, bumping into people, knocking others down. He stumbled, and when he turned around, I was there. He snatched off his jacket, balling it and clumsily wrapping it around his right arm. I had him cornered.

"I'm sorry Bobby, man! Say, man, pleeease!" He pleaded with Nigger Tarzan, holding his wrapped arm up. "Don't cut me, man, I'm sorry!" And from my crouching, stalking stance, slightly moving the Iron Mistress back and forth, I lunged. He held his coat-wrapped arm up, trying to block the knife. I held my attack stance; the next would be the fatal blow.

"Bobby, Bobby!" It was Donna's voice. I did not look around. I had Lupe.

"He's going to kill him! He's crazy!" someone said.

"Please man, Bobby, I'm sorry, man. I'm sorry. I won't fuck with you no more, pleeease."

"Bobby's crazy, man!" the voices were saying. "He's going to kill."

"Bobby, don't do it," Donna pleaded.

I came out of my attack stance, standing straight, still holding the knife, mad, staring Lupe down, my chest out. I said loudly, "If you *ever* fuck with me again"—pointing the knife at Lupe—"I'll kill you! I'll cut your god damn guts out, motherfucker! You got that!"

I looked around at the crowd. "And that goes for all of you! Motherfuckers!" I shouted loudly.

About three months had passed since Steve had joined the Army.

I asked Mama to give me some money to buy pants and gaucho shirts, suede shoes and a jacket. I got a closer, neat haircut and let the process in my hair go back to a natural. I began to talk to Willie Ward and Roger Hammond. They did not bother people, so here and there I would hold conversations with them to ease my friendless, lonely, inner rage, not wanting to suddenly get mad at people.

In Christmas vacation time, Willie Ward and I were walking in front of the Rivoli Theater and there was Steve! Coming down the street in the splendor of complete Army dress, with one stripe on his shoulders, shined combat boots and all, and a cap.

"Hanpi!" He smiled.

"Say, Steve, man, Watanka!" I said, and we reached out our right hands and gave each other our Indian forearm-gripping handshake. "Say, Jack! Look at you!" My language had changed a little. "You really in the Army, man. How you make out learning combat?"

"It's ok. But one needs real battle experience."

"Where you headed now?"

"I was going to your house. I'm leaving tomorrow for Korea."

"Korea! Man you sure look good, Jack!"

We walked down the street. Willie Ward said nothing, but listened. He smiled one time at the way I carried on and talked about how Steve looked in his Army suit.

"Watanka, man, Jack! You remind me of the first time I ever saw an Army suit. My cousin one time—shit, I sure wish I could have joined."

"Hanpi, I see you have taken to the white man's dress and ways."

"Aw, I still got my clothes—my moccasins and everything." I felt embarrassed. "I just dress like this, man, to keep people from fucking with me," I explained. "I almost killed Lupe, he was fucking with me one day about the way I was dressed, calling me Nigger Tarzan—I don't know—I just lost my head."

"But Hanpi, you let them get to you."

"Yeah, I know. But Steve, it's good to see you, man." Damn it, I called him Steve, I thought; I should have called him Watanka.

Steve commented about people moving out of the Village.

"Yeah, they finally got people to leave, man, this place is gone," I said, remembering the big fight the people had with the police over the eviction.

We walked all the way back to Steve's house. Steve and I sat in his low-level, basement-like room, talking for hours and remembering, looking at our now-fading marks of the word *Sioux* on our arms, and bragging about our stamina and endurance. I told him I was still going to try to get a job and go to South Dakota. "Somehow, I'm going to make it there."

Steve looked at me. "You probably will, Hanpi. But you are changing. You'll probably be better off living here." Steve stood up. "I don't know, maybe I'll see the land of the Lakota someday. Now, though, I got to go. To the bus station, back to the base."

At the bus stop, Steve said, "Hanpi, man, you are all right. Like I said before, you are the best and only friend I ever had." Under the streetlight I could see Steve's face and all the serious meaning. "You are a great warrior," he said. "If I don't ever see you again, I just want you to know that I love you like the only real brother I ever had. You gave me all the confidence I ever needed in myself."

"Yeah, man, but, well——" I saw the bus was upon us. Sad now, I said, "I'll see you Steve——" We shook hands, Indian fashion.

"Don't let people make you lose your temper, Hanpi."

The bus door closed and it drove off. My real friend. I saw him standing up in the bus, then walking, then sitting down.

A week or so later, after school, thinking about my partner, Steve, and what he said about me being his friend, I went out into the courtyard and threw the Iron Mistress at the big tree trunk, sticking it in time after time. The sun had gone down and it got darker.

In the dark I threw the Iron Mistress angrily and wildly at the tree, again and again. A stunning pain caught me in the center of my forehead. When I grabbed my forehead with the palm of my hand, I felt something wet. The knife must have bounced and hit me. I groped around—I finally found the knife. The blade had popped and broken in two pieces, beyond repair.

Three days before graduation I was called to the principal's office. I sat there in a wooden-bottomed chair wondering what he wanted me for—did he know about the banister? About the fight with Lupe?

"Step in here," the principal said.

"You know, Bobby, you have a very good school record up to now." I suddenly hoped—maybe I'd be presented with an award or something at the graduation. If I got an award, Carol would like me then. If I do get something special, Mama would like that. Then he looked up at me standing in front of his desk. "Well, your grades are very good all the way through, except for these last reports. I'm to inform you that you will not be graduating."

"Not graduating?" I asked, really surprised. "What do you mean? It's only three days to graduation! Look, I already bought the robe, paid for graduation pictures, and been rehearsing, and you sit up here with your——"

I knew I was totally let down and wanted to leave right then. I stood a moment looking at him. He had unconcern written all over his face.

"Fuck you!" I angrily said to him. "Fuck it all!" I turned and stormed out of his office and on out the reception area into the hall, thinking to myself, twelve years of school for nothing.

Mama, heartbroken, stood over the kitchen sink and tears welled in her eyes. I couldn't be there and explain why, as her crying was about to break me apart. I changed my clothes.

"Bobby!" Mama called to me. I stopped and turned around. "Where you going?"

"I don't know, Mama. I'm just going."

I roamed the hills all alone that day. In strict solitude, sometimes trying to figure out what to do and knowing I had to leave since I was no longer in school. George would certainly put the pressure on me to work for him, and I knew I would not. Never!

That night at home, my father called to me. I went into the kitchen where he was and sat down at the table. I knew that he was going to ask me about working for him and that Mama had told him by now that I would not be graduating.

"I'm going to pay you," George said. "I'll pay you for your work. I'm going to buy one of them project buildings and salvage it and we can make——"

I stood up and stepped away from the table while George kept talking. I turned to Mama: "Say, Mama, I want to tell you-all something."

"What Bobby?" Mama asked.

"I'm going to join the Air Force tomorrow." I looked at George.

"Bobby! You don't need to be joining no Air Force. Why you want to go off doing that?" George was getting louder. Dislike for the idea was in his voice. "You ain't joining no Air Force! I ain't signing for you."

"Bobby, I don't want you joining no——" Mama started.

"George, I don't need you to sign. I can join on my own. I'm eighteen. So that's what I'm going to do tomorrow." I turned and walked away to my room.

"You ain't joining no Air Force. Shit!"

"Now, George," Mama was saying, "don't start nothing with Bobby." I shut the door.

I signed the papers at the recruitment center. Then I went to the induction center in San Francisco. There was not a thing about the whole examination process that bugged me, because I was glad to be there. We filled out papers and took IQ tests and aptitude tests, being herded from place to place in groups of fifteen. Our physical exam started with the head, eyes, hearing. Then the doctor walked down in front of us, from one recruit to the next, looking directly at our feet. He stopped abruptly in front of me. "Ah, what's this, an injury?" He stooped down looking at my foot, then touched it. "This is a skin graft, huh? Step back."

I thought while I waited, worried about the Air Force not taking me. I would tell them that I could hike twenty miles on this foot, and I could run five miles nonstop. That would convince them that I was good Air Force material.

God damn, I was getting nervous wondering when he was going to talk to me. The doctor had gone into an office. I stood there impatiently. Then he came out.

"How did this happen?"

"I was hit by a car. But I can do anything anybody else can do. I can hike——" The doctor stood up.

"We can't take you. You can get dressed."

At home, I walked up and into the hills, again in my Nigger Tarzan dress, wallowing in my friendlessness, rejected, ungraduated, tormenting memories of not making it—in anything. What's happening to me? Maybe I've sinned too much. Naw! I don't believe in God, the Great Spirit, nothing! I had to get away. I had to leave the house. Go somewhere. Where would I—could I—go. There was nowhere, no one I could turn to.

Then it hit me. I could go to L.A. Yeah! Look for a job and stay with Ann—no, Alvin, my cousin. I could run with Alvin. He could maybe help me get a job. I left the hills headed for home. I'd have to get Mama to give me some money to leave.

In Los Angeles, things were looking up for me. I looked for a job during the day and went to school at night. Ann gave me money to buy books. I did the schoolwork and looked at television and dodged my Uncle Walter, who had a tendency to preach and give me Bible lessons whenever he caught me sitting around. "Don't you touch that thing down between your legs. That's sinful," he would say. And he'd carry on: "Going to school ain't going to save your soul, Bobby. You'll see things that you don't understand about life at prayer-meetings."

"Naw, Walter, I just want to get myself a job and go and do what I want to."

"You see, Bobby, you ain't going to get no job unless you try and be a man of Christian faith. You won't get a job even from the state unemployment place unless you got my blessing. I can tell you how to get a job, because the Lord showed me in a dream. You got to follow my Christian knowledge."

"Later, Uncle Walter," I said disgustedly. "I'll get a job without all that."

I finally caught up with Alvin—against Ann's advice—Alvin worked part-time in a bowling alley, setting pins. I went to his job and waited for him to finish his hours, then we left. I inquired but there was no job opening at the bowling alley. Alvin and I talked and made plans about getting ourselves a two-bedroom apartment and having girls over and having parties like some of our other cousins had done.

One Friday evening Alvin and I went out to see the Globetrotters. I had heard about them and the fantastic basketball they played.

We sat up in the high bleachers, and at the break we went down and bought ourselves hotdogs and milled with the crowd, talking about getting our apartment.

"Say, Alvin—look, man, ain't that a purse laying there?" I pointed at it, peering between the steel supports of the bleachers.

"Yeah, sure is," Alvin said. Then we looked around to see if anybody in the crowd was looking.

"Let's get it man, it might have some money in it."

"I am!" Alvin quietly exclaimed. He reached and picked it up.

"Let's go," Alvin said. "We got to get somewhere and see what's in it."

We went into the men's room. We found twenty-seven dollars.

After searching the purse thoroughly, we put everything back in it except the money, closed it, and Alvin wiped our fingerprints off. Then we set it down in back of the toilet and left the men's room. As we came out the door, a janitor appeared in the aisle. We went back to our seats to watch the Globetrotters play. They put on a hell of a show.

When the game was over, and we were milling around on our way out, a guy in uniform stopped us. "This way," he said, pointing for us to walk in front of him. "Move, boy!" He moved us into a room with other uniformed armed guards.

I leaned to Alvin's ear. "What you think they got us for?"

"I don't know, don't say nothing about that purse we found. Anyway, we ain't done nothing."

Another guard brought in a white woman. I looked at her face. She staggered and wobbled in her steps. She was torn up, drunk as a skunk, about to fall.

"Are they the ones?" the first guard asked her.

"Yeah!" she said, almost falling. The *Sky* held her. "They're the little black bastards. See, they took my purse, they got all my money."

Another guard brought in the janitor we saw by the men's room. He had the green cheap alligator purse in his hand. "Is that them?" one of the *Skies* asked.

"Yeah, it's them."

The cop said, "Snatching this purse got you boys in a lot of trouble."

I was enraged! No! I stood up, saying, "We ain't snatched that purse, we found it!" I was yelling, looking at the cop in anger.

"Bobby, sit down. Be quiet, man!" Alvin said, putting his hand on my arm. "Don't say nothing!"

"Found it!" The two cops laughed at the idea.

We sat there for a while, quiet, and Alvin reminded me again not to say anything if we got split up going to jail. After a while the *Skies* came in and cuffed us, squeezing the cuffs tight. I wanted to cuss them out, but I said nothing, and we were taken out and put into the back of a paddy wagon.

We wound up at the Wilshire Street Station in L.A., in a ground-level but seemingly basementlike jail where some ten or twelve bars separated cells with two bunks in them. We were moved to another jail late Sunday night.

Alvin woke me and told me we were ready to go to court. We filed out and were taken to another large holding cell. All the bench seats were taken, and just as many prisoners were lying out all over the floor, asleep, and numerous others talked about their cases. After a while Alvin struck up a conversation with another, older prisoner, who, from his talk, had been in and out of court and jail.

He asked us what we were busted for. Alvin told him and I interjected my angry feelings of being busted "for nothing," emphasizing and explaining all over again that we "really found the purse." The old dude went over and over our case with us, and gave us advice from his experience.

"Your best bet is to tell the judge, 'Your honor, I don't know, ah, we don't know how to plead.' The judge is going to think you're a dumb nigger kid. Act like you're waiting for your mother, and you casually say you're only seventeen. You guys say, 'I ain't never been in jail and I don't know how to plead.' It'll work. Oh—don't forget to say, 'My mother is here.' She can ask to let you go in her custody. That way you can get out and maybe, just maybe, the D.A. will drop the charges, since you ain't never been busted down here. You can get a warning from the judge when you return to court. But go in there and act like two dumb kids."

We got it in our heads what to do, and he assured us we could beat the rap like that, nine times out of ten. "If you don't say no more than what I hipped you to, then you might get cut loose when you're called in that courtroom."

Alvin got out that day, but it was fifteen days before a judge let me out, telling me never to come back to L.A., to go and join the Air Force and serve my country. I had fifteen days there of learning about jail—jail food and prisoners, being sprayed around the penis and the ass in case of bugs, cell doors slamming, guards. I had gone off into a quiet, don't-bother-me, strict solitude.

Within hours after I was let out I was on a bus on my way back to Berkeley, glad I was out of jail. But as I got closer and closer to Berkeley, that friendless, crippled, rejected, unloved, jobless, depressing attitude came over me again. My lonely Nigger Tarzan rage crept inside my thoughts, and a depressing nothingness of self dominated me.

I got off the bus at the Oakland Greyhound station at 5:00 A.M. and walked six miles down San Pablo Avenue to our apartment—"F"—in the village, pondering with disgusted feelings on being a *failure*. What to do? I did not know.

The racetrack was closed that time of year. I couldn't even get a jive paper job anywhere. I tried the many factories near and about our Village and way beyond, and was given a flat no.

I went home and sat at the kitchen table. "Mama, let me have five dollars."

"For what, Bobby. I ain't got no whole lot of money."

"I got to find a job. I want to have some money on me. I want to go to San Francisco, then down to San Jose and look for a job. I can't find nothing around here."

"Well, let me see." Mama raised her apron and unpinned her dress pocket, pulling out a crisp five dollar bill. She walked over to the kitchen table and laid it down, saying: "I hope you find something." Then walked back to the sink. "We got to move, but we ain't found no place. And George ain't making no money with that truck." Mama paused then said. "Lord, I wonder what's going to become of us. I tried so hard——" Mama began to cry. "Just, oh me, I just don't know what we going to do."

I got up, picked up the five dollar bill, and walked out the door. I went to San Francisco. I wandered through the crowded downtown area and beyond, up past the Mark Hopkins Hotel, noticing all the rich-looking white people driving up in new cars. I walked on, feeling I did not want a job where I had to beg white people for tips or anything like that. I walked and walked; then I noticed I was on Van Ness Avenue, right in front of the armed-forces induction center. I watched some large groups of seemingly new recruits come out of the building. I figured they must have just got in the Air Force and must have been sworn in. I wished I was with them, leaving.

Shit! If I go inside and really explain, get somebody to listen to me, get the guy at the entrance counter upstairs to let me really tell a doctor what I can do with my foot and tell them how I can hike twenty miles and throw knives and how I learned to shoot when I used to go hunting with high powered rifles——I stood there and dreaded the lonely state I was in. Shit! Give it another go, Bobby!

I raced up the stairs and walked in front of the counter. A man in uniform stepped to the counter asking, "Can I help you?"

"Ah, yeah, remember me, my name is Bobby Seale and I'd like to see a doctor about getting in the Air Force. The doctor wouldn't listen to me before. He didn't know that I can hike twenty miles and I can run five miles. I used to do it everyday——"

He cut me off: "Wait a minute, I remember you. You were rejected. What's your name again?" He walked away to a file cabinet. I kept talking fast to him as he searched the files.

"Yeah, man, look. If the doctor would listen to me or I can show them, I'm tough, man. I used to hike twenty miles all the time. I rode bicycles two hundred miles in three days. I used to wrestle and have lance fights. You know, rugged, knock-down lance fights all the time—and my foot don't give me no trouble. I, man, I, I've lived a rugged life, rode horses. And I can shoot, man! I've hunted deer and bear up in Mount Shasta and all over California."

He walked back to the counter. I didn't know what else to say. Then I thought, I'll show him as he said, "Well, I don't——"

"Wait, man, let me show you!"

I snatched off my jacket and stepped back away from the counter. I stood sideways to him with correct posture, my chest poking out.

"Now count and see how fast I do them!" I leaned a bit, my body still erect. "Now watch my left foot. It won't bother me."

I was falling straight forward as though I would slam into the floor on my face, stiff. My falling body gained momentum. The airman hollered out, "hey!"

Before my body slammed to the ground, the palms of my hands hit the floor in front of me and broke the fall. I started doing a succession of pushups, "One, two, three!" I knew they were correct, straight-back pushups as I counted rapidly aloud, moving with speed, "Twenty-one, twenty-two——" I kept going, going all the way down to the floor, letting my chin and chest slightly touch the floor, going on and on. I stopped at fifty, still in a pushup position, holding it. I told myself to do five quick extra ones. I pushed them out fast and stopped, still holding my position. Then I put my foot up under my belly and stood, straight, and walked to the counter breathing hard but controlled.

"See, what I mean, man? I'm strong, and I'm tough enough to survive any training. I bet very few people can do what I just did——"

He was looking at me in disbelief, first smiling, then with a serious look on his face. He said: "Rugged—I guess you are."

"I can do anything, man! My foot don't bother me. Just let me see the doctor and I'll do the same thing . . . I'm ready! I can——"

"Wait, wait hold on! You see, the Air Force don't need the rough rugged guys so much. They really want guys with skills, like——"

I cut him off, talking fast, explaining how I knew carpentry, my father having taught it to me since I was a little boy, how my father had a cabinet shop and used to have government contracts with the Navy and Army, and how I got As, nothing but As for four years in drafting, always a B-plus in machine shop. My math was excellent. I rattled off a lot of technical jargon of making tools.

"I can read any kind of blueprint and use all precision measuring instruments such as micrometers, telescope gauges, dial indicators and rule calipers. I can run a ten-foot-bed planer, turret lathes, six-foot-bed machine lathes, surface grinders"—I had his undivided attention as I went on explaining—"I grind tool bits of any shape and size for any job. I know tempering and heat-treating processes and all my metal alloys from cold-roll soft steel, to tool steel, to copper and different hardnesses of roll sheet and extruded aluminum. Say look, just call my teacher. You can call Berkeley High School and ask the machine shop instructor, Mr. Lindstead. He'll recommend me, go ahead, call——" I stopped, looking at the dude, wishing, then said: "Just let me see the doctor man, and I'll show him."

I looked around. A couple of other airmen were standing there looking at me, a woman airman behind the counter was looking at me. I looked at all of them with a wish and hope that they would see what I meant.

"I got to do something. Let me see the doctor. Let me get in, man," I pleaded, trying to rise above the sorry feeling I had for myself.

"Ok, I'll give you an appointment to see a doctor. You'll see a foot specialist. Ten hundred hours tomorrow morning, I mean ten o'clock."

"Ok, right! I'll get there. I'll be there!"

He wrote down and explained the directions and time to me then said: "Now, if they let you in, you might as well be ready to leave tomorrow."

I walked out the door with a grin and smile on my face, hoping and praying I could convince the doctor.

I was sworn in with a large group of about thirty other recruits the next evening. After being sworn in, raising my hand and all, we were told we were now in the United States Air Force, and then to police the building of all trash and coke bottles. Did I work around there until we left that late evening!

It was night time when we arrived at Parks Air Force Base. I had really done it, left home! I was happy. Finally *gone*!

PART IV

The Bed-Adapter Kid

"HUP! TWO! THREEUP! FOUR! Hup! Two! Threeup! Four!"

The training instructor's southern drawl rhythmed out the pace of our sixty-man marching cadence. Marching at the head of our flight, I kept in time to "Hup! Two! Threeup! Four!" with a sharp sheer accuracy that I'd never done or heard before. "Hup! Two! Threeup! Four!" Our training instructor paused to listen, so he could hear the blended single *bump-thump*, the unified sound of the sixty heels of our sturdy and spit-shined boots as they struck the blacktop pavement of the road. A sixty-man marching *bump-thump* that just wouldn't quit! I felt proud of myself, proud of my own accuracy, listening to the sixty heels behind me.

"Hear me now! Hep—hawp!" He loudly drawled it. "All right then!" he bellowed. "Keep it together!" And I could hear each and every last one of the sixty heels in back of me, striking the pavement at the same time.

After the one month I had been in the Air Force, we were really beginning to sound sharp. Sharper than a mosquito's peter, the saying went—and that was sharp! I was right-hand guide, and I was ready to be the best and do everything that I was told.

After learning about clap—V.D.—and seeing pictures of syphilis-ridden bodies, which all shocked me, basic training was over and I was given orders to go to Amarillo, Texas, to be trained as an aircraft sheet-metal mechanic. I would try to be one of the best sheet-metal mechanics there was. I arrived at Amarillo Air Force Base a day early.

I got saddening letters from home, meantime, from Betty and Mama. I didn't want to write to them. Mama was always telling me in her letters to

79

pray and do right, and Betty had nothing to say except John was in and now out of jail again and had joined the church also.

Their letters frustrated me with memories and lost dreams. So I wrote Mama a one-page letter telling her I was not a part of the family any more. I told Mama not to write me at all, that I totally disassociated myself from them, that I didn't believe she and George were my real mother and father and I had changed my name to Robert Crane—just to forget about me. I wallowed in my lonely, disgusted friendlessness—but with a certain acute sense that I thought they were all behind the times, and didn't understand the world as I did. I had a strong need to feel I was starting my life all over again from a new perspective that would propel me to another and greater self—Robert Crane. To be one of the smartest, most knowledgeable persons around. I wanted the future.

Two weeks later a captain called me to his office and asked me why did I write such a letter home to my mother. I could not and would not answer. I stood at attention as he explained that my mother had written and sent the letter to him and that she was worried about me, writing such a letter home denouncing my family. "Why in God's name do you want to do something like that?"

I stood there looking straight ahead, pissed off at having to stand there, partially embarrassed, and at the same time feeling trapped. Why did she have to do that? Why did I feel this way?

"Answer me, airman!" the captain shouted.

"That's just the way I feel."

"Well," he bellowed, "I'm going to order you to write home twice a month. I'll have the mail clerk check to see if you are writing home and report it. Twice a month. Is that clear, airman?"

"Yes, sir."

"That's all. Dismissed."

I left feeling foolish and confusedly angry at everybody. I wrote home a half page, saying that I'm doing all right, don't worry about me so much, and tell John to write me. I was angry, and I was friendless. I went to movies and I studied, and I desperately wanted to break loose from this dreadful lonely foolishness I felt about myself.

Standing in line one day in the chow hall, a white boy accidentally bumped into me and I suddenly began cussing him out.

"Come on, motherfucker! Come on outside so I can break your God damn neck." I stepped out of the line. "Come on!" I said, walking. He followed me as I went out the door angrily beckoning to him, hopping down the stairs standing ready, but he stopped at the top of the stairs.

"Come on, you son of a bitch! I want to show you who I am. Get your white *Sky* ass down here, motherfucker. I'm going to teach your southern white ass about Nigger Tarzan!"

He stood there looking at me, then his partner pulled on him.

"That guy's nuts! Fuck him. Let's go." And they turned and walked back through the door.

I walked off back to the barracks, raging inside, and another white boy bumped into me there. "Watch where you going, motherfucker," I said. And I stepped back, braced myself, and yelled an Indian war cry, startling him; then quickly, with my fist balled, I crashed right into his gut, making him double over, and quickly again—*wham!*—I caught him hard on the side of the head with a low right hook. I stepped back, saying, "Now, stay out of my way, motherfucker!" And I walked off, leaving him stunned and doubled over as I walked fast to my room.

I felt rotten later, knowing I had really hit that boy for nothing. I was trying to make myself believe that white people had shot and killed Negroes and my Indian brothers just because they felt like it, and now it was their turn to get their asses kicked. But I had to face the fact that somehow it was wrong for me to beat on the white boy just because *I* felt like it. Feeling immature and lost, I wondered what was becoming of me.

In class I would lose myself in the training; and I convinced myself not to let my temper get the best of me. A few days later, I saw the white boy I had hit and I apologized to him, stopping quickly and looking him in the face and saying, "Look man, I'm sorry. I hope I didn't hurt you. I was on edge. If you don't want to forgive me—well, fuck it, I'm still sorry." And I walked right off to my room, trying to figure out some other things to do to relax, to get rid of the tension within me. My body was always tensed, I realized. I became ambivalent about my ready strength.

I was dressed in new civilian clothes. I had not spent any of my money, so one day I bought clothes, records, and a record player, and then went to a Base movie after that day's Tech School training. Coming from the Base movie that afternoon, I passed an open barracks window, and heard one black dude and three white boys playing cards and calling off poker hands. The big black dude was in my Tech School class—his name was Alvin Dubois. I stopped, saying, "Hey, what you cats doing, playing poker?"—trying to sound friendly.

"Yeah, you know how to play?" one white boy said. "You want to join in?"

"Yeah, I guess so."

"Say!" Dubois said. "How you know all that shit in class. I can't get that shit for nothing."

"Aw, man, I just like the layout work. It's like drafting. I used to do it in school. I always got A's in it. Anyway, all that stuff's really easy."

I won a few hands and lost a few until I was nearly twenty-five dollars in the hole. Dubois seemed to be winning the most. I sat there telling myself I would just appear to be sharply dressed and cool, knowledgeable and wise—tough if necessary—and act like I'd been around a little bit.

Dubois was a pretty tall, muscular dude who rose higher than six feet, maybe six foot one, and seemed adept at poker. He had a short forehead and knotty, kinky hair. The four white boys tried to josh him somewhat, but they stayed within their limits, smiling.

"You big tough son of a bitch. You did it again. How do you do it, Dubois?"

"All in the game. All in the game." Dubois smiled.

"Hell, I'm pretty near thirty dollars down," another white boy said. "You want a drink, Seale?"

They poured me about two shots in a cup. I picked the cup up and tried to turn it up and drink it like I'd seen done so many times in the movies, and I quickly swallowed about half the whiskey in my cup. The shit nearly killed me as I tried to feign I could take the terrible taste and the burning sensation, but I couldn't fake it and began to cough like crazy. They all cracked up looking at me.

"Oh, shit! That shit tastes nasty." And I coughed a little more trying to sit up straight and get myself together.

"Here," the white boy said, handing me a cigarette as he laughed. "Take a smoke, that'll ease it. He.e."

I took one. Another white boy lit it.

"Take a deep drag, Seale."

I sucked in the smoke again, inhaling the smoke into my lungs, then let it out, coughing; but it did ease the burning bourbon whiskey.

"Man, shit, that whiskey——" I said, trying to be hip and with their laughter I felt they were my friends—something I needed.

I felt real nice—relaxed and sort of happy—after a short while. I played poker and talked on how to make it through the class. Drinking, I seemed to remember a lot to talk about.

I got pretty high and Dubois pulled me to the side and told me I ought to go to my barracks to sleep it off, that I had already lost thirty dollars or more, that he was just trying to beat the white boys, not me.

The next morning when we waited to fall in and march, Dubois walked over.

"You was tore up last night," he said.

"Yeah, I guess so."

"You remember what I told you about what I was doing?"

"Yeah."

"That's why I didn't drink anything."

"Did you win?"

"Yeah, man. I broke them. They was drunk."

"You do that all the time?"

"Yeah." Dubois stood up. "Say, look. I'm sticking with you."

"Huh?"

"I'm just sticking with you. You a pretty smart motherfucker. You really know this sheet-metal stuff. I just want to be around somebody who knows all this shit!"

"Oh, yeah. Ok, yeah. I'll hip you."

"Fall in!" A corporal hollered out.

Dubois—"Dubby"—and I struck it off as sort of quasi-friends. When we had a big barracks move, Dubby and I became roommates along with other black airmen. I now smoked and drank and killed whole packs of Pall Malls whenever I drank—also smoking early in the morning, always getting a short two-minute buzz from two quick deep inhales. I bought more records and clothes, read, hipped Dubby to everything he said he didn't understand about Tech School training. I found out Dubby was a lazy sleepyhead, but he was my friend and I woke him every morning.

After six months I graduated tops in my Tech School class, an honor student. We had a few choices of bases to go to where our specialties could be used. At the bottom of the list I saw: *Rapid City, South Dakota, Ellsworth A.F.B.*

"Hey! Man!" I exclaimed. "Shit! South Dakota!"

"What?!" Dubby said. "South Dakota! What the hell's there!"

"The Black Hills! The land of the Lakota!"

I had never seen so much snow in my life as at Ellsworth A.F.B. I mean it was cold.

Three days after I got there, to my surprise, Dubby arrived. When I left Amarillo, Dubby's orders had not been cut. We readily became roomies—roommates.

Some more new troops hit the base a couple of days later and were assigned to our barracks.

Webster, a slim five foot eleven, partially curly-headed dude from Washington, D.C., was always trying to joke, but coming up late.

Green, from Mississippi, was my size. He looked upon the big cities where everyone else came from as really being somewhere to be from.

Snake, from Detroit, standing a slim, long six foot one, was always talking about getting back home to his girl.

Rabbit, who got his nickname the same day he arrived, was a slim skinny six foot one, and could he run! In back of our barracks this dude had actually chased, outmaneuvered, outran, and caught a live wild jackrabbit!

We were all young, between eighteen and twenty years old. Besides Dubby and I, the rest of the new troops were fresh out of Basic Training, not Tech School. But we were all considered young troops by the others who had been stationed at Ellsworth for two and three years.

Ellsworth A.F.B. was said to have some four hundred black G.I.s on it, and the white enlisted men outnumbered the blacks four to one. In downtown Rapid City there was only one club where "colored" were allowed to go and drink—the Fire Island Club. The other numerous downtown clubs would not serve us, nor would the white prostitutes sell black G.I.s any ass. There were no women for us black G.I.s to chase or even to buy some ass from except a small handful of Indian girls, who would cater to blacks.

I spent the majority of my free time at the movies or checking out some information about the Sioux Indians. I resolved to be a top airman, and set myself a goal to become a sergeant. I just might possibly re-up and make a twenty-year career of it—but only if I made the rank of staff sergeant before my four-year tour ended.

I went to the Black Hills periodically off and on to observe and know the landmarks. I could see the Black Hills from the windows of the barracks; I could see them from the flight line of the B52 bombers I worked on; I could see them, they were always present with me. These were the hills that Steve and I had dreamed and talked of.

One Sunday evening, I was told that the C.O. had a message for me. There was a telegram for me from Betty.

Slowly, I lowered the telegram, as shock came over me. I just couldn't believe what I was reading. An upcoming funeral—Steve—Watanka—dead? No! He had been killed in Korea by a rifle shot. I read and reread the telegram, standing there in the C.O.'s office, trying to tell myself that it wasn't true.

The C.O. asked me, "Anything wrong?"

I didn't even half hear him, but just stood there, then turned and walked out the door past the chow-hall entrance, out the building, downstairs to the exit and out of my barracks.

I walked to the rear of the barracks, looking out beyond the flight line at the late evening sun turning red as it set over the distant Black Hills. I wondered why they appeared so black when one saw them from a fifteen-mile distance. Watanka was dead. He never got a chance to see and roam the great, beautiful land of the Lakota. My friend, my best friend. I thought about all the times Steve had spoke of dying a young warrior.

I had decided to hang out at the Fire Island Club—a basement, off the main street—with its out-of-the-way dirt parking lot and rowdy, bad-mouthing cut-and-shoot atmosphere. The men who hung out there were all blacks, and there were a few Indian women, all alcoholics and whores. I tried one evening to hit on a half-breed chick named Zelda. But she was like all the rest. Being used by hundreds of G.I.s.

Early one night, as I was making my way around the sparse grove of trees that partially hid the Fire Island, I heard some cussing. I peered through the trees and saw people in and around parked cars; I tried to identify the cars, and then I was moving under the vague front light of the Fire Island. With a fast-walking pace I turned right into the dirt drive-way, and heard a woman's voice: "You God damn son of a bitch!" Then—*boom!*

I stopped in my tracks as another shot went off—*boom!* I couldn't make out much except two dudes hopping up some nearby stairs. They were laughing and shouting, "Man, get away from this bitch!" The woman was beginning to cry, shout, and curse with seemingly strained drunken heartbreak, and as I came closer I saw it was Zelda's sister, Gloria. I had heard she carried a gun and would at times go wild and start shooting it off.

"God damn it. Fuck it, fuck it, fuck it!" These Indian girls cursed like white people to me. Like *Skies*.

I stepped up to her. "Say, girl——" She was half drunk, leaning against a parked car. "Why don't you put that gun away? Say, look, let me buy you a drink, ok?"

"Sure, fuck! Yeah, buy me a drink."

I got her to put the gun in her purse and found out her sister Zelda was in the Fire Island. We went in, downstairs, an almost empty place with a bit of curling smoke lingering in the atmosphere. The jukebox blared—"Lonely Teardrops." Zelda was talking to an old black dude; I liked Zelda's quiet manner, her reserved way of looking unknowable, and she was the prettiest Indian chick around, with the best shape and all.

Zelda got up to sit with us in the wooden booth seats. Shit—I was feeling glad and lucky to have come to town early and now suddenly have two of these Indian chicks to hit on before any other G.I.s arrived. I readily rapped to Zelda, trying to talk cool but nicer than most boastiferous conversations I heard in the Fire Island. And I found right away that Zelda sort of liked me, my conversation about my knowledge of American

Indians, jazz music. She looked at me, and when I paused, she'd say, "Go on, huh?"

Gloria caught the next dude that came in, named Lou, getting up and asking him to dance with her. I noticed he wasn't dressed as nice and cool as I was. In the desolation of South Dakota, where four hundred black G.I.s were attempting to make it with not more than twenty Indian girls, I realized I had to set my scene with Zelda now, early, before the crowd of wild-talking fools and fighting nuts came in. I didn't want to have to shoot nobody—my personal protection was a twenty-five pistol either me or Dubby carried every time I came here. But tonight I was thinking Zelda could be mine to screw. My penis was already hard as a rock; I was anxious but coolly reserved, speculating that I might not even get to screw Zelda, but wanting to, bad.

All four of us wound up at a one-bedroom motel apartment. I hadn't really asked Zelda. There was that bit of cover-up shyness on my part about that.

Gloria and Lou went into the bedroom. A half hour later, Zelda said, yawning, "I'm going to bed. You coming?"

In the bedroom we were uncomfortable, cramped in the space Gloria and Lou left us on our side of the bed—and me still playing the reserved game, still in my shorts and T-shirt, she totally naked. I finally began to hassle the scene, trying to get my dick in her vagina, but I couldn't seem to. Everything I did seemed to hurt Zelda, which made me pause and stop. I tried to talk softly to her, and she started dropping off to sleep; so I went at it again, only to find I couldn't get my penis in her—me pushing hard, she grunting in pain. Feeling bad that I wasn't doing something right, that I wasn't really fucking. I lay there, deciding to let her alone, and she fell off to sleep. It came to me to screw her while she was asleep, so I waited a long while and then, in the dark, I lightly felt around the hairs of her vagina and took my penis and guided it, searching, anxious again. I pushed hard with the tip of my penis, entering, and then waking Zelda.

"Why you have to have it that way," she moaned. "I don't like that, ok?"

"Yeah, yeah, ok." I got off her.

Two weeks later Lou told me that Zelda didn't like me. Laughing, he said, "She don't like the way you tried to screw her in the butt!"

"What!" My face got hot. "Naw, man, she wrong, it was an accident when we first started——"

I had been a corporal for five months and I felt a greater worth about myself. Tech Sergeant Parrot took an interest in me. I led my flight-line teams during aircraft repairs. I had no problem with the authority, or with Master Sergeant Lawson, who headed our shop. I got along. The second master sergeant under Lawson was somewhat of an asshole, but he and I hadn't had any run-ins with each other. The few white G.I.s I could talk to were the kind who were able to hold decent conversations without expressing their racism in any overt manner. I told Staff Sergeant Gene I had been thinking about re-enlisting, but he told me I should wait awhile, that I might find I didn't like it enough.

I had been smoking for a year, and I'd learned to play whist fairly well. A number of other G.I.s would gather in Dubby's and my room nearly every night to play cards or penny-ante poker, listening to records and drinking. I bought all the latest sides. I even bought some bongos, as I had begun to like Cal Tjader and Tito Puente and to pick up rhythms to the songs while they played on the box. I dug jazz greats from Miles Davis to Dinah Washington, and I especially became interested in the jazz drummers, like Shelley Mann, Max Roach, and Art Blakey.

Paydays, our whole field maintenance squadron reported a half hour early to the dispatch building. We would get information, instructions, and verbal orders on everything from our Strategic Air Command Base safety rules and status to places that were off-limits downtown. Major King, our squadron commander, even told us which loan companies downtown would give us good deals.

On the safety orientations, I stood in agreement with Major King, because we had had a number of plane crashes on the flight line. He would repeat our responsibility to see to it that the planes flew without malfunctions and how our jobs were just as important as the pilots and flight crews who took them up. This all gave me even a greater sense of my own worth, as I knew I was not one of those airmen who was negligent. I made it a point to know every new mechanical technique and innovation on old and new aircraft.

For over a month, I had been assigned and dispatched to the docks along with Buck Sergeant Haynes. I worked rapidly, expertly, and consistently on stacks of gig sheets and completed the jobs with ease—everything from a popped rivet that needed replacing to minor or major structural repairs or modifications. But Haynes and I had a run-in, over some bullshit. There was cussing and talking back and forth, but the result was fine: I not only won my point, but Sergeant Haynes got taken off from being in charge of the work crews. All the work crews except the sergeant and his partner were put under me.

The next day Haynes passed me mumbling something under his breath. I couldn't quite catch what he was saying except the word "black." I quelled my desire to bash him in the mouth.

I ran the five crews at the docks for the next week. We cleaned up the work in four days. Then one morning I woke up late, feeling bad with a hangover. I rushed out in the sudden late-spring snow to the shop. When I spotted Haynes coming toward me, I said to myself, If he says that "black" shit to me again, I'm going to kick his white ass. Haynes passed me, and then said, "You little black-ass nigger!"

Woooh! I was about to explode! I wanted to kill him. I quickly stepped over and grabbed a four-foot-long, sturdy piece of aluminum metal extrusion, the heavy kind. I gripped it tight, swished it to feel the weight of it, and turned around and ran up behind Haynes. *Wham!* I knocked him a blow that was cushioned by the hood of his heavy, fur-lined parka. He turned around, surprised, and *wham!*—I caught him upside his head again.

Now I hit him all across his back and arms as he ducked and dodged, trying to get out of my way, running between the work benches; then he stopped and whirled around with a stool in his hands. With my next raging swing, I struck the stool and Haynes rushed me. I grabbed the stool, letting loose of the metal extrusion, and we both tussled with the stool.

Suddenly Sergeant Parrot appeared and grabbed Haynes, pulling him away and shouting, "Hold it! Hold on!"

"*Yeeeiiieee!*" I gave out a loud Indian war cry and ran with a tight, ready, right-hand fist, leaping high into the air, coming down at Haynes's frightened face as Parrot kept pulling him back. The knuckles of my hand sank into Haynes's flesh, against his bone. With that blow, Haynes, Parrot, and I hit the floor. Parrot let Haynes go and grabbed me from behind. Before he could drag me too far away, I lifted up my leg and furiously kicked Haynes a blow to the stomach. That made him double over in pain.

"Seale! Cool down! Cool down! Hold on! Hold——" Parrot held me in a grip. I kept my eyes on Haynes as I struggled to get loose from Parrot.

"Let me go, God damn it!" I yelled to Parrot. "Just let me go!"

"Ok, ok, but cool down, you're messing up on the promotion. So cool down!" Parrot then let me go. "You got to be cool, Seale."

"And if you fuck with me again, motherfucker," I shouted to Haynes, "I'll kill you. I'll blow your God damn brains out, son of a bitch! Don't you never call me no black-ass nigger, never, motherfucker, not as long as you live!" I huffed and puffed, panting.

"Seale, just cool down!" I turned, and Sergeant Lawson was saying, "Slow down, just hold on."

Parrot was holding me by the top of my shoulder. "Say, Seale, man, this might mess up the promotion, so just cool it," Parrot said again.

"Fuck a stripe! I'll promote that motherfucker into bad health." I didn't care about any promotion at that point. But I finally cooled down.

The very next morning I stood before a captain who read off what I was charged with. He asked me did I have anything to say.

"I don't like white airmen calling me a black-ass nigger, that's all I got to say."

"Well, I'm going to sentence you to thirty days in the stockade, busting you to airman basic, and forfeit your pay for a month."

"You mean I have to go to jail?"

"Thirty days. That's all. Report back to your squadron headquarters."

I was back at the shop thirty days later, working diligently with a white civilian, with Sergeant Parrot still behind me, coaxing Sergeant Lawson to let me do major repairs. In another month I was promoted back to airman third class with one stripe. But Webster and Green began to run with Snake more now, and they didn't hang with me much after I came out of the stockade. I'd trained Green and had always treated him fair, and Webster had been my friend. Snake was pissed seemingly all the time because he had not been promoted yet. I had lost those three as friends.

Six months after the stockade and after two years in the Air Force, I was up again for corporal—and made it. Feeling good, back at the shop, I overheard Webster talking to Snake and Green.

"I got my leave pay. Let's go to town tonight. The drinks is on me!" Webster boasted.

"I'll drink and fuck anything!" Green put in. "We ought to make one of them Indian chicks sell us some pussy."

"We going to town tonight!" Snake exclaimed. "And get o-ver! See, we got to get them whores drunk."

As they talked and bullshitted, I thought: Webster's ready to spend money on Green and Snake, but he forgot about the fifteen dollars he's been owing me for over a year. And he was supposed to be my friend.

"Say, Webster." I smiled and walked up to him and patted him on the back sarcastically. "Ah, what about that fifteen dollars you owe me from when you needed your license for your car?"

"Ah, man, I *paid* you!" Webster lied.

"Say, man, later," Snake told Webster.

"Naw. Now, just wait. Old do-good, tight Webster is treating you-all, and all I'm asking is for you, Webster, to pay me my money. We don't run with each other no more, so pay up."

"Hey, come on, Webster," Snake said, walking away, "don't give him your coins." And Webster started walking away.

"That's all right, Webster. Now I know how you don't never pay nobody back!" I said loudly. "Whatever you borrowed from me, you can just keep it." I walked back to my work bench, mumbling under my breath, "Motherfucker. A two-bit jive motherfucker."

Webster, Green, and Snake came back a couple of hours later. They huddled on one side of the shop for a while, then Snake walked up to me.

"Hey Bobby!"

"What?" I said, not looking at him.

"Webster said he ain't giving you shit and if you ask him for that fifteen dollars again, he going to kick your ass."

"He *what*!" I stopped what I was doing and looked at Snake.

"Say, man. He can fuck you up."

"Man, Webster can't kick my ass and I don't even want the money. He can keep it 'cause he's a chicken shit motherfucker; so, you know, fuck it!" I turned my head.

"Oh, yeah, I think he can kick your ass," Snake nastily put in, looking at me like he was tough. "But, ah, he said you better not ask him again about——"

"Aw, later, man." I waved Snake off. "Fuck the fifteen dollars."

I felt mad, rage coming on. I knew that Webster could not beat me. We were the same size, but Webster most of the time had been scared that dudes would jump on him. God damn! I thought about the situation some more and concluded that Snake was the instigator and Webster didn't even say that.

At noon Webster walked in the shop and up to Snake. Then he hollered out loudly to me, "Don't bring that shit up to me no more, motherfucker, 'cause I'll kick your ass!"—trying to sound bad. Snake and Green were standing there smiling at me. I felt embarrassed, as I looked around; all eyes were on me.

"Aw, man, later!" I raised my voice, waving him off, saying, "Later, you can keep the money." But at the same time I wanted to let him and everyone else know I wasn't scared of him.

"I think he scared to fuck with you, Webster," Snake boasted. "He knows you can whip him."

I turned sideways, looking at Snake, then at Green. They were all laughing at me. I wanted to jump back at them. I looked at Webster with my serious, curled-up old Indian expression, then looked around the room for something to pick up to whip all three of them. I turned my head, driving the thought away, telling myself, No! I got to just ignore them. I remembered Steve telling me not to let people get to me and make me lose my temper. I'll just forget them—fuck them—fuck them.

In the shop, later, Snake, Webster, and Green were at it. Snake had spread the story to Dubby and Gene. It was up at the parachute shop and throughout the dispatch building. Stanford and Dan had heard it. Dubby, who worked in the docks all day, came up to me and said, "Man, Webster threatened to kick your ass if you asked him for that money he owes you."

"Aw, Dubby, man, Webster just talking. I don't care, man. I ain't going to lose my head."

Gene went over to try and talk some sense to them, tell them not to be talking about me all up and down the flight line.

"Naw, if he asks me again for the money, like I said, I'll beat his God damn ass!" Webster looked at me.

Gene shook his head and walked toward me, saying, "Silly motherfuckers."

It was at this point that I somehow *calmly* made up my mind. For the first time in my life, a controlled type of rage was within me—very controlled, with a conniving sense of vengeance, to stop them for good, but on my terms. I suddenly *knew* I was going to kick Webster's natural ass. As Webster looked at me, I had a half smile on my face.

"Say, Webster," I hollered out. "It's all right. Just forget it. It's all right." I waved at all three of them as I walked closer to them at the gate. They were slightly confused, lessening their threatening stares. I smiled righteously now, showing teeth, thinking: Webster old buddy, your time is just about ripe.

As a rule, I did not initiate fights. My confusion had been a lack of confidence to deal with situations, believing I'd be counted last and rejected, beat, or killed and would die and go to hell. But that was all part of my honest past. I had always been scared to start trouble. Sometimes, in a rage or just mad, I'd say things to get people off my back—and people had cheated me, and that would make me the aggressor—but no, no Bobby, you were even scared then. And now, I wasn't. I'll show them my dignity when they think I don't have any.

As they walked ahead of me, I held back and feigned away the pulsing need to just go off into my old rage. There was a time and a place for everything. And I realized and was afraid of the thoughts and remembrances of going into a rage. I was scared of myself and what I might do. So I had to calculate exactly when and how to literally beat the hell out of Webster. I'd try to beat him within limits, though.

I stepped faster, caught up, and walked alongside of Green as we now walked four abreast. I smiled as they talked. Yeah, you're still my friends, my facial expression noted. I kept my hands in my pockets, making sure I did not flex up in any way, keeping my face meek and friendly, listening to them and laughing when they laughed, knowing I was being cunning.

I glanced at a large rock on the ground, thinking I could quickly pick it up and knock shit out of Snake. I knew Green would be shocked by the blood gushing out of Snake's slimey head, with his face smashed. But no— I'll just wait. I'd have to do in all three of them at the barracks. I'd have to get something to beat them with. Hey, I know! I'll get a *bed-adapter*—that's it! It's a good two feet long, just like a steel pipe.

We walked in front of our barracks, and when we got midway I stepped toward the entrance. They kept walking ahead toward the chow hall. I went inside, into my room, and quickly stooped, looking left and right to find a bed-adapter. There was one, under my bed. I hopped over, crawled on my knees on the waxed floor, and got it. Then thought—after chow, I'll come in my room. Maybe I'll ask them in my room, to fake there's no hard feelings.

I caught up with them, got my food, and sat down at the table with Snake, Webster, and Green. I ate very fast but very little, as I did not want to be full and sluggish. Ironically, they started talking about going downtown.

"If I can catch one of them squaws tonight, I'm going to get over!" Snake said.

"If you catch one, I'm fucking her after you," Green said, grinning and looking at Snake as if he was all-powerful.

"What if the whore don't want to fuck you when I get through?" Snake said. " 'Cause I do some tall fucking."

"Then I'm going to Bogart some pussy," Green spouted.

Webster laughed and said, "Green, nigger! I'm next and I know the whore going to be in love with my dick when I get through."

I laughed when they laughed, thinking and knowing that when I got through with their asses, they were not going to town, or anywhere else, for a long time.

I followed them as they put their trays in the open section where the eating utensils were to go. I even held the door for them. In the barracks, they walked on past my room and I quickly stepped into my open door, moving fast. I opened my locker door and picked up the bed-adapter, gripping it tightly in my right hand and holding it straight down behind my leg as I walked into the hall.

"Hey! Webster!" I said, stepping fast. "Ah, look, man. I just want to ask you something." I was not smiling, but looking Webster dead in the eyes as I approached him. "You told me not to ask you again for that fifteen dollars you owe me!" I stood half sideways to him, gripping the bed-adapter tight behind my leg. I wanted that same talk from him.

"Look, motherfucker, I told you that I'll kick your ass if you messed with/me again about that!"

Snapping the bed-adapter up, I gripped it with both hands and reared back to release the blow that carried the violent strength that filled me, swinging at Webster's skull as he turned and suddenly jerked his head with shock and fear in his eyes—but it was too late.

Whamm! I could feel the bed-adapter connect across his face, knocking the natural hell out of him, his head thudding between the wall and the bed-adapter. Blood gushed from his mouth. I jumped to a more sturdy position; I came back and solidly connected again, almost in the same place. More blood splattered. His stunned body weakened, and he slid slowly to the floor. *Whamm! Whamm!* More body-blows as he sank farther. I beat him again and again across the back. He doubled up into a knot with his hands and arms all over his head as I beat him. I hit him four more hard licks as he covered up his head, and I caught his wrists. His fingers quivered from the impact of the blows. He had no choice but to loosen his grip around his head.

I stomped him with my boot in the head twice, then kicked him in the stomach, striking his knees. I stepped away with furious fiery eyes, tensed and flexed, looking for Green. Green stood by the doorway, ready to run, looking at Webster's downed mutilated bloody body, then at me, and shaking with fear. Slithering, moaning pleas cried out from Webster's bloody mouth. "Help me, help me!"

"You want to back him up, motherfucker?" I stepped toward Green, gripping and raising the bed-adapter, getting ready to lunge forward and strike.

"Naw! Bobby, *please!* I'm sorry, man!" He backed up. "Please, I'm——"

"Help, help!" Webster's bubbling mouth was spitting blood-words, but I kept going toward Green.

"I'll beat your God damn ass too!" I yelled to Green. "You low-lifed son of a bitch! And I was your God damn friend!" I pointed with the bed-adapter. "So go tell Snake, so I can *kill* that motherfucker!"

I heard Gene's voice. "Bobby! Say, man!" Gene had come out of his room. Dan was looking over Gene's shoulder.

Green quickly left.

"God damn! This cat's got to go to the hospital!" Dan said, looking at Webster on the floor in a puddle of blood. I stepped back, listening to Webster mumble something. I raised the bed-adapter and came down across his side.

"Bobby! Bobby!" Gene jumped back—*wham!*—"Bobby! that's enough man, you going to kill him! Bobby!"

Wham! The last blow carried a certain finality.

I stopped. "You two-bit motherfucker! The next time——"

"That's enough," Gene yelled.

"You talk about——" I huffed in heaving breaths.

"Shit!" Dan exclaimed, stepping back in his room door.

"—kick in my ass, I will kill you," I said, looking down at the moaning Webster.

"Bobby, that's enough! Now, go on to your room, man. I don't blame you. But cool it. You got him and I'm glad."

I walked off back to my room and stepped in the middle of the floor, heaving breaths of air, feeling a relief, a sort of victory but with a confused sorrow that told me I was dangerous, a killer. Webster's bloody face flashed in my mind. I walked a circle in the middle of the floor, the bed-adapter still gripped tightly in my hands. I jerked it with short gesturing blows, telling myself I ought to go back down the hall and kill the motherfucker. No! I pleaded with myself and stopped in the middle of the floor. My rage had gotten out of hand. Snake flashed in my mind —Snake! Yeah! I'll get him, too. I'll kill Snake's ass! He needed to be shot!

I reached in my pocket and got out my keys. Then I stepped to Dubby's locker, opened it, and got his gun. I stuck the gun down in my fatigues pocket, snatched the door open, and looked down the hall.

Green had come back and was trying to help Webster get up. Gene tried to dab at the blood on Webster. Dan walked quickly into the latrine. I started walking fast down the hall, bellowing, "Naw! Your kind of motherfuckers think you can fuck over people, but not me." I was looking at Webster and Green. Furious anger was still riding high within me. "So the next time you even think about beating my ass, you'll think twice, motherfucker!"

"Come on Bobby, man, that's enough. Leave them alone!" Gene said.

I walked into the day room. Three white G.I.s were staring at me. I looked out the front day-room window, hoping I'd spot Snake, then walked back toward Webster. Dan had got a mop and bucket and was walking toward the bloody hall floor.

"I'm—I'm not paying you shit," Webster mumbled. "I—I—I'm going to get—get you, motherfucker."

"*Yeeeeiiieeee!*" I lunged forward and my tightened balled fists simultaneously caught him in the head. Then a left, a right, a left-right, beating his head again and again. He had no defense and I kneed him in the gut as he doubled over.

"Bobby!" Gene hollered out. "Hold it, man! Cool down!" I stopped. I had great respect for Gene: he was all right. I left that scene and returned to my room, uptight to the max!

"*Woooh!*" Dan exclaimed, looking at Green and Webster as Green again attempted to help Webster. "That's what you simple-minded folks get for fucking with Seale. Now you done got whipped with a bed-adapter!" Dan laughed at the idea as he swished with a mop, trying to clean up the bloody mess on the floor. "Yeah, you going to learn that you going to get killed trying to bluff and fuck with people. Now Seale done whipped your ass good with his bed-adapter! Ha, ha, ha. Yeah, Webster, you damn near got your ass killed. You think Snake's bad?" Dan continued his serious-joking teasing. "Aw, naw! Boy! Seale's the baddest—the Bed-Adapter Kid!"

Gene came in and shut my door. "Keep cool! Bobby, man! I mean I knows how you feel, but you done whipped that nigger's *ass*!" Gene was smiling and grinning. "Sit down man, relax."

I sat down on my bunk, still shaking from the nervous, riled tension that had built up within me.

"You stopped that shit cold, man!" Gene said, as though he were elated. "You hear Dan out there, letting them know some more? Motherfuckers. Ooh, shit! And calling you the Bed-Adapter Kid!" Gene cracked up. But I was worried.

I opened the door and walked out down the hall. Dan was still cleaning the blood off the floor, teasing Green and Webster, who were walking slowly down the hall to the door which led upstairs. "You better not fuck with me either," Dan told them, "simple-minded motherfuckers, 'cause the Bed-Adapter Kid's my friend and I'll tell him on you!" Dan slung the mop across the floor, laughing.

In my room I shut the door and lay down on my bunk, remembering Webster lying on the floor, then wondering what Snake was really going to do when he found out. I heard Dubby coming into the hall.

"What's happening, in this motherfucker!" With this gayful saying, Dubby came into our room. "B.G.! I just heard you and Webster got into it. What happened?"

"Aw, ask Gene and Dan, man. I don't want to talk about it."

Dubby walked out the room and I heard him asking Gene, "What happened, did they beat my roomy?"

"Shit, Naw!" Gene exclaimed. "Your roomy damn near killed Webster!"

"Yeees, sir!" Dan exclaimed. "The Bed-Adapter Kid—your roomy—showed them silly fools where it's at! Bobby whipped Webster so baaaad!"

"No shit!" Dubby said in disbelief.

"Man, you ought to see Webster's head. The right side of his head done swelled up bigger than a God damn basketball. He must of knocked half his teeth out! There's six of them right there on the table."

"Damn! Where's Webster now?" Dubby asked.

"I think he's upstairs. Him and Green. In they room. He better go to the hospital."

"I got to see this shit!" I heard Dubby walk out of the room and down the hall.

Gene and Dan commented and laughed some more about the whipping Webster got as I sat there on the bed, listening. I now had another reputation, one I did not want. I felt myself beginning to dislike it already.

Webster was taken to the hospital. I stayed in my room for awhile, then walked outside the barracks—worrying, thinking. Gene asked me was I all right and I told him, yeah, I was just trying to think, calm down and relax, and I kept walking.

Finally, late that night, I took off my clothes and got into the bed. I lay there thinking and remembering Webster on the floor and how his blood had spewed all over the floor, then remembering his face. I thought for a long while, looking up at nothing on the ceiling. How Webster was lying there moaning for someone to help him. The man was beaten. I beat poor Webster unmercifully and then went back to beat him again. I wanted to kill him. Why?

A totally sorry feeling for myself crept over me. I could have killed him. I wouldn't even help the man after I'd downed him. He was pleading, moaning for help even from me. His image stayed in my mind and I silently cried. I tried to convince myself that I was right, but at the same time confusedly hating myself for what I had almost done, the way I had brutally done it, and what I was capable of doing.

I wanted to pray to the Lord to be a better person. What kind of sin had I committed? What kind of sin had Webster committed? Thou shalt not kill. What if Webster had *died* there, lying in that gruesome pool of blood on the floor. I knew I did not want to die. I asked myself did I believe in God, and couldn't answer yes or no. I didn't know, I just didn't know.

I felt so lost and tensely alone. I didn't want to feel that way. Did I want to hate people? I felt like a mass of inner fear. I found tears running down my face. I stayed closer and closer to my barracks.

Several days went by, then Webster opened the door to my room. He had a sort of forgive-me expression on his face, paused, then slowly approached me: "Here, Bobby, here's your money, man."

I stood up, pushing the chair back from the table, surprised, as Webster held the money out, then he laid the money down.

"That's what I owe you—I——"

"Yeah, ok, man——" I had a croak in my throat.

Webster stepped back to the door.

I heaved in a breath, looking away out the window, and said: "Webster, man, I got to ask you—to—to please man, forgive me? I'm sorry I beat you like I did—really, I'm really sorry man. I lost control——" I would not look back at Webster, I stared out of the window. "See man, it's like, if you don't forgive me for not helping you when you was bleeding"—a rush of tears was on my cheeks—"then I don't know what's going to become of me—I mean—just forgive me man, please."

"Ah, Bobby, man—don't—— Yeah, ok, you all right. It's over—I forgive you, man. It's all right. It was my fault. Don't worry."

I still looked out of the window. We were silent a moment, then I said, "Thanks. Thank you."

Webster left, and I stood there a long while.

Six months later, Rabbit, who played valve trombone, began to play with the Base jazz band. I had bought a brand-new set of drums. Rabbit and I got some gigs downtown at the U.S.O., playing backup.

A nationwide Air Force talent show was to take place. Rabbit and I found a black bass player and hooked up with a piano player. We entered the talent show and won locally; we were cleared to compete at Travis A.F.B., thirty-five miles from Oakland. The night of the talent show, we lost; and we returned to Ellsworth.

By this time, I had only a year to do before I finished my four-year tour. I was bent on getting out of the service and becoming a jazz drummer. Every evening after work I was practicing, rhythmically swinging out, sharpening my skills. I could lose myself in those drums, mad or happy. But I had overloaded myself with debts and a collection agency sent me a "final notice" to pay on my drums or they would be repossessed.

When I got to see an agent, he told me I had to pay off the whole five-hundred-dollar balance. I just couldn't understand that. I was only two lousy months behind. The drums had run near seven hundred and sixty dollars, and they would not accept the fifty dollars I tried to give them for the two particular payments I was behind. They sharply cut off any explanation and told me I had thirty days to pay off the whole five hundred dollars.

They were some chicken-shit bastards, I thought as I left the downtown office, worried now about having the drums repossessed. I tried to get a cosigner for a credit union loan—it had to be a sergeant. I attempted to get each and every sergeant I saw and somewhat knew; they would not do it. I tried gambling and won; I now had one hundred and sixty dollars. I went back to the collection agency, but they would not accept the hundred and sixty as partial payment, nor would they extend my time.

My squadron commander told me I had better pay off that five-hundred-dollar balance on my drums. This was Lieutenant Colonel King, recently promoted. I told him I needed a little more time to get a cosigner.

But he said I had to pay the money now! He cussed me and told me I'd better pay off that damn bill. Why was he putting on the pressure? A rumor was that that particular collection agency was run by Lieutenant Colonel King's relatives. That was something! I really believed it, the way King was putting the pressure on me.

When payday came, I had exhausted every avenue. I had three hundred and seventy dollars.

I gambled for two days that weekend. I was winning and losing but always coming back to the original amount I had. Finally, as I continued to gamble, trying hard, I ended up losing. By early Monday morning I had a hundred and seventy dollars to my name. I was totally disgusted. Noon that Monday, Lieutenant Colonel King threatened to put me in the stockade if I didn't pay off the five hundred dollars.

God how I hated the Air Force and King. It just wasn't fair—it was all a calculated pressure game, and at the expense of my future. I was definitely not going to give up my drums. No! I would not give them up. That was the basis, finally, of my present and future.

I went to do a U.S.O. gig that Thursday night, worried like hell about losing my drums. Afterwards I went to get a couple of drinks at the Fire Island Club.

I felt everything was all going backwards. I despised the Air Force and felt hatred toward Lieutenant Colonel King as I got drunker and drunker. Then I was to report for night duty, which meant standi rg by to do any emergency repairs or jobs. Back at the Base, I drank some wine I had in my locker. I walked, drunk, the four long blocks to the shop.

I went to sleep on top of a workbench. The next thing I remember, I was being awakened by a loud banging on the locked door coupled with the noise coming from the loudspeaker—the bitch box, we called it—from dispatch. Some dude wanted me to repair a bracket. The part was damaged badly: the ninety-degree corner socket was cracked in all directions, and the type of part I needed to fix it had to be ordered.

The dude came back cussing me. I got mad and chased him out of the shop with a hammer, threatening to kick his white ass.

I lay on the bench to go back to sleep. Then the bitch box started up again. That was it. I snatched the bitch box from the desk, ripping the cord loose. A minute later the phone rang and I ripped all three phones loose, now raging. I didn't stop there, but kept on, tearing up the office, turning over all the desks, and cussing Lieutenant Colonel King aloud. I walked out into the shop and turned over all the worktables. I turned over and picked up workstools and threw them into the windows. This was it! This was really it! I just didn't care any more. I knew I had tried hard to be the best, maybe too God damn hard.

Rabbit came to the door, banging on it loudly. I opened the door for him and went right back to wrecking the whole place. Rabbit was astounded as he tried to talk to me. I stumbled, drunk, throwing my tools across the floor. Rabbit grabbed me but I pulled loose again and again. Then I guess Rabbit must have hit me because I was out cold.

I came to in my bed in the barracks. I got up and walked for I don't know how long in the night, then went into the day room and sat drinking the last bit of wine out of the bottle—glad I had torn up the shop.

The first sergeant came out from his office. "Seale." He was looking at me. "Come on. The Colonel wants to talk to you."

I walked in through the narrow hall, in front of the Sergeant, past his office and into Lieutenant Colonel King's large office.

"All right, Seale," he angrily shot out, "where are those drums?"

I would not answer. I wouldn't say anything. He looked at me and it was registering on his face that I was mad at him.

"So, you got pissed or something last night. What happened down there?"

I would not answer.

"Ok, tell me where the drums are and I'll forget about you being drunk last night."

This low-lifed bastard, I thought. All he wants is the drums, so he and his relatives can make money again and again, reselling them when someone gets a month or so behind in payments. Hell, no!

I ended up in the stockade.

PART V

Baptism of a Lonely Rage

OAKLAND, CALIFORNIA—the train's last stop. We passed our old village, and when we passed the Berkeley station the train had slowed, rolling on by factories and back streets, trestles and overpasses. I could see the Oakland station. It was early morning five years before when Steve and I had walked more than four miles to the adjacent freight yard; we were headed to Wyoming and the Black Hills of South Dakota. Here I was, now, actually returning from there after four years in the Air Force, with a bad-conduct discharge. We were the righteous wild ones, Indians, in the five years before that time. We were the Sioux, Lakota, black boys wanting to be something better than what everybody had prepared for us. Vaguely, I relished the memory and the need, that we were supposed to fight the white man for this land—but I had lost that desire.

Suddenly I felt an acute unease about Steve's death. The idea that Steve was dead never set right. And I knew I had blocked it out. Ignored it.

In the station I claimed my swanky three-piece Samsonite blonde-brown luggage. I tipped the Red Cap a dollar, watching people get on a bus to go across the bridge to San Francisco. I shook my notions of despair. A grown man, I thought. I'm beginning all over again.

I quickly looked myself over—wearing a three-button charcoal-gray sports coat, an old medium-gray English-design silk-weave shirt. I looked down at my pants, satisfied: light gray slacks, still neatly creased, with tweedy pinstripes; my cuffs rested just above soft black leather Florsheim shoes. I had cultivated a neat pencil-thin mustache.

I saw the number twelve bus coming up in front of the train station—shit, I thought, I ain't taking no city bus, not with a thousand dollars in my pocket. I'm taking a cab.

The cab let me out in front of the address I gave him, the hotel Mama and George were managing. It was two stories high with an old weather-beaten rundown neon sign, in the heart of the second worst cut-and-shoot district; how in the hell did Mama and Daddy wind up managing that place? And she a staunch Christian.

Two overdressed chicks—prostitutes, I bet myself—were suddenly looking at me, smiling with a gesture of acceptance of my appearance. A few older and middle-aged women with shopping bags walked up and down the street. I looked out across and up and down the street.

"Well, I'll be——Look here—— Bobby!"

I looked up. It was Hilda's mother, walking up to me. She was in her late thirties—foxy, short, smiling, dressed very neatly. She brought back memories, memories of some up and down and sideways bullshit two years before while on leave.

"Well, I'll be!" she exclaimed. "Woooh! I mean, a man!" She walked toward me. "And sharp and looking good!" She stopped and smiled lustfully, looking in my eyes. I figured, remembering her, she wanted me to return a lustful look. "Nigger man, what is you into?" Looking me up and down: "And dressed to kill!"

"Aw, I just popped in. You looking good yourself." I lowered my voice. "Good enough for me to really get to know you this time." I eyed her for acceptance of what I meant and suddenly felt I wanted.

"Wooh!" She stepped up to me and moved to kiss me as I controlled my shock. She shot her warm, long tongue into my mouth, putting her body close to mine, standing right there in front of the Ritz Hotel embarrassing me as she squeezed me close to her, moving her tongue and closing her eyes. I kept my eyes open, darting them from left to right, thinking, shit! Then she stepped back, looking at me again, and said, "Boy, if I could just get you!"

"Ah, girl," I said, feeling embarrassed. And we arranged to meet up as soon as I had seen my Mama, and let loose of my luggage.

I stepped inside the hall of the hotel. "Bobby!" Mama said. We went through the tight narrow hall to the two rooms where Mama, Betty, and George stayed. I listened to Mama carrying on about how I should have written and let them know I was coming home, as I looked the place over. "Let me call Betty so she——"

"Naw, Mama, don't call her. I want to surprise her myself." I was talking to Mama, but my eyes were compelled to look over the apartment. Mama and George's bedroom was also the kitchen. Everything they had owned was somehow jumbled up and junked up in this stifling place. Our old worn couch and coffee table were there, another rollaway bed, boxes of old clothes and a few pieces of George's unrepaired furniture junk. The same old rundown rabbit-eared television was sitting at one end of the living room. It was too tight, crowded, and filthy.

For the first time since walking into the hotel door, I really looked closely at Mama. She was wearing glasses and her hair was gently gray-ing—she was much fatter now. A print housedress shrouded her stout frame and she had on old worn houseshoes.

"Is you hungry? You want something to eat?"

"Naw, I'll eat later." I sat down in a chair next to the table, thinking I didn't want to eat here.

"Betty is sure going to be surprised to see you. Betty Jean stays down at that church all the time. Betty Jean is *saved*, Bobby. She doing good work in that church."

"Where's George?"

"Lord, George Seale is probably over yonder at that old pool place."

"What's his junk business doing?"

"Oh, Bobby, I don't know," Mama said disgustedly. "George don't seem to do nothing with that old truck no more. Lord, but we just barely making it round here. And this place here!" Mama's voice got loud. "I wish I was someplace else. Lord, Bobby. These old nasty-ass nigger men and women, whoring and carrying on—I done told George over and over that we got to get out of here, but he just want to stay here, messing around with these old pimps and prostitutes. Lord, Lord, sometimes I wish I was dead and gone to see my Savior!"

After some more talking I stood up, going into my pocket. I moved two twenties and a ten off the thousand dollars I had from savings, handing it to her. "You keep it for yourself. Don't give it to George."

"Ooooh, Lord, don't worry. He'll never know I got it, Bobby. If the Lord struck me dead tomorrow, you, Betty Jean, and John Henry would get everything I got. I got it arranged that way. The little savings I got, I got it set up so Betty Jean can draw it out, just so George Seale can't get a penny of it. Bobby, I got it so George Seale can't get his low-down nasty hands on it."

"How much you got saved, Mama?"

"Well, Bobby, it's just a nice sum. But don't worry about it. I'm still poor." Mama smiled.

I was feeling how Mama was a good mother to us all her life. And turning over in my head how she stuck with George all these years. Now she was starting to get old, stuck here in this filthy rundown transient hotel.

"Say, Mama. You-all still cutting on the owner of this place?"

"Lord, Bobby. I hope and I prays that the Lord'll forgive me, but I ain't got no other way to make it round here. Every once in a while I checks to see if the sheets somebody uses is still clean, then I just keeps the two dollars."

"But Mama," I teased, "ain't that cheating and sinning?"

"Well," Mama dragged out the word defensively, "all I got to say is, them whores renting the rooms and the old white man who owns this filthy place is the real cheaters and sinners and we's got to live! I don't pick up more than twenty or thirty extra dollars in a month's time. I keeps what I gets. George, he's always getting somebody to give him something extra. I just tries to make it," Mama ended sorrowfully.

Someone knocked on the door. Mama came up to it and opened the top half. There was a white man and a black woman there.

"Yes," Mama said. "Can I help you?"

I had a rotten, hateful facial expression for the prostitute, looking at her like she wasn't shit.

"We just want it for an hour, Mrs. Seale," the prostitute said to Mama, then cut her eyes at me.

"Oh, yes—I forgets your name."

"Mable, Mrs. Seale," she said politely to Mama.

Mama gave the man their key and shut the half door and put the two dollars in her pocket. And I asked her, "You going to be able to keep that?"

"Yes, Lord, and I thanks Him every day for making a way for me," Mama said, and walked back into the kitchen-bedroom.

I went on across the lobby area of the church and pushed the doors open and stepped inside the empty auditorium full of wooden pews. A short feeling of guilty nervousness came over me—I turned to leave.

"Can I help you?" a lady's voice pleasantly echoed, a sanctifying sound—conjuring up more guilt.

I stopped, turned around. "Ah, yes Ma'am." I spoke politely reserved. "I'm looking for my sister." She looked at me closer. I wondered did Betty and I still look something alike. "I was just looking for Betty—Betty Seale. She's my sister. My mother said she was probably here."

"Oh, yeah! You're *Betty's* brother. But she has two brothers. She talks about both of you *all* the time." We went through the exit door into a hall and another room.

"Someone is here to *seeeee you!*" She was almost singing it as I stepped through the door and readily saw Betty, with her plain but light skinned face, sitting down behind a desk, almost gasping, with eyes big at the sight of me, which let loose a happy grinning smile from me for her.

After the greetings and the askings and the explanations of where each of us was at, Betty was then saying, "Wait a minute! Look at you! These clothes! I got to show you off to everybody. Come on. You've just got to see Reverend Anderson."

Aw, shit! "Naw, Betty, I'm getting ready to split. Look, I'll——"

"No!" Betty said, opening a door. "Come on!" I followed reluctantly into a sort of lounge, carpeted, with expensive-looking couches and a highly finished table with a twenty-cup coffee pot setting on it.

Betty opened another door, dark mahogany, and Reverend Anderson was sitting behind a large, curved, swanky desk. All this along with my mounting guilt elicited a feeling of sinking to my knees, asking for forgiveness. Be cool Bobby! Blotting out the fact that I had a gun on me, in church.

"Reverend Anderson. This is my brother Bobby."

"Oh, yes, Sister Seale." A staunch mother-authority in a manly tone that could be pleasantly brisk, gripping you with each pronounced word.

Whooh! This preacher got some cuts, I thought, admiring the sharp clothes he was wearing. The suit must have cost two hundred dollars, I imagined.

There was a whole lot of embarrassing back-and-forth about if I was more "settled," and how a young man becomes wiser when he comes into the house of the Lord. I didn't want to say anything wrong to Reverend Anderson in front of Betty. She was happy to see me. I wanted to get away, not paying any attention to the Reverend's words, blocking them, un-til——

"It's like your friend who killed himself," Reverend Anderson began. "He shot himself because he was without the Lord."

"Who?" What was he talking about?

"Steve, Bobby," Betty said, sadly.

"I had somewhat known about that before it happened." Reverend Anderson spoke deliberately as though he wanted to get to me quickly. "I told Betty before it happened. The Lord God gave me a vision."

That hit hard. I was confused. They were saying Steve had *killed* himself?! No! They were wrong! They had to be! He got killed in action. He would never——

"Yes, the Lord God told me that a tragedy of some kind was going to happen to someone who was close to your family. And it turned out that this young fellow was close to you, a very good friend of yours."

I started to get very nervous. What kind of mumbo-jumbo bullshit was this?!

"So, the world around you, if you are as wise as you seem, should let you guide your feet and soul here Sunday morning. We get along fine here, and your own Christian mother is probably the best thing that ever happened in your life." The underlying, believeable truth in that statement got to me. "And that trouble you were in before you came home—in the stockade jail. It must have made you wiser," the Reverend said, assuringly. "I'll be willing to bet that you had to wonder about how you were wrong."

Now why was he assuming *I* was wrong. Let me get the hell out of here.

Outside, when we could get there, I said, "Betty, just tell me what they say happened to Steve."

"Well, he shot himself after he burned down a building."

"When? Where?"

"In Korea. Larry Page said he got into an argument about a Korean girl he was in love with. Then she was supposed to be sinning—you know, laying up with some of the other soldiers—and Steve was going to kill this one soldier and he set the place where soldiers sleep on fire. Then they came after him, and while he was shooting back at them, he took the rifle he had and shot himself in the head."

"Aw, naw! I don't believe that!"

"Well, Steve's grandmother said it was so, too, Bobby. Steve was your good friend, and I hated to hear about that, but he was just like Reverend Anderson said——"

"Reverend Anderson didn't even know Steve!"

I felt sad, a knowing feeling of guilt and no other way to turn, and remembering my awful state and my need to save Steve, but figuring that someday he *would* die fighting white soldiers, the very ones who would train him to fight.

She had on a negligée that fell just below her butt. She shut the door and stood right up to me, reaching around and through my sports coat, pressing her soft body against mine. Then I pulled away a little.

"Say, let's sit awhile. You got any records?"

"Yeah, I got a couple. Want some wine?"

I sat down on a stool in front of a dressing mirror.

She had a cold glass of Thunderbird and had sunk back on the narrow bed against the wall, resting her back on some pillows. "Well, this is me, Bobby, sweetie."

"Yeah, girl, it's all right."

She was relaxing on the bed, letting her legs rest in a partial part.

Looking at me with that lustful look, letting me know that she wanted me to screw her.

My dick was hard, but my jockey shorts held the hard-on down, then I crossed my legs so as to keep it from showing.

"Come over here," she said, patting the bed beside her. I stood up. "Take off your coat, let's get cozy, since you want to talk."

I took off my coat. Then thought, fuck it. I unbuttoned my shirt, pulling it out of my pants.

"We going to relax, huh?" I began taking my shirt off.

She got up and pulled her panties down to the floor, stepping out of them. Then reached up behind her back and unsnapped her bra and pulled it out from under her negligée.

Fuck it, yeah! She's ready, I thought. This was going to be it, my first real fuck—there'd just been Zelda in South Dakota, a real bust; one other somewhat earlier, which also was a failure; and nobody else except back when I was twelve years old. I stepped to the bed. She lay back on it with her negligée over her, covering the crotch of her parted legs. I dropped my shorts. Then looked at her. She smiled. Then I got on the bed and put my knees in between her legs and raised up her negligée and sank forward, laying my body over hers and getting ready to put my penis in her vagina.

"You got to get me worked up a little, sweetie."

I figured she meant to put it in. My hard penis was on her vaginal lips and coarse hairs. I wriggled my penis around past the hairs that covered her lips, and proceeded to try and push it into her dry vaginal hole.

"Bobby, honey, let's first, ah——"

I pushed harder, only an inch or so in.

"Oh!" she moaned.

I thought it was feeling good to her. I pushed harder. It wasn't going in right. I became somewhat self-conscious and proceeded to move my butt around, with the head of my penis doubling her hairy lips back into her vagina. I wanted to bust my nuts now.

"Wait, Bobby, wait! Let's play a little first. You in a rush. You're hurting me. It don't feel good like this, sweetie."

I yanked my penis out of her and then sat back. Shit, she's telling me I can't fuck!

"Well!" I was irritated, thinking I just want to fuck her and leave. "I thought you wanted to get with me."

"I do. I do, sweetie. But I want to—oh, nothing. I don't want to upset you."

I looked at her. Damn! She still got that look.

I opened her vaginal lips with my hand. It felt dry. Then I rubbed on her fluffy soft lips, then stuck my finger down in her vagina. It was getting good to me! I rammed every bit of my penis in her all the way, holding her tight, pushing my penis hard. She moaned, "Oh, oh," then, "Baby, sweetie, don't hurt me, real easy." But it was too late for me and my penis and mind to take it easy, as my whole body was tingling with total tension—and then with each ramming, jamming move, my penis in the bottom of her vagina, I ejaculated as she tensed up in pain. Again and again, and in a few seconds her pussy was sloppy wet. I let my penis rest in her, laying there on top of her.

"You got off. I'm glad, Bobby. How long has it been?"

"A long time, over a year and a half."

"That long——"

"Yeah."

"Oh, I see, you was just needing some."

Getting away from Oakland in my front-seat night ride to something new—the Greyhound Scenicruiser was speeding down Route 99, the valley highway. I watched the distant lights of oncoming cars on the highway, splitting and dividing myself from my family—from Mama, George, and Betty—from the contradiction of Christianity and filth. I knew the lonely desire to start something anew, I knew how to wallow in the feeling of my need to be a Bobby Seale more intelligent than Superman—Superman only had strength. A Bobby Seale able to run to any corner of life's activity, different from that childhood fear of death and fools and selfish concept of love I damn near believed did not exist for me.

Brotherly love, as for my brother, John, was not at all the deep friendship-respect that Steve and I had had (at times almost making myself believe he was still alive somewhere). And fatherly love was a misconstrued identification and revenge. With my mother, it had happened quite a while ago that to receive her love and know it was to find myself in the loneliest, most bewildered state of inner and outer tears. These rambling thoughts and feelings were with me on the ride going to L.A. to live with my first cousin, Alvin.

"Say! Bobby!" Alvin called out, stepping up to me fast. There he was. Six feet tall with a processed-straight head full of hair and a duck tail, having combed his hair like some white boy. He had a slap of scars on his face—as though some chick had put four razor blades in her hand between each finger and slapped him twice. His dress seemed flashy to me, nowhere near the sharp, neat quasi-conservative businessman style I had and valued.

We greeted each other and I was overjoyed to see him, suddenly feeling the fast-paced hip life I figured he must live. Alvin talked on, telling me he had a job at the airport as a janitor and would crack up laughing at the title of his supervisor—"maintenance engineer."

We got into his polished and shining, white-wall-tired car and took off. "You still playing drums, ain't you?" Alvin swerved the car recklessly around a corner, ducking in and out of traffic. "I'm singing, playing rock 'n' roll. I'll be glad when I make me a record. I got one demo already." The car hopped through traffic. "Hey, remember when we went to jail together?"

"Say, Alvin, any fine fat devils around where you live?"

"Fat what?" Alvin laughed heartily.

"Fat devils! Fine good-looking chicks. I mean, I got to get me a good-looking, smart chick. Somebody who digs where I'm coming from. But she got to look good."

"Oh, yeah." Alvin laughed. Then asked, "Why you call them fat devils?"

"Aw, it was just slang I picked up in the Air Force."

"If we can get a band——I'm going to organize a band, and you play the drums—you know, come up with some new beat, then cut a demo and we make big money. Then I'm going to quit my job. I can make money, then—won't need no job. I won a lot of talent shows already."

Alvin speedily drove up to and stopped in front of a house and opened the door. "Come on."

"Just a minute," a woman's voice called out. I heard footsteps, then the door opened. "Alvin!"

"Say, girl!"

Darlene was looking at me—this was another cousin of mine, one I'd never seen, at least since I was little. Children were everywhere, noisy. One jumped past us out the front door.

"Bobby, boy, I ain't seen you since way back in Jasper. You was a little old bitty boy. You sure done growed up. You-all sit down." Darlene went to the bedroom door off the short hallway and opened it. "James, honey, you asleep? Come on, James, I want you to see who's here."

James came out and he talked fast about everything and anything. He was sturdy, muscular, two hundred pounds, but bald-headed at the front. Much older than Darlene.

I was very impressed with their family. My cousins, with a home of their own, backyard and frontyard, children—which all made me like and respect their welcoming, fun-loving, down-home kind of ways.

"Say, you-all!" A near six foot three, curly-headed black-skinned dude smilingly stepping in the door.

"Get on in here, Clovie," James said. Three more tall dudes followed Clovie in. They were all my first and second cousins.

"Say, you-all," Darlene said. "You-all know who this is?"

"Oh! Hey! Bobby!" Clovie excitedly stepped to me.

I became acquainted with them all and their country-style, open friendliness, and found they were sort of proud to have me as their cousin. They went on about me a little as though they were all happy to have me there. When they found out I would be living in L.A., they exclaimed over and over about the fact that since I had a trade—"Bobby let me tell you, you got it made. You got it made boy!"

I hooked up a sheet-metal job, fabricating and assembling framings for windows, being praised by my numerous relatives with "Shucks" or "shiiit" or "Lord, Lord." I even later shifted jobs, for better pay and heavier skills, doing template fabrication for experimental aircraft sheet-metal work—which really bolstered my "smartness" to my relatives, having such an employment title attached to me. I was doing my best, being the best on the job, finding myself in another realm, seemingly beyond the twists of my lonely inner consciousness.

Alvin and I ranted, speculated, and dreamed of becoming millionaires someday, furbishing and refurbishing fantastic notions of soon making that big leg-wiggling record of his, him singing like a colored Elvis. We were rehearsing and arranging Alvin's songs. I whipped the sheepskins of my rented trap set, fooling myself into believing his original songs were good. There was a seeming closeness to making a hit—we cut five demonstration records of colored-Elvis music in three months, and I was running back and forth from a jive outskirts Hollywood studio, always trying to spot big-time movie stars when passing Hollywood and Vine—hoping one day to get a chance to see Marlon Brando, whom I always admired.

My cousin Clovie became my good friend—he would stand up with his tall, big feet, seemingly clumsy, but grinning and laughing with delight, and say, "Boy, boy, Bobby here! I mean, he knows some words. He can break them down too, boy." When we went out gambling, we grew to be, here and there, running partners in a fast-paced lifestyle. Ultimately, sitting in the kitchen over at Clovie's, Clovie asked me to teach him to read. To my surprise I saw he could only read "the," "but," and "is." He had been trying secretly to learn from a Dick, Jane, and Spot first-grade reader. So my enthusiastic personal instructions with Clovie gave me a worthy feeling.

The first few months I wasted some of my money going out to clubs, buying an old no-good car, making it to more and more talent shows with Alvin, and dropping seventy to a hundred dollars some weekends playing poker and blackjack. Falling into the trap of projecting an air of having some cool, well-kept hustle. It wasn't really me, but it allowed me to feel more relaxed around other working-class hustlers.

We put on a dance and show, featuring Alvin's singing, with me playing master of ceremonies and host—telling jokes that, surprisingly, had people bending in their chairs and cracking their sides—and playing drums. And in the break periods for the band I found women were hanging on to me, especially one cool, fine-looking, brown-skinned lady who sort of let her body, soft and smelling good with mellow sweet perfume, fall into mine with a conservative rubbing, making my penis hard as a rock. With me saying to myself, ok, she wants to fuck me—good. Now I had two chicks at one time, the first time I would fool around with two.

And in that peak time, after living in L.A. for some six months, I was agile and ready for my future of moving involvement. My mode of behavior had changed; I loved being busy with people and friends. I felt worthwhile performing both superficial and necessary functions—from telling jokes to explaining to Clovie how to read, from helping Alvin to lending money, from gambling to driving back and forth to work across L.A. and noticing one day I had spent my whole one thousand dollars.

Then, late 1959 the situation reversed itself: a nationwide steel strike hit. I had quit my job because an old white worker made reference to me being the "only nigger" and me trying to know too damn much. Instead of letting myself get worked up to a desire to kick his ass, I calmly terminated my employment there, believing that there were plenty more jobs where that one came from.

I found out, though, that there were none for sheet-metal workers at all. And without a job I was drawing unemployment insurance, my friend Peggy—a stripper and prostitute who was earning her way through nursing school—actually giving me money for rent and food, everything I owned having already been pawned. Without a "job title" or a job itself, I dodged my relatives.

I hooked up with a mean-looking, six foot, black-skinned dude who did house wrecking.

But again I felt a total rejection. I wanted to leave town.

One Monday morning I packed up what few things I hadn't pawned and split for Oakland, longing for a home, with my first plan of action being to convince Mama to move out of the Ritz Hotel. I always had the feeling that I was not defeated so long as I could feel I was starting anew on a Monday. Here I was, settled back and rolling on a Greyhound.

It stopped to pick up passengers in Burbank—I looked around, looked to the rear. Shit, all the seats on the whole bus were taken up, now someone would take the last empty seat, next to me—some old white person probably.

I glanced to the front again and was surprised to see a pretty black-skinned girl coming slowly down the aisle, stopping halfway, scoping from right to left for an empty seat. I couldn't help but slowly look her up and down. She was young, her hair was hot-combed and shiny and hung neatly, brushing the tops of her shoulders. She had on a light blue silk-type dress that made her seem shy and very innocent. I smiled and her eyes quickly darted away. She just seemed to stand there, two bags in her hands, not knowing what to do.

"This is the only seat," I said, and smiled. I stood up. "Let me help you, ok?" A scared, shy smile encompassed her lovely face.

"Ok," she said timidly. "Thank you."

I stepped down in the narrow middle aisle of the bus and proceeded to put her bags neatly into the overhead racks, then got back into my window seat.

Her large innocent eyes really beguiled me as she sat down, checking and making sure there was enough space between our legs as she pulled in her flaring dress and sat as far as possible away from me. The light, shy blue of the dress upon her soft, smooth, black skin made her seem like a pure virgin.

Now, let's see, Bobby. Just sort of introduce yourself and sound real intelligent and pleasant, and pronounce your words right.

She began to turn her head toward the window again, and just as quickly I said, "My name is Bobby." With a pleasant tone.

"Hi," she said quickly, smiling but hiding her teeth. Her mouth seemed to protrude a bit. And by the way she was smiling I sensed that she was ashamed of showing her teeth in a smile.

"What's your name?"

"Amelia." She held her head down.

"Ah, that sounds like a real nice name," I said, "for a real nice looking girl like you."

She blushed, looking at me a bit taken aback, then turning her head away with a questioning expression, nervously trying to hold a smile. I guessed she thought she didn't look good because she was dark skinned. I thought about how Mama used to say, "When you-all grow up and get married, I hope you-all don't marry no dark black person. Dark black folks is evil and mean." But I had long since rejected that notion. And anyway, this girl sure was pretty, and her scared, shy blushing emitted a natural innocence I had never seen before.

I tried to draw her out in an awkward conversation, and pretty soon she had told me, with one-word answers, that she was coming from Mississippi. She was going to Fresno. "I'm going to go and stay with my Auntie in Fresno." She was opening up. "You live in Oakland?"

She was talking pretty freely now. I could see in her eyes and face that she actually liked me. That quick, my rather conceited twenty-three-year-old sureness told me she was falling apart. But damn, I had never caused a girl or woman to start liking me that fast. But that I-like-you look was coming through strong. It instinctively made me feel the desire to screw her, to protect her.

She was only seventeen years old and would be eighteen in a couple of months. She had just finished high school in Mississippi and now she intended to stay in California and go to college to be a nurse.

I told Amelia about all my trades. That I was a jazz drummer and that I had done some professional comedian work at the Brass Rail Club in L.A. That I was a skilled carpenter and a journeyman aircraft sheet-metal mechanic, but since the steel strike I had been seeking another type of job. I told her my dream of someday designing and building my own house—a mansion—because besides being a carpenter, sheet-metal mechanic and parttime comedian and musician, I was also a draftsman.

When we had traveled over a hundred miles past the grapevines, we were damn near boyfriend and girlfriend. She easily embraced my hand when I reached for hers as we got off the bus for a rest stop. She wouldn't let go, nor would I.

I'd definitely come down to Fresno and see her. I'd call her soon as I got to Oakland. This girl was nice and wasn't corrupt. Then, I began to wonder how many boyfriends she had had. Probably not many, I speculated. She was not at all the fast, hip type of girl, and a hundred miles from ever being a whore. Then again, I really didn't know her.

Eventually I asked:

"I bet a nice, pretty girl like you has had a few boyfriends. They probably look better than I do."

"You? No!" She was smiling, gazing at me. "Bobby, you the best looking, handsomest person I ever met."

"You didn't have a boyfriend back in Mississippi?"

"Boys don't like me. I had one, but he just found somebody else."

"One!" I smiled. "Is that all?"

"Bobby, you the only man I ever met like this."

"Yeah," I said, smiling at her. Maybe so, she just might even be a virgin, I told myself. But naw! There ain't no virgins any more in the world. It's damn hard to find a woman who's *not* out selling ass or just trying to use somebody. Oh, hell, shit—I know I like Amelia.

"Say, Amelia, you know, I just met you and I really, *really* like you. I mean, at first, I just wanted you to like me, but I'm sort of checking you out in a way I ain't never did before with anybody."

"Oh, Bobby." She was blushing and smiling, still hiding her teeth.

She seemed happy, with an almost questioning disbelief. I looked deeply into her, coming closer to her, and kissed her soft cheek. She was so warm and smooth it aroused me. I sat back and just looked at her, allowing my honest feelings to be expressed, letting myself go ahead and get mentally involved with a loving feeling beginning to burst inside of me. I seemed to forget about my hard times in L.A., and the hard times that surely awaited me at home, and I was engulfed in the feeling that for the first time I really felt love—for a young, naive beautiful black girl.

The time flew by, and before we knew it, the bus was pulling into the Fresno station. Amelia called her aunt and we waited at the restaurant dining counter for her to arrive. I said I'd come down next week to see her and, "Amelia, you know, ah, wow. Say, honey, look here—I feel sort of real love is already growing between you and me. It's funny, but that quick——"

"I know." She paused. "I feel that way too." And slowly a lone tear came out of her eye. "Oh Bobby. I don't want to leave you now."

But as things developed, Amelia's aunt—a sharp- and snappy-dressing woman about thirty—invited me to her house.

We drove up in front of a righteous *house*, a nice, comfortable little home with a front yard. There were two black-skinned children playing there and a white-skinned, straight-haired baby sitting on a blanket in the front yard. The shade of the afternoon was casting its shadow from the row of trees along the street.

Two days later, Amelia and I seemed to greet each other every passing moment, each expressing deep feelings of affection. And just like me, Amelia would be passionately hot when we kissed, but she, trying to hide *that* feeling.

I went out to seek employment each day, but couldn't seem to find any.

The fourth night while downtown at a movie, I couldn't resist the urgent feeling I had any longer. I sweetly but gently talked Amelia into going to a hotel with me. In front of the cheap transient hotel Amelia got nervous as I coached her through the front entrance. Now I knew Amelia was really a virgin. I kissed and held her a long while to ease her. I took off her panties in the darkness of the room as she clung to me, her heart pounding.

"Bobby, I ain't never done it before."

"It's all right, honey."

I took my shorts off, Amelia's arms clinging tightly around my neck, her head buried in my chest. She seemed afraid to even look at me. I tried playing in her vaginal area to arouse her, but it only seemed to arouse me more. I forced entry into her. She tightened up—stiff, afraid. I couldn't seem to help myself. I guess I wasn't very gentle with her, because she began to cry as I reached a climax, busting my nuts in her sweet, juicy, warm pussy.

We got up and I got a towel, telling her to wipe the blood off.

"Honey, if you get pregnant, don't worry. I've always wanted a baby. And you know I actually love you enough right now to marry you and— I'm sorry it hurt you."

"It wasn't really that bad, as long as it was with you."

"I'm sorry, Amelia, I just wanted you so bad—I had to."

"Oh, Bobby, I'll do anything you want. We can do it all the time. Anytime you want."

"Well, it won't hurt next time."

"It won't?"

"No. I'll make it feel wonderful, like you do to me. See, baby, you were mostly scared and, being a virgin, it's like that the first time."

"It is?"

"Ain't nobody ever explained that to you?"

"No," Amelia said, shaking her head.

"Well, don't worry. You know, I think making love is a special aspect of being in love. I mean, I'm really finding that out with you."

The very next night we came back downtown to that same hotel. I took my time with Amelia, playing with her, getting her to know it would be wonderful. Amelia got righteously hot. She asked me, in a soft whisper, "Bobby, you going to do it now, huh, please?"

And we tripped royally. It was the first time I ever enjoyed making love so much. I relished the fact that Amelia was filling this craving need I had to love and be loved. I wanted nothing more than to marry this pretty, young black girl.

Later that evening I dropped Auntie off at an old but well-kept apartment building, which I'd brought her to before. This time she and the baby would be spending the night. Good, I thought, now maybe Amelia and I would have a chance to——But, naw! We couldn't sleep in the bedroom, not with Hubbie there, Auntie's silent and seemingly henpeck-ed husband.

Later on the idea popped into my head again. Amelia's sheer, soft, cotton pajamas that revealed a teasing portion of her breasts conjured up the desire that I was trying to hold down.

I couldn't help but wonder about Hubbie. Every night he would fall off to sleep just after the national anthem finished playing on TV. Didn't he and Auntie ever get down? I asked Amelia and she said that even that one night I had gone back to Oakland, to get my unemployment check changed to Fresno, Hubbie and Auntie didn't sleep together.

Hubbie was looking at TV. Fuck it, I thought. "Uh, Hubbie, can I ask you something? Is it all right if Amelia and I go into the bedroom? We're not going to do anything." I put that in real fast before he could answer, trying to look nonchalant. "We just wanted to talk some and we're going to leave the door open and all."

He was staring at me and as soon as I stopped, he said, "Look, you and Amelia can do anything you want. You can sleep together." Then he turned his head back to the TV.

Shit, he didn't even care. Damn! What kind of house is this?

The next day about three o'clock Amelia told me, "Auntie said to get Hubbie to buy these groceries I wrote down, and for all of us to come up where she is to have dinner there."

When Hubbie arrived from his warehouse job around four or five, Amelia told him and we were off with the two children. We went to the supermarket. For the first time I actually saw Hubbie happy. He doublechecked the grocery list to make sure he had gotten everything.

We piled into the car and drove to the apartment house where I had dropped Auntie off. Hubbie was driving and parking like a madman, rushing and anxious. He knocked on the apartment door just as Amelia and I stepped up behind him with the children.

"Oh! Here you is!" It was Auntie's voice. She stepped into my view.

I was shocked, looking back at Amelia to see if she was seeing what I was. Amelia threw her hand over her mouth, flabbergasted. The only thing Auntie had on was a super-sheer negligée that only teasingly covered her ass. Full legs, bouncing breasts, even the hairs of her vaginal area could be seen silhouetted through the nightgown.

Auntie reached for Hubbie, hugging him for the first time that I had seen. She pushed her body all up against his in a forthright gesture of just what she had in mind; and Hubbie seemed to be loving every minute of it. Auntie then kissed Amelia and beckoned us in.

I saw Amelia stop in a cold stare after walking about ten feet down the inner apartment hall, and I walked behind Auntie to where Amelia was. There was a certain distant feeling I had now for everyone except Amelia.

"This is Amelia, Harold," Auntie was saying as I finally stepped into position to see what was going on.

My shock was uncontrollable. Harold, whom Auntie was introducing Amelia to, was a white man. A fiftyish white man in a bathrobe sitting totally relaxed and smiling and acting as if he were geniunely happy to see and meet us. I started to check his body for any signs of Negro features—

he might possibly have just been a light-skinned person. But white was coming through loud and clear. I was fighting for breath, trying to say hi, trying to act like I was cool and this whole scene was really nothing.

"This is Bobby, Harold honey, he's a wonderful young man and he and Amelia are going to make a lot of money, yes, yes." Then Auntie turned to Hubbie. "Hubbbieee, baby!" And went over to him. Hubbie smiled as Auntie whispered in his ear, and he softly caressed her naked ass, not caring about anything.

"Have a seat," Harold was telling Amelia and me. "Make yourselves at home." He smiled.

The children got down on the floor, playing with their ten-month old little brother. Now I could see why that baby looked just like it was white! There was no doubt the baby was Harold and Auntie's.

Hubbie went to unload the grocery bags on the eating table, and Auntie sat on the arm of Harold's chair, crossed her legs over, and slid down into Harold's lap. She kissed him and whispered something in his ear. Then she got up; her round, shapely behind shook a bit as she walked.

"Amelia honey, I want you to cook the spaghetti."

"Ah, ok, Auntie," Amelia replied quietly.

"I'll help her," I said quickly.

"Oh no, that's woman's work. You and Harold get to know each other." And Auntie turned to Amelia and said, "Hubbie and I are going to be in the bedroom if you need anything."

And Auntie walked to the closed bedroom door where I noticed Hubbie awaiting, looking happy, with his right hand in his pocket. No, I was mistaken! Hubbie's dick had gotten hard! Auntie opened the door and entered the bedroom. She smoothly began to caress and squeeze Hubbie's dick on the outside of his pants as he rubbed her naked ass vigorously, closing the door behind him.

Harold never looked their way as I began, with a crack in my voice, to make phony conversation with him. Harold was calm. The children paid no attention to it all. As though it were a common occurrence to be there, playing mindfully. Only Amelia and I were quietly and coolly astounded. I wanted to be away from there. Somewhere with Amelia, in our own world.

I began to hear Hubbie and Auntie beyond the door to the only bedroom of the apartment. They were fucking up a storm in there. Hubbie's grunts, Auntie's sweet-talking in muffled sound—none of it seemed to bother Harold at all.

I loved Amelia and I knew she loved me. I looked at her busy in the kitchen. This whole scene threatened our two-week-old, blissful, pure affair.

Harold said, "I really love her, you know."

"Huh?" I asked, confused more.

"She's everything in my life."

"You mean, ah, Auntie—ah, Amelia's aunt."

"Yes. We have the baby." Harold looked at the baby playing with the other children. "And ever since I knew she was pregnant, it's just been a wonderful life for me. A woman like her. She makes me know I'm still a man and not just a machine, wasting my life away."

Late that evening we got back to the house and Amelia and I made love, but this time with a special closeness; as if we were reaffirming our love for each other. I knew now I wanted to marry Amelia and get her away from around Auntie. I listened and thought for a long time as Amelia slept. I had to hurry up and land a job. I'd build a home for us.

A few days later, in the afternoon, Auntie told me she was expecting company and would we go to the store and pick up a six-pack of beer.

That evening about nine o'clock, while we all sat watching TV, there was a knock at the door.

"Answer the door, Hubbie," Auntie said. "And let Geraldine and them in."

There were three women, not looking too well. They all seemed as if they'd been working hard keeping house all day—possibly welfare recipients who came out of the house in a rush with only enough time to throw on a little lipstick.

And another knock sounded and Hubbie readily got up to open the door.

A tall, lean, red, southern-looking white dude around forty-some stepped in, followed by a shorter, stocky Mexican, also fortyish; and finally a black dude, fiftyish and looking broken in the face, entered.

"Ah, have a seat," Auntie said. "Bobby, get a couple of chairs out of the kitchen. Hubbie, get three beers for everybody."

The three men chugged their beers as Amelia and I watched attentively to see what was going on.

"Ah, you got my money?" Auntie said snappily to Geraldine.

Geraldine handed her some rolled bills.

"Ok, go ahead," Auntie said.

"Come on," Geraldine said, beckoning the white man as she stepped to the hall in front of Auntie's bedroom door. The lanky southerner followed her into the room, shutting the door.

Once again my mind was blown! I was cool as hell, trying to act as though I had been around, but Auntie's exploits were nothing short of amazing to me. More than ever I wanted to get Amelia away. It gnawed at me. I had to find a job. I had to marry Amelia.

That night I slept on the couch. I was watching television. I really worried as I watched the TV sign off with the National Anthem.

"Oh, say can you see, by the dawn's early light——"

And I thought of Amelia's aunt. Maybe she's just trying to make it the best way she can. Hubbie attends to her needs like a puppy, gives her his weekly check in full. His wife, a god damn whore. I guess the world is just a tough, hard place to live in.

"——O'er the land of the free, and the home of the brave!"

Sunday morning, Auntie asked me, "You ain't got no job yet, see, and one of those chicks who was here last night, ah, she thought you was cute."

"Me?"

"Yeah, boy, you a good looking young nigger. Anyway, see, I could set it up and introduce you to a couple of others. I mean it could be some real money if we set up an operation."

"What you mean?" I asked, but I was hearing her loud and clear.

"Say, no shucking—you could work some young girls. They'll do anything you say when you do it to them right. Say, once a week, and then keep them on the street. Like Amelia. You know, I found out a couple of those guys who came here would pay twenty, twenty-five, thirty dollars if you'd tell Amelia you-all got to have money. See, Amelia would do it."

"Oh no, ah, I wouldn't do that." I was really dumbfounded, hating her, still trying to feign I was a hip dude, but— "I ain't going to pimp Amelia. I love her too much." I looked down at the floor. I wanted to take Amelia and leave right then and there. "See, I want to marry Amelia. She's everything I've needed to have a life with somebody.

"Well, look—not Amelia, ok; but I can get some fast chicks to dig you. We can still——"

"Naw, I ain't doing that—I just—No!"

I told Amelia later, "I'm going to leave and go to Oakland today. I got to find a job so you and I can get married."

"Oh, Bobby!"

That next night, in Oakland, I called Amelia.

"Oh, Bobby, Auntie said I can't marry you." Amelia started to cry.

"Yes you can, Amelia. In two weeks, as soon as you're eighteen. Like I told you."

"But she says I have to be twenty-one here in California." She sounded like Auntie had really convinced her.

"Amelia, she just wants you to stay there. She wants you to be a prostitute to make money off you! Use you! Please, honey——"

"But Auntie say she don't want you to stay here no more, and I don't know what to do."

"Now look, honey, we going to get married as soon as you turn eighteen and as soon as I get a job—ok, baby?"

"Yeah—ok."

"Now, I love you and all you got to do is leave with me when I come for you, ok?"

Amelia was scared as hell and I knew it.

She called me the next day. Auntie really had her head turned around. Auntie told her that if she left with me, she would have her put in a reform school. Amelia just wouldn't believe that she could marry me at eighteen.

This thing was weighing heavy on my mind. At the same time, Mama and George were moving—in the process of carrying all their junk out of the Ritz. "Ah, you ain't got that damn thing situated right! Ah, ah, we got a better place right here."

I was mad at Auntie—feeling I was going to lose Amelia—wanting Mama to move to someplace better—George breathing down my neck about this damn bullshit. I just couldn't take it anymore—I exploded.

"Fuck you, George!" I grabbed a worn chest of drawers, heaved it up in the air, and threw it off the truck, trying to hit George.

"Fuck you! Stay here, son of a bitch!" Shouting as the chest crashed to the sidewalk. "Move it all or stay here in this rathole!"

I got off the truck, turned and walked off steaming down the street. I walked the streets most of the night, making my way to the hills and sleeping in the deep billowy grass of the warm summer night.

On Amelia's eighteenth birthday I drew my unemployment insurance and boarded a bus to Fresno.

Amelia was crying her heart out. "Bobby, no. I can't. I don't know. What if Auntie say to the police that I ain't eighteen like she told me she'd do. Bobby, I'll go to jail. Auntie told me how bad it was 'cause she done been there before. I can't—not now. I don't know."

"Amelia——" I stood there looking at her tear-filled face. I loved her so much and I was now feeling sorry for her, wanting her to understand her freedom. It was a further indication that she knew nothing of the world, just like my mother. I was heartbroken; so much so I felt my insides would burst. I had no job. No real money. But she just had to leave with me.

"Amelia—please, honey."

"Auntie don't want us to see each other no more!"

How in the world did this happen? How? How! Just because I didn't want to pimp Amelia or anybody else?

"Amelia, you ain't going to leave with me?"

"No. I can't, Bobby. I want to, but I can't."

"Ok, ok, ok! Shit!" I stood there a moment in silence. I wanted to break up crying with her. God, I hated Auntie. Loved Amelia.

I stepped away from her.

"Amelia, I'm going to leave. I don't know what I'm going to do. You won't leave with me. I can't hurt your aunt. But look, remember what I said, don't let your aunt turn you into a prostitute. Please honey, don't do it!"

"Oh, Bobby, I ain't—Bobby, I love you." Amelia was broken up with tears.

I slowly walked off, trying to brace myself. I stood deliberately straight, walking away, not looking back. I walked until I got to the end of the long block and stopped on the curb and looked back. Amelia was still standing in the yard, looking in my direction. I stood there one minute staring at her. I let tears roll down my cheeks. I had no job, no home, no Amelia. All I got is a dream—a God damn dream—and that ain't shit.

To love someone and lose them. It was still fresh five grieving months later. I walked the streets aimlessly, didn't even go up in the hills for a more soothing solitude.

The crummy, tight apartment we had moved into didn't help my feelings of despair any. It was only just less dilapidated than the Ritz Transient Hotel. I became more introverted. Not giving a damn about anyone or anything.

Fuck the world and all the people in it! Pain was achingly easier with that feeling stated, fuck the next dude! To hell with some jive chick! Fucking women! Shit, they aren't pure and I'm going to be out to prove it!

I couldn't figure or connect my thoughts, feelings, and beliefs. This was new behavior that was anti-me. But I wanted it. I wanted to give my last goals and dreams of a house, education, and a woman away to the devil.

I started hanging around Reverend Anderson's church, surprising Betty that I would even come at all. My purpose was certainly not a spiritual one. I was there to check out chicks, screw them, and drop them—all to prove my point.

John, in the Air Force now, came home on leave. This was a happy relief.

Mama called Betty at the church and she was home in a jiffy, excited and happy to see John. Suddenly George came into the house. George had really been bugging me about paying Auntie's phone bill, which I had run up talking to Amelia. I knew I didn't want to hear any more shit about that.

George spoke to John, then came into the living room and sat down on the old, worn maroon couch.

"Bobby!"

"What?" I shot back. I was pissed off just being there, remembering, all cramped up, no job, no Amelia. My body gritting, tensed, as I thought, George better not ask me to do some job with him.

"Ah, ah, you know that phone bill you left that woman with, that girl's aunt? Well, that woman called back up, talking about her phone bill was forty-five dollars and she want you to pay it. And I got a job——"

"Say, wait a minute, George!" I raised my voice. "Don't tell me about no jive phone bill of that damn woman!" I spoke in a demanding tone. "She ain't shit! So fuck her."

"Ah, look, God damn it! You don't talk to me like that." George braced up to let me know. "You got to *pay* that woman!"

"George, you don't pay no God damn body!" I stood up. "So don't say that shit to me no more! You hear me, God damn it!?" I was shouting with a vengeance, and George got up out of his seat.

"Who the God damn hell you think you is!" He rumbled the house in a roar that spelled out my past fear of him. But no, George—I'm bad too, now.

"I said, don't bring that motherfucking shit up to me no more. Fuck that God damn prostituting bitch's phone bill and her God damn niece; and if you come at me nigger, I'll hurt you, George."

"Nigger!" George stood up, steamingly angry, but I was also on fire as he continued. "I'll kill your God damn ass!"

That was it. I moved to the doorway of the kitchen.

"Hey, Bobby," John began to say, "why don't you-all——"

"Bobby!" Mama distressingly hollered out.

As I stepped across the kitchen floor, I shouted, "Fuck you, George! And ain't you, nigger, or nobody else"—I stopped, shouting and pointing back at him in a nervous rage—"going to fuck over me!" And now I was thinking I had the right to kill George as I'd promised five years earlier.

"I'll break your God damn neck!" George stood at the doorless opening. "You don't cuss me in my house!"

I had stepped over to the fifty-year-old cabinet drawer and snatched it open. The eating utensils were jumbled, and in a noisy, quick search, I spotted the old Bowie knife I had made for George. But I didn't want that knife. I was looking for Mama's knife. Where was it? There.

Now totally disassociated from right and wrong, I told myself I was going to kill George. I would finally end it all. I didn't give a damn. Let him and the whole world know how much I hated him. I turned and took one bracing, stern step across the kitchen floor toward George. Mama's stained, dishwater and grease soaked, wooden-handled butcher knife was firmly placed in my right hand, and I was in a killing rage.

"Now, come on, George. So I can cut your motherfucking guts out. You going to get your ass killed!"

"Bobby!" Betty pleaded, but I stared straight at George's angry face.

"Say, Bobby, man!" John frustratedly warned.

"Oh, Bobby!" Mama was almost moaning. "You-all, please! Oh, my God."

"Come on, George!" I was nervous but in complete control.

"Say, Bobby, look man." And John stepped into my view, sort of placing his hand out in front of George's chest. John was pleading disturbingly and Betty started crying.

"Lord, I tries so hard!"

"Naw, he want to kill me. Let him come on, John!"

Mama's and Betty's pleading and crying was getting to me. But now, it didn't make any difference. George had threatened me for the last time.

"God damn!" John spoke in a grieving tone. "Shit, man!" He raised his voice. "Bobby! Look at you-all. I come home to be with my family a while——" I could feel what John was saying, and a tear rolled down his face and another down the side of his cheek. "I mean what am I supposed to do? I don't like the shit George is doing either. I ain't got nobody else but you, man, and Mama, Betty, and George, here, man. God damn, Bobby!" John was really crying with a demanding angry plea. And Mama and Betty were crying hysterically.

I was beginning to feel wrong because of their agonizing pleas and crying. I wanted to speak further against George but I couldn't.

Suddenly George's face appeared withdrawn, remorseful, disturbed. "Ah, ah, I don't know why you-all want to treat me like you-all do." And a tear came down George's face. He paused, not knowing what to say, then said, "I, I ain't got nobody but you-all either." And George broke up crying.

"Lord, please, all we got is each other." Mama whimpered. "Bobby, Please. George don't hate you like you doing now."

"That's right, Bobby," Betty whimpered.

"Man, Bobby, please don't do this," John cried, his face full.

I was on the brink of tears. George's feelings of being unloved were my own as I shakenly tried to hold back my own pent-up feelings. But I couldn't. Moisture began to fill my eyes. I wanted to be a part of them so much.

"I'm—I'm——" I was croaking in the throat. "I don't know. I'm sorry, Daddy, man." I raised my voice. "I've always loved you. I'm sorry. You used to be everything to me. I'm sorry, Daddy."

And George walked off into the living room saying, "I'm sorry too."

I sat in the kitchen as we silently let our tears express what we couldn't say. I realized that I was suddenly happy. I had feared but also admired my father, loved my mother, brother, and sister—and I had never told them so.

I was the last to stop crying in the few minutes that followed.

An hour or so later I told George I would work with him on one of his house jobs. And with a rejuvenation, I felt—Damn!—I had finally arrived back home.

"A house!" I said to Mama and Betty. "You-all mean *buy* one?"

"That's what we ought to do, Bobby," Betty noted sadly, in a way that let me know she misunderstood my loud reaction.

"Yeah! Sure! You right! But, ah, we got to have a down payment. We got to save——" I paced around the kitchen floor.

Life was treating me very well since that traumatic incident with my family. I had obtained my high school diploma. George had paid me for the drafting work on the last two jobs. I had found a job at a carwash.

"Well, Bobby, now what I'm going to tell you," Mama said, "you keep this to yourself. But I got near two thousand dollars I been saving since I left the Kelly Field back in San Antonio."

Did I want us to buy a house?! My answer was one I had heard many times in the Air Force. Do a bear shit in the woods? Answer—Yes, sir! And a couple of months following we all moved into a two-bedroom, five-room, wood-frame home with a small back porch, a separate rear garage, and a driveway, in a quiet residential street in Oakland.

With the comfort of living in our own home, I readily enrolled in Merritt College, taking evening classes. I became exuberantly involved in acquiring an education as an engineer draftsman. I'd pop home in the afternoons, barbecue in the backyard, and sit down to design additions to the house—a lower-level den, an extra-large upper bedroom and bath for Mama and George. I bartended at a local night club for a short while and then was hired as a standup comedian at the same bar.

When John F. Kennedy began running for president, I had a hopeful notion that things were really changing in the world. "Ask not what your country can do for you, but what you can do for your country." Fantastic! The whole black community loved him. To see Kennedy on the move, with his agile way of getting things done, inspiring. He also had a good-looking wife, Jackie. When Jackie would get in the car, she'd cuddle up to him and he'd put his arm around her. "Get it on!" I spoke aloud to the TV news. I went out and voted for the first time in my life. The backdrop of the civil rights movement, Martin Luther King, and the NAACP attempts to put new laws on the books made me feel I was a first-class citizen.

*

I bopped across the street, headed to the college for one of my classes. A crowd of people were on a corner watching this one man.

He almost danced as he walked and spoke, interjecting comments in a rather boppy, hip way, back and forth for twenty feet, up and down the sidewalk near the corner. As I walked on I heard: "Chinese people go to the Chinese schools to learn about Chinese people." He emphasized this with a stop and a gesture, looking at and talking to the thirty or more students. I thought his mannerisms rather comical.

"White people go to white schools to learn about *white* people." Bringing home his meaning with an artistic oratory, eliciting a laughing acceptance from the crowd. "And *black* people go to white people's schools to learn about *white* people!" That really broke up the crowd with laughter.

He continued with a similar analysis of black people shopping and buying from white businesses because all black people owned in the "ghetto" were barber shops and Bar-B-Q pits. Right, I thought, he's right. But what was *ghetto*? It was the first time I'd ever heard that word.

From the line of dudes against the store-front wall, a tall, curly-headed dude on the end stepped out.

"Hey!" I said aloud. "I know him." That's William Brumfield, Steve's brother. Oh, shit. If he's with them, these cats must be Communists, something I didn't want to have anything to do with.

William spoke about some dude, a writer named Richard Wright, who went to Paris, France. The white people ran him into exile. I stayed to listen because I wanted to say hi to William.

Another dude began talking now about white people; about what they had done to us black people for hundreds of years. I walked toward William Brumfield, and he calmly noticed me, saying, "Hi, Bobby."

I stepped next to him, standing against the wall.

"What's the rally really about? Who's the dude who spoke before you. He's out of sight. He can, how you say it? Blow? That cat's out of sight."

"He's Donald Warden, the head of the Afro-American Association."

"The Afro-who?"

"Oh, Bobby, this is John Thomas." William spoke slowly. "And this is Huey Newton." This brother, Huey, reached to shake my hand, and I extended mine. "And that's Kenneth Freeman speaking."

"Yeah, you-all blow good."

"You should come to some of our book discussions."

"Yeah, maybe," I said, reluctantly. I didn't want to come to any book discussions. I thought they might be discussing Communism and plots to overthrow the government.

When the speaking part of the rally was over, I stood around listening to William explain things to a group who had questions, and I listened to Huey Newton and Kenneth Freeman argue a few points with others about the Afro-American Association. These dudes seemed very intelligent to me. They left me trying to understand the meaning of so many words and trying to figure out what was the black bourgeoisie?

A couple of months later the Cuban missile crisis hit the front entrance of Merritt campus with a gigantic rally led by what Kenny Freeman called "a socialist group of white boys."

The speaker talked about Castro and Cuba and scorned the blockade by Kennedy that could cause a war. It was all very confusing to me. I rejected the speakers as a bunch of Communists who had no right to be supporting Castro against John F. Kennedy. The content of the speech shifted to civil rights. I was half angry at the white speakers already, then this white boy said, "So, black people have no rights. They are second-class citizens!"

What the fuck is he talking about. I'm a first-class citizen, I told myself.

"Not one of you can speak out in this very country. In the South black people do not have the right to free speech." He paused. Communists, white people, I thought in anger. Before I knew it, I shouted out, "I'll speak anywhere I God damn please! I got free speech 'cause I know I'm a first-class citizen!"

The crowd laughed slightly and responded with a few *yeah*s.

"And ain't nobody going to stop me from speaking nowhere in America, 'cause I know I'm a black man and I ain't no Negro and I ain't *cullud*! And ain't you or nobody else going to tell me what to do! Ain't no racist, ain't no Communist, ain't *nobody* gonna stop me from speaking or I just got to *die*!"

The crowd roared *yeah*s, clapped and raved with response. They made me feel I was right telling those white Communists where to get off at.

I saw Kenny Freeman standing across the street on the outskirts of a smaller rally of black students. Huey Newton was in the middle, arguing. I decided to go listen. I edged my way through to listen to Huey argue in seemingly very philosophical words about the civil-rights laws the NAACP was trying to get for us—all being a waste. The laws that were already on the books weren't serving black people, and what was the use of making more laws?

I really liked Huey's intelligent way of articulating his opinions. I was so caught up with my newfound knowledge, my head was whirling.

Later that day I popped into Spike's Cafe to order a hamburger. My eye caught a dude at the next table.

Damn, that's Robert Jr. Sure, it's him. It had been so many years. And Robert Jr. was scanning the room from face to face until he saw mine.

"Man! Shit! It's been, wow, years since I seen you. Ah, what you doing."

"Nothing," Robert Jr. said.

"Well, ah, how's Woodie and Sis?"

"They're ok——" He slowly looked away.

"Ah, and your mother?"

Robert Jr. slowly turned back to me, paused, then said, "Mama, ah—died."

"Oh!" I was a little stunned. "Ah, yeah, that's bad."

Another thing that I had heard dawned on me. Robert Jr. had gone to prison.

I went on with small talk, trying to get him to talk to me, to reminisce with me about our times and childhood friendship. Robert Jr. just listened remotely until I wound up with nothing to say but: "Well, what you been doing, man. I mean, all this time."

"Aw, nothing." He relaxed a little. "I been to the joint, Bobby; and, you know, standing around on the block."

"The joint? Prison. Yeah, ah, Betty told me."

We were silent. Then I said, "Yeah, well, ah, what happened to your mother? I mean, I always loved to see your Mama and Daddy dance, and you and Sis. Man, and when we used to go to the movies and I didn't want to go to Sunday School. Ha, ha!"

"Yeah, I remember, and one time you thought you was a Christian."

"Yeah, something else. Ha, ha, ha! Ah, where's Sis?"

"Oh man, ah, Bobby, she's on dope. You know. And Mama, well she died of the same shit. It's all, you know——" He coolly waved his hand, as I could see he didn't want to talk about it.

"Yeah." I had to think of something else to talk about. "Man, do you know I can't get over how everybody is gone. I mean, just like, why did they have to tear down the projects—that was our village. Remember all those long walks we use to take to the Berkeley Hills, and raiding fruit trees?"

"Yeah, all another time. And in the summer, every Monday morning was a new week for you."

"Who, me? What you mean?"

"You had six days every Monday, to do what you want before it's Sunday again." Robert Jr. gave a cool, quick, closed-lip smile, looking at me, then away, saying, "Yeah, man! I used to sit in the joint remembering all the good times we had when we were kids."

"I wish I could remember it all."

"Yeah, man. It's the shits." Robert Jr. stood up. "Ah, hope you do good on this scene. I saw you talking out—you pretty good."

"You saw me?"

"Yeah. Ah, I got to move."

"Well, say, Robert Jr., I live around the corner." I was up and following him out the door. "And Mama would like to see you, man. John's in the Army and Betty, she's stuck off in the church. But I live right around the corner, right there, turn right three doors and across the street." Robert Jr. was walking off. "And drop by sometime, ok?"

Nothing could tear me away from the world that was opened up to me through the Afro-American Association. I wanted to imitate Donald Warden's snappy, boppy, hip gestures and overemphasis. I even asked him could I speak. I found I could hold the attention of a crowd with my own boppy gestures.

I read the material diligently. I made every book discussion. I believed in the doctrine that we black people had to have our own. I understood who Marcus Garvey was; I read about Booker T. Washington and W.E.B. Dubois. I learned to debate, to argue logically according to the newfound knowledge I had achieved. I had identified with the American Indian's struggle wholeheartedly; and now that the realm of black oppression was opened up to me, I was quickly delving in with an aura of dedication and inner meaning of purpose.

The AAA gave "Soul Parties." Everyone greeting with the new hand-shake, doing African dances that looked like overexaggerated gyrations. I had made friends; I was close, really, with everyone in the AAA. Being a member stole me away from the desire to be any part of the black bourgeoisie. I gave up the notion of ever building a house up in the Berkeley Hills. I'd build it somewhere in the black ghetto.

One night with our AAA group, I asked Don, "Well, William Brumfield and Huey Newton and, ah, Kenny Freeman—why don't they come around anymore?" Everyone was quiet at the table. "How come they don't blow at our street meetings? I mean, I thought they were all good, and it seems to me they would make our organization grow faster and——"

"Well, look, let me explain. See, Brumfield and Huey Newton, ah, they really shaky. And Kenny Freeman, all he wants is power. So don't you worry about them dudes, they shaky."

"But Huey Newton and Kenny, I mean it just seems like they would be good for the AAA."

"Naw, *you* good! Say look, see, we going to give you a permanent speaking spot, ok?"

"Ah." I hesitated. "Yeah, ok." Brumfield, yeah—but Huey Newton and Kenny Freeman? I sat back in my chair. I had opened some kind of can of worms. The way everyone was suddenly acting edgy. I sat quietly, thinking about how Warden wanted me to see myself as a speaker. A promise—

a gift not to say anything about Kenny, Huey, and Brumfield. But why?

The next night at the scheduled Soul Party, when I arrived—the hand-shakes? I received none. The talk and exaggerated brotherly friendship? There was none for me. I tried to talk to people but they only shunned me. I danced a couple of fast records by myself when a couple of sisters refused.

Kenny Freeman dropped in and stood against the wall, looking, not saying anything.

The question in my head was, Did he know he was shaky? Then I began to understand something. To them, I was now shaky. It pissed me off realizing they were ostracizing me from them, from the AAA. I got up and decided to talk to Kenny Freeman. I mentioned what had happened, the ostracisim, then I said, "I mean, man, that ain't right, you know?"

"I *know*!" Kenny busted out with laughter. "Ho, ho!" In his half-squeaky voice. "Say, look, let's step outside."

That night and the next day at Merritt College Kenny ran down to me about when the AAA first started. Kenny explained how Warden, going to the University of California, joined the AAA's book discussions and from there he swung to his side all the six or seven dudes who weren't too bright. Kenny told me that right after the Missile Crisis rally Warden more or less split the AAA. He said the disagreement stemmed basically from one group saying black people needed to start cooperatives and Warden believing individual black businesses were the answer to the problem.

I liked William Brumfield, but his manner was too distant and different from mine. I liked Kenny Freeman, who seemed to have a storehouse of information. I very seldom saw Huey, though, who seemed to have a lot of chicks chasing him when I did see him.

I began to rap and hang with two young dudes, Ernie and Isaac. They and I agreed on things and we would crack jokes about the AAA and here and there criticize their members who were enrolled at Merritt.

On the TV news I saw Malcolm X talking of white people being devils. I had heard the Muslim doctrine but I only had Elijah Muhammad's image; Malcolm for some reason seemed different in his stance. It shocked me how much Malcolm X favored Steve, with his large forehead, facial structure, and lips—only Steve's lips were a little thinner.

Isaac, Ernie, and I went to hear Malcolm X speak in person. I listened to Malcolm X with a mesmerized enthusiasm, having a front-row seat and looking around to see disciplined, ready Muslims everywhere lined against the wall.

Malcolm had us captivated, over a thousand, jampacked, on the edge of their seats, as he thundered on eloquently, teaching us, constantly reaffirming his allegiance to the Honorable Elijah Muhammad.

Watching Malcolm, he was the man! He was the only one who could really tell it like it is. He was a better speaker than Warden or even Martin Luther King. But what fascinated me most about him was his resemblance to Steve Brumfield. I couldn't get over it. I even began to toy with the possibility that reincarnation really existed. I found myself trying to imagine that he was really Steve. I found myself choosing Malcolm X as the real leader of black people, and my leader.

When Malcolm finished, the whole audience gave him a thundering ovation, everyone rising to their feet. I hopped out of my seat, seeing him surrounded by what seemed like fifty Muslims, going down the right aisle, headed to the lobby.

I found myself studying everything about black people and reading *Muhammad Speaks* every week to find out what Malcolm X said. No one could tell me anything against Malcolm X.

Kenny, Ernie, Isaac, and I formed our own small study group; we read and digested a lot of material that opened up a realm of knowledge for me. We read James Baldwin's *The Fire Next Time* and Ralph Ellison's *The Invisible Man* and Jomo Kenyatta's *Facing Mount Kenya*. I began to read everything I could get my hands on concerning African history and the present-day problems of Africa.

For a few months we were even off into the politics of Africa, protesting and supporting the freedom of a black leader imprisoned in South Africa for simply speaking out against apartheid.

In 1962 I discovered the existence of a man named Robert Williams, who'd been forced out of the country to Cuba back in 1959. He'd been head of the Monroe, North Carolina, NAACP. We sent Ernie to Cuba, with some money a white radical group gave for the purpose, and he came back with a pamphlet, "The Crusader," about revolution in this country. It was getting confusing to me if they wanted to get down to revolution. But the big surprise to me was when Kenny told me of our plans to send Ernie to Cuba. I couldn't figure that because Cuba had turned Socialist-Communist. I still couldn't grab the concepts of Communism and deep inside believed that it was wrong.

The three children were bombed down south—all the killings being done by vigilantes—murders of civil-rights workers—Kennedy's assassination. I wasn't too much for any kind of white president any more, but I still felt a loss at Kennedy's death. Malcolm X said publicly on TV that "the chickens had come home to roost." Which I interpreted to mean that revolution was bound to come sooner than we all thought.

One day, while reading a speech by Malcolm—in which he talked about guerrilla warfare being the essence of strategy for black people to obtain their freedom—I got into a small argument with Kenny, Ernie, and Isaac about us at least getting guns and then learning how to shoot them.

"Yeah, man," Ernie said, "but first we got to get Mao down. We got to know——"

"Ernie, I don't think Mao is the point——" As I began to argue Frantz Fanon's view. But between the three of them I was more or less told that I had my ego out front of the revolution.

That only meant to me we weren't going to do a God damn thing. I felt that, really, Kenny, Isaac, and Ernie were just not up to the idea of black guerrilla revolution. And when the revolution did get heavy, they would not know methods nor would they have the stamina to even move to fight white racists. I imagined Steve and I organizing a group of mighty black warriors. I also began to imagine joining Malcolm's new Organization of Afro-American Unity in New York.

One day I got my paycheck and talked Ernie and Isaac into going with me to Sears to buy a thirty-three-dollar rebuilt English-made 303 bolt-action rifle; telling them they had to learn how to shoot and that I'd teach them.

I took Ernie and Isaac into the Berkeley Hills. I loaded up, showing them how, then I paced off the distances to our targets and got both of them to fire at least twice. For the two days that followed only Isaac seemed interested in learning how to clean and break the rifle down and put it back together. Ernie ignored my contribution, later telling Kenny I was going about this guns business all backwards and that I had too much of an ego to even be handling guns. That ego shit was beginning to get on my nerves. I ended up damn near pleading with Ernie to understand.

"We talking about revolution in the future. Ok, man, what is revolution? It involves guns, man. If guerrilla warfare comes, then what are you going to know how to shoot? How to stay underground? And Malcolm X is talking about long hot summers of possible riots and you can't do nothing because you don't know how to shoot and all you want to do is study."

I got nowhere with this type of talk.

Three days later they hid the gun from me. I asked them about it and they shrugged their shoulders—this was their method of bucking me.

*

131

I let Kenny drive and I sat in the front seat next to him. I was thinking of the two years I had spent running with these cats. I was really disgusted with their do-nothing attitudes. My youthful fervor was riding high. I believed in revolution and wanted desperately to do something, shake up something—anything—to help promote black people's freedom. But this group constantly talked about I-had-an-ego this and my-ego's-getting-out-front that. I realized that they were younger than I was and had had different experiences than I— Ernie and Kenny's families being relatively well off. I felt I couldn't make it with them any more, but I was trying again.

It just seemed as if ignorance abounded, and that my black people were destined to wallow in it, because no one was either ready or willing to do anything. With the exception of Malcolm. And now more than ever I seriously toyed with the idea of going to New York, introducing myself, and joining the group Malcolm had started shortly after leaving the Muslims.

Kenny and I picked up Isaac and stopped in front of Ernie's house, waiting for him, having blown the horn.

"So you saying," I said to Kenny as we waited, "you, me, Isaac, and Ernie are the Revolutionary Action Movement in California here?"

"Ah, West Coast, not just California."

"That's a lot for just four of us."

Isaac said, "All we have to do is go every place there is, then find out where black people live, each city."

"Yeah, I guess so. Well, look, how are we supposed to organize. I mean is Robert Williams the leader? I mean, do we tell people that Robert Williams down in Cuba is the leader if we—how do we get——"

"It's RAM, maaaan," Kenny interrupted, "West Coast RAM, and all we have to do is stay underground; keep everything underground, and we've been chosen so you got to do it."

"Well, as long as we really going to *do* something, that's what I'm after. I don't want to sit around bullshitting."

"Ah, man, what you mean?"

"Kenny, I mean that I'm really dedicated, like I said before. If we are going to organize black people, then let's get down to it. So if Isaac and Ernie—well, they good, but I ain't living with nobody."

"Say, maaaan, why you bring that up? See man, we got to get our egos straight."

"But I ain't talking about no egos." I raised my voice, refusing to be dictated to with some quick intellectualizing, wanting to first and foremost express myself to them so Kenny, especially, would know where I stood. "I'm talking about bullshitting! Robert Williams, you, Kenny, whatcha name back in Detroit. Ok, you say we black revolutionaries. It means to me that we got to do something."

"Yeah, that's true, but we got to stay underground. We got to have fronts. We got to move inside the other black groups and take them over. We got to have the shit down and——"

"So what you saying is that we don't tell people about Robert Williams. We keep that underground?"

"Say, man, we got to or the FBI and the police will have us all in jail."

Yes, I could fathom the dangers that the FBI represented, but I was still dedicated and wanted to know how we could organize this shit, get it rolling; so I asked Kenny, "But how we going to do it, man?"

"We give out the info to brothers who are interested. Say, man, now you say you ain't got no ego?"

"No, Kenny, wait. Listen—look—what I'm saying is that you-all got to trust me. But first, you got to hip me to what we going to do. And if we got some righteous work to do for black liberation, whether it's with guns or if it's just recruiting brothers who are interested, then let's get it on; and if it's having some front that the *man* don't know about, then let's put it together; and if we going to get inside black groups and take them over, then ok. But I swear, I ain't going to sit around, supposedly a member of RAM—like I'm just now finding out we were already RAM ever since Ernie got back from Cuba. Let's just do what we say."

I looked up to see Ernie coming out of his front door. He looked bewildered.

"Say, what's wrong with Ernie?"

Kenny and Isaac looked back as Ernie crossed the street. Was he mad? His face was red and he was seemingly nervous. I couldn't figure him, noting just five minutes before he'd seemed happy. I tried to imagine him having a fight with his father or mother, but that wasn't a part of his nature, nor did it fit his family.

Ernie said nervously, as he approached us, "Man—Malcolm X has been shot. They killed him! It's on the news."

"Malcolm X?" I asked loudly.

"Yeah, man." Ernie was nervous as hell.

"No!" I sat back in my seat, noting the impact of it now. But I was finding myself vaguely lost, lonely.

"Did they say who did it?" Kenny asked.

"No. He was speaking and they shot him when he got up to speak. Ah, say, Kenny, man. I don't know—what we going to do?"

I sat looking out the front window, silently raging in thought.

Ernie got in the back seat behind me and Kenny took off driving. I didn't want to believe what Ernie had said. I turned around and looked at

Ernie, who was slumped down in his seat with his head buried just below the windows. Fear was written all over him.

I looked at Isaac, who was sitting silent, watching out of the window. Then at Kenny, who said nothing. And it was the God damn truth. These God damn cops—Lyndon Johnson——

"That's it you-all. The motherfucking white racist president and the FBI killed him!" I was mad. I turned in my seat to ask Ernie something and quickly noticed him peeking just above the window and looking back as though he might have thought someone was following us. He slumped back in his seat, keeping his head below the window.

"What's the matter, Ernie?" I asked.

"Nothing, nothing!" He coughed and swallowed and answered, not looking at me, his face red as a ripe watermelon. He was scared, scared as hell. Because he had been to Cuba and talked to Robert Williams. Maybe the FBI would be after us. Underground, was my thought, angry, having to face the reality that Malcolm was dead.

"Shit!" I said, loudly. "Fuck all these racist motherfuckers! They need to be killed! We need guns, God damn it! Guns and underground operations to get some real righteous revolution on. They killed Malcolm! Shit!"

Malcolm was my personal friend. My leader. My unknown partner. Malcolm's rebellion was mine and Steve's. I was wishing I could talk like Malcolm X, think like him, as the car came closer and closer to a parked motorcycle cop. Suddenly, I raised up, sticking my head and body out the window, and yelled, "You racist white motherfucking cop! We going to kill you! You-all *killed* Malcolm!"

Kenny jammed his foot into the accelerator, getting the car up. "Bobby man, you'll get us killed!"

"Fuck them white-ass cops. Fuck them!" I was ranting in a verbal rage that would not quit. "I'll kill they ass! 'Cause I tell you one God damn thing—if I had a rifle now and the way I feel, I'd get even with these God damn racists. I'd let them know they can't kill my leader."

"Man, we know, Bobby."

"Naw, you don't. Naw, you don't know how to do it. I can't get used to just not doing what's supposed to be done."

"But it got to be done right."

"Right? Right! Fuck, I can do it right, but we got to be ready to do it. We ain't going to never get no kind of power to stop oppression until we get people like my old partner Steve, he's dead now. Oh, nothing, shit! Son of bitches! They trying to kill our spirit. But they ain't going to kill mine."

"Say, man, see, your ego is out."

"Ego! Don't talk that shit to me. Let's talk about shooting the God damn FBI. If we going to organize West Coast RAM underground or on top of the ground, either way, we got to let these dogs know that we stand behind Malcolm and all he taught us."

Everybody sat quietly until we drove up in front of my house. It dawned on me we were supposed to pick up Kenny's brother and ride up in the hills somewhere to begin to outline some structure for West Coast RAM.

"Why we come here, man?" I asked.

"You upset, Bobby, man. So we got to cool it today."

"Aw, shit!" I opened the door. "Man, you cats ain't ready to do nothing." I slammed the door and walked up into the house.

Isaac, Ernie, and Kenny sat around the table. I went and got Frantz Fanon's *Wretched of the Earth* and a pamphlet on Malcolm X and came back and sat down as Kenny was saying, "We got to find out some more about it before we can do anything."

And Ernie said, "Bobby, man, you got to be cool!"

"Cool, my ass, Ernie. See man, I don't blame you for being scared, having gone to Cuba. But being cool don't mean I'm going to do nothing."

"But, Bobby, man," Isaac interjected. "What you did back there, hollering at the cop. They'll put us in jail—they'll kill us."

"Fuck that cop!" I flipped the pages of the pamphlet trying to find where Malcolm said every man had a right to keep a shotgun in his home.

I got up, pacing, listening to the background noise of the radio in the kitchen and the TV in the living room, then I heard a special bulletin interrupting the TV program: "Today Malcolm X was gunned down and slain——"

I stopped in my tracks. I turned, stepped to the front door. Before I knew it I was pulling the red bricks out of the ground that I had put there to neatly decorate the flower bed, cussing racists aloud, stacking six bricks in my arms. A brick for Colonel King—A brick for Lyndon Johnson—a brick for Bull Connor—a brick for a cop—a brick for an FBI agent—a brick for——

I hurriedly walked to the corner, and watched the traffic passing on the four-lane street. They all seemed to have black people in them. Then I saw one coming. It was brand new. It had white people in it. A block away. I readied myself to move out into the street. I stepped off the curb, the car coming too fast. I couldn't get them to stop as I ragingly slung back my brick, heaving with my right arm and whirling the brick at the oncoming car, watching the brick hit the car with a thud, landing on top of the car, the white people shocked, looking at me as it whizzed by.

I was throwing the bricks as if they were javelins, striking cars. I was caught in a storm. I was cleansing myself.

"Bobby, man!" It was Kenny behind me. He grabbed me and I jerked away.

"Let me alone, motherfucker!" As I saw a car coming, I threw the brick hard, causing the driver to jam his brakes to a squeaking halt, another car stopping abruptly behind him. "Motherfucker! You racist rotten motherfucker!" And the lone white man got out of the car.

"You going to die. You glad Malcolm X died!"

I reached to the ground ready to knock the shit out of the man. I was crying by now, mad, enraged. I threw the brick, aiming for the man's head as he ducked. Isaac, Kenny and Ernie grabbed me, telling me to "be cool, Bobby, man."

I cried, and trembled, mumbling things under my breath. I knew I was wrong, but also right, and I was telling myself, Kenny, Ernie, and Isaac as I jerked loose from them, "Whatever I do from now on, it's this racist society's fault. It's their fault." And I let the tears cloud my bewildered, lonely, confused existence.

I walked off down the street, looking for something—anything—Kenny, Ernie, and Isaac calling to me.

I walked on another block, saw a rock, and whirled it in a window of a white man's business. I went into a sandwich shop and said I wanted a hamburger. I saw two white men in suits inside at the short five-stool counter. I sat on a stool, feeling it would be wrong to continue this hate rampage. But those two white men just had to be sitting there right at that moment. I spoke deliberately to the black girl behind the counter. "Say, sister. Did you hear about brother Malcolm X being killed by the FBI and Lyndon Johnson?"

"Huh? What you mean."

"White folks done killed Malcolm," I said loudly, as I looked for a response from the two white men eating their burgers. They just kept staring straight ahead.

I ran it on a bit, arguing with Kenny Freeman about I didn't want to leave. The black girl served me my hamburger. I was looking at it, not hungry, and arguing with Kenny. One of the white boys got up from his stool and stepped away, wiping his mouth with a napkin, and I stepped up and almost before I knew or understood what I was doing I took my hamburger with its bun and lettuce and mayonnaise and onions dripping and I run it over his white face. Kenny and everybody grabbed me out of there. When we got back to the house I put my fist through the porch door. The weight of Malcolm X's death had finally just hit me. Then I sat at the kitchen table and I said, "Fuck it, they killed him—I'll make a God damn Malcolm out of me." That seemed idiotic to Kenny and the others. I bandaged my hand and felt after an hour or so that I had bandaged my soul.

PART VI

Uncle Sammy Called Me Full of Lucifer

I PICKED UP THE PHONE before it could ring again.

"Bobby." A sad voice came over the receiver. It was Artie, a young, nineteen-year-old girl who followed me around at school every day.

"Yeah, girl, what you want?"

"I left home," Artie sadly pronounced, and there was no playing in her voice and manner. It made me believe her. Something must have happened—she must have finally rebelled against her super-strict father who made her be in the house by 5:30 P.M. "I'm at the corner of Grove and Ashby. I ain't got no place to go. That's why I called you."

"Ok, ok. I'll be right there."

In a few minutes I drove up to the corner and Artie was standing there with three large bags.

"Artie, what in hell are you doing! Where the fuck you think you going?"

"With you." She picked up one of her bags. "I ain't got no other place to go."

"Me! Shit! Look, say, you better—you ought to go home, girl."

"My Daddy kicked me out." Artie stepped from the curb and proceeded to get in the car with her smaller bag.

"Well, look, come on, let's go to my house."

Artie explained that she had an argument with her father. He hit her in the head with his fist and then told her to get out.

"Now where you going to stay?" I asked.

"With you if you let me."

"But Artie—oh shit! Say, look girl. My Mama and Daddy stay here. Now I know you ain't talking about sleeping in my bedroom. I know my Mama ain't going to stand for that." Anyway, I didn't think of Artie in that type of relationship.

"Well, I just wanted to stay somewhere until I can get a part-time job and maybe get an apartment I can share with somebody."

"Who?"

"Well, I don't know. I thought about you."

"Me?" I shook my head—this was amazing. "I don't believe this shit and yet I do. Just a minute." I left her in the living room and headed for the kitchen. "Say, Mama——"

"Yes, Bobby."

"Look, see, Artie just got kicked out of her house and she ain't got no place to stay so is it all right with you if she sleeps on the living-room couch? It's just until she can get herself a part-time job and get her own apartment with one of her girlfriends. For two or three weeks. She ain't got nowhere to go. Her Daddy knocked her in the head and kicked her out of her house."

"Ooooh!" Mama sadly exclaimed. "Why sure, Bobby. You mean that girl's father hits her with his fist!" Mama was astounded. "His own daughter. Lord, Lord—oh, me," Mama sighed.

And Mama politely explained to Artie it was ok, and after asking Artie what happened, Mama listened and sympathized with a rather unknowing but partially shocked, disgusted air: "Lord, these old menfolk just driving their chilluns way from 'round them." And, "Artie, you just stay here as long as you need. And you can share what little we got. You is welcome." Mama went on to talk and get Artie a quilt and a couple of sheets, and went back into the kitchen, working at the dishes in the kitchen sink.

By this time RAM was a thing of my past. After Malcolm X's assassination I had got a gun, while Kenny, Isaac, and Ernie were only talking fear—the FBI disguised as Muslims would be trying to kill us, West Coast RAM, the way they did Malcolm, or they could be in the form of a college student or a truck driver or any form at all. I felt the fear the same as they did, but I felt that once again they were doing nothing and that anything at all was used as a reason for doing nothing. I wanted to be moving on some programs, and I also believed with my whole self that if somebody was coming to kill me, I needed to have a gun. None of that was their kind of thing.

We fell out over "bourgeoisie" too. "Being black ain't no phony shit," I told them, "it's real to niggers who live in direct oppression every day. You so hooked up trying to look dirty and live in the nastiest rathole in the ghetto, trying to be a ghetto black; and being bourgie ain't what you believe it is. You so bourgie, you trying to rub off your own past bourgeoisie life, you come down living in the ghetto with garbage and shit all over your floor. Man, black people ain't going to follow nobody who's going to keep the ghetto filthy. Shit! When niggers got old worn-out, dirty couches in the house, they'll get a sheet or an old spread and wash it and tuck it neatly all over the couch to try and make it look nice and clean. Just because black people have a need in their minds to keep things neat and decent, you call it bourgie? Naw, they *poor*, man! So you can play the dirty ghetto game if you want to, but you got to at least dress up. Like Malcolm X—was he bourgie? He put ten years in prison. I brought Huey Newton over, you mistook him to be bourgie.

"Niggers want to get out of the filth. They want homes and nice things and cars and they always attempting to get it. In my mind the struggle is about getting this shit turned around, to clean up our houses and get homes."

I was working at a "poverty job," working for the community. There was a man there named Mr. Low, around fifty years old, who supported my ideas against the jive the college students put out, even though my thoughts were incomplete. I'd allow that Saul Alinsky, who the college dudes took as all-knowing, could say what he wants to, but our situation in Oakland was people were starving, going day-to-day without a job, and these college students wanted to pay dudes a dollar twenty-five an hour to sit around and talk, sit around and listen to the college students talk. My feeling was to put dudes to work, teach them carpentering, plastering, plumbing—give them a way to get some skills for their dollar twenty-five. I was going on the thought that the more people have, the more they'll fight for. Mr. Low was backing me up. Then we discovered one day that we had a tie-up in the past—he was one of the organizers of the people's actions in my former village, when people tried to keep the government from taking them out of their homes. I remembered people had turned over police cars, people were righteously standing up for their right to live decently and not be shoved around. Then I learned that Mr. Low was a Communist, a black Communist, and I really had to think about whether all those programs about "I Was a Communist for the FBI" were truth or jive, that Communists were the enemies of America. Mr. Low didn't look like no enemy of America—he was working hard to help people's lives.

Five days after Artie moved in, I got a paycheck from the poverty gig and I took Artie to a party, mostly feeling like her big brother. But she, not knowing how to act, sort of envisioned me as a boyfriend. I bluntly told her I was not her boyfriend and explained that when she got an apartment I was going to "Fuck you, Artie—and I'll just be shacking with you to give you some idea about the world. Anyway, sooner or later you going to fuck somebody."

But Artie was still too silly to understand that and resolved to keep looking forward to getting an apartment with me; and me telling her that she had to hurry up and get a job and that I'd go ahead and pay half the rent. Artie more or less ignored my words, following me around and even going to my job.

Now I was running back and forth, from my afternoon poverty gig to college and my morning six units, cramming, studying with the Negro History Fact Group I had organized, Artie coming in my room to wake me up each morning to start the whole day over again. The weeks became more intense. George did not want Artie there and it seemed like every day there would be a new argument as to why.

"Ah, ah, Bobby, ah, you know that girl is got to go home."

I was pissed to hear that over again. "Say, George, look, that girl is *nineteen years old!* She does not have to go home."

"Well, I called that girl's father, and her mother is worried about her going out at night with you."

"Say, look, George, stay out of——" I paused, feeling like I was suddenly in some kind of nigger soap opera on TV. "Man, you ain't got no right to call nobody. Stay out of our business. If Artie and I want to go out together, you and nobody else ain't got nothing to do with it."

"That girl's father is going to send the police over here to get her. I told him he ought to get her!"

"Now, just wait a God damn minute! Fuck her Daddy. Beating her up with his fists."

"Well, I told her father that he ought to get her home, out of this house!"

"In other words, you told her father to call the police—right, nigger?" I loudly shouted at George. "All right." I picked up my nine-millimeter pistol. "Let me tell you, George." I held the pistol's barrel straight up in the air near my face, looking dead into George's face and eyes. "If any God damn police come here that you done got Artie's father to call, they'll have to take her out over my dead body, nigger! You stupid ignorant nigger! She has every right to do what she wants to. And any God damn way," I shouted. "How in hell you know—we just might be planning to *marry* each other. See, nigger?" Wondering if the lie I was telling was getting through to him.

"Well, ah, if that's what, ah, you-all want to do, is get married, I guess it's all right." George was looking beyond me and I turned to see Artie standing in the kitchen, looking and listening.

"What the fuck you mean it's all right?" I said continuing my rebellion. "I don't need your approval. Shit! I'm twenty-eight years old, nigger. I'll do what I want to." I stepped into the kitchen, looking at Artie. She was smiling.

"What you laughing at, Artie!" I said, still puffed up with anger.

"At what you said."

"Oh—George? Shit. I can't figure why he's all of a sudden got to think he can run me."

"I mean, about getting married."

"Damn! Girl, look. I don't want to be married, and anyway——" I paused, suddenly imagining and thinking what if I did marry Artie? Shit, the way everything is going now—ain't no real black organizing going down—I could just as soon be married as not. Anyway, Artie is probably a virgin chick and I have to teach her everything about the world. Artie was looking at me, so I said, "Say, look, I'm a black nationalist—a black revolutionary—and I figure I'm going to be that for the rest of my life. So if you really want to get married to me, ok. But you got to accept my life commitment to the struggle for black liberation."

"I don't care," Artie was smiling.

I was giving myself to somebody. Share and share—share my life? Yeah.

"Ok, but *now* I'm serious. Do you want to get married?" And I was thinking if I really did this, it would make George shit.

"Yeah, I do."

"Ok, then we'll get married." Anyway, it'll be something new to do. And I'll build her a house—— My previous frustration had eased.

"When?" Artie asked, excitedly.

"Oh, I don't know." Maybe if it works, we'll even have a baby.

"But when?" Artie pressed.

"Ah, when I get paid next week sometime." Yeah, I'm going to do it. Why the hell not.

I thought strongly about getting married without that head-over-heels love that I had cherished in the past. I believed I couldn't ever be in *love*, not after Amelia. But marrying Artie, I realized, was more of a reaction to the way my father and Amelia's aunt had interfered. Parents and older folks would mess over us younger ones if they had half a chance. I was now more determined than ever to marry Artie.

I got back home and found out that George had called the police and had them take my nine-millimeter pistol. George didn't arrive home that evening, but Sunday morning he pulled up his car out front.

God, I was steaming. I wanted to yank George out of the car, but I kept reminding myself he wasn't strong now, he was now slightly crippled. I shouted to George as I walked up to the open window: "You ain't shit, nigger! You stupid old ignorant son of a bitch! Why you call the God damn police and give them my gun?"

"You ain't got no right with no gun," George shouted back at me. "Threatening me, God damn it!" I noted a small degree of fear in his voice, reminding me that my formerly brave father was crippled and old now and couldn't defend himself. I couldn't strike him. I knew I couldn't, even though I was to the boiling-over point. I felt this time he had really wronged me.

"Fuck you, George!" I got overbearingly loud. "And you know that I ain't threatened you! You ain't no good! You ain't never been." I knew I wanted to stop. My father was being humiliated as he listened to me and a film of tears jumped into his sad eyes. But I couldn't seem to help continuing.

"You ain't going to never do right by nobody!" George started the car engine and backed out the driveway as I followed along, cursing him, calling him ten kinds of simple-minded motherfucker.

I stormed into the house, slamming the door, still cursing George aloud to myself, walking back and forth from the kitchen to the living room, Artie following me. I tried to ease myself but couldn't. I stopped abruptly in my tracks and Artie bumped into me. I turned to say, "Ok, Artie, look! It takes three days. We going down to the court, get a judge and you and I are going to get married, all right?" I had this surging thought to show George what it meant to care for a family in the right way, but more than that, to actually carry out what I had told him, to prove that he was wrong. To prove to George that I was better than him, that I had the philosophy of being a forward, rightful person toward people. That no one had the right to suppress Artie's rights and we would not let Mamas and Daddies—nobody—stop us.

Artie asked, "Can you fix the table?"

"What table!"

"This one. It's wobbling."

I went out into the garage for my tools, still uptight a bit, and noticed George's toolbox. Then with all my angry strength, I slung George's toolbox off the bench. The tools spewed out from the garage, along the concrete driveway. I decided I would repair the table and I would eat before I went back to pick up George's tools.

When we were half-finished eating, I heard George's car drive up, and a couple of minutes later George's car drove off. Artie and I got talking about going to San Francisco; Artie had never seen the San Francisco planetarium and I wanted to show her the pendulum that swung back and forth, giving one the feeling and understanding of the earth's constant spinning movement.

We both heard voices coming from the driveway. Artie stepped to the window and abruptly turned to me, with amazement on her face, saying, "The cops are out there!"

"What?" I exclaimed, as I stepped to the window, looking out to see three policemen and George.

"He called the cops on you," Artie said in amazement.

I heard the front door opening and I stepped to the dining room, seeing George with two policemen coming in behind him; I was standing there with Artie beside me, pissed to the hilt. I looked back through the kitchen door to see two more policemen coming in the back door, and I shouted out, "All right! You are on private property. Now get out of our house!"

"Bob," the black policeman started off, "your father here called us out. He's lodged a complaint against you."

"Say, wait, first of all I got a complaint against him. But more than that, you get off this property." I looked back as the two white cops behind me stood ready. I began to have the leery feeling I'd be beaten up, and jerked around to say: "God damn it, George! This house is private property. You simple-minded——"

"Well, it's your father's house, Bob," the black cop calmly said.

"It's not *his* house. It's our house. Me, my sister, and brother own this house."

"Now come on, Bob. Let's go quietly." He reached for my arm.

"Get your hand off me!" I shot out. "You invading my house. He don't own shit!" And I was grabbed from behind by the two white cops.

"You know God damn well, George, it's our house! Did you tell these damn cops you built this house? Well, you ain't shit." The cop pulled me. I resisted slightly only to tell George: "It's our house and that's why we made sure your God damn name wasn't on it. So we could have the home that you never took the time to build." I was going out the front door. The two cops practically carrying me, as I kept looking back at George with all the hate I could muster in my expression. "Our home! You simple-minded moutherfucker!" Then I was carried down the front steps, and the police proceeded to handcuff me, telling me that I was being charged with threatening my father with a deadly weapon and malicious destruction of private property. They put me in a car and I shouted, "Artie! Say, Artie!" She finally heard me. "Get Mama to get me bailed out right away when she gets back from church."

The white cop looked into his rearview mirror at me angrily. Then shook his head and said, "When you people going to stop killing each other?"

I thought about that. But fuck him—what does he know? White people don't even know the half of it when it come to us black people.

Two hours later I was bailed out by John, and as he drove me home, he and I scorned George, but with the scorning, I suddenly made up my mind that George really didn't see what he had caused. Because of his injury, he must feel we, his children, have to take care of him, like I remembered him trying to do for his father in his last days, and now here I was bucking him in this final stage of his life, rejecting his advice in the most crude way, even though George was wrong.

I took in a deep breath as we drove up in front of the house. I resolved that the house was as much his as it was mine, even though his name was not on the title, to keep him from botching that up. He was crippled—so was I. He was headstrong—so was I. I'd move out of the house. He could have it. I'd just move on and build my own house.

I apologized to George, and with Mama and Betty both after him, he said he was sorry, too. He dropped the charges Sunday night.

That Monday morning, Artie and I boarded a Greyhound bus. I felt that newness of something surge inside me as we watched the countryside and then the great High Sierra Mountains—those same mountains I believed I saw the very first time I had come to California back in 1945.

Artie and I were married in Reno, Nevada, that evening.

"Well, how do you feel, married now?" I asked Artie.

"I don't know. We just married and I'm glad," she said.

I smiled. "We going to stay here in Reno tonight. I'm going to show you about the world of gambling and let you see how and why so many people can grow addicted to it and lose their life's savings within this gigantic capitalist operation. It's the epitome of what I know to be the basis of how capitalism functions: that is, we never win when we're hooked to this system. Come on, girl, you got to keep up with me—I move fast."

I hung out at the college cafeteria. I had begun to acquire seniority at Merritt College. I was now one of the "old heads" around the college campus, being consulted by students concerning the black liberation struggle.

It was a new winter semester and Negro History had been expanded to a six-unit, two-semester course—the credit for this falling to Huey and me. Richard Ioke had even arranged for me to lecture on the past crises in the Congo, which I had diligently followed and studied.

One day I argued scornfully with Isaac Moore. He was wrong, it seemed to me, for belittling black playwright Leroi Jones for being married to a white woman. I held my position, telling Isaac that, regardless, "the white woman is still the mother of those black children, fool! You would have them hate their own mother according to your jive cultural view. Running around here saying that Leroi Jones should take his children and divorce his wife. Just because she's white!"

Isaac made me realize even more that RAM and its do-nothing group were way out of my bag of reasoning. They would pay no attention to Malcolm X's new thoughts—those he had toward the end of his life—that revolution had to be for everyone, black and white both.

Sitting in the cafeteria one day with about twenty others, I suggested that a campus group should be organized. A few seemed very interested. I told Huey about it and Huey explained to me how he did not believe it would be worth much unless some nonstudents, "brothers off the block," were in it or at least attracted to it.

Huey ran down how such a campus group would need some street sense to give impetus to the do-nothing activity of the blacks on campus. I ran down how he and I would be the ones off the block to start it off. He agreed. So after various suggestions and a couple of days' argument, I came up with the name "Soul Students Advisory Council." Our immediate issue would be that of black men being drafted into the service to fight in Vietnam. Our campus was over fifty percent black, so the issue took hold.

We put the work out, got the new black-history instructor to sponsor us, and we had the Soul Students Advisory Council officially launched on the Merritt campus. We scheduled a rally in the main auditorium and I recited a poem called "Uncle Sammy Called Me Fulla Lucifer." The poem brought the house down, and at our next meeting following the rally we had over one hundred official participating members.

Organizing whist-playing college students told me something I had not realized before. That some of them could do something if it was in their interest. And I was trying to figure what was Kenny's sudden interest— Kenny Freeman, who led West Coast RAM, a do-nothing group.

One evening Huey and a close friend named Weasel and I sat in my hog out in front of my house, drinking and killing a second six-pack of malt liquor as Huey went on to explain how one should study ancient sociology via art and the facial expressions in it. We got into a discussion of cultural nationalism, then talked about the inner soul of the brother off the block, which Huey interpreted best by citing his like for the folkloric, down-home sounds of T-bone Walker and John Lee Hooker. Huey suggested that we go up to Telegraph Avenue near Cal campus and we might be able to find some of those down-home songs in some of the hippie boutiques of that area. So we took off just to see.

The six-to-eight block section of Telegraph near Cal's campus was crowded as usual, even though it was 9:00 P.M. It was late spring and the student and hippie night-activities were at their bustling height.

After we went into a couple of record shops to listen to a couple of down-home songs, we milled for two blocks down Telegraph, with all its night lights and activity and hordes of students in an array of colors—Chinese, black, white, Chicano. Suddenly, Huey asked me, "Yeah, Bobby, ah, say your Uncle Sammy poem for Weasel." With people bumping into and walking in between everyone. "Say it so everybody can hear you and watch, Weasel, see if some of these hippies and students don't stop and listen to him."

"Ok, here goes." And I said, "Uncle Sammy called me fulla Lucifer!" I was loud and boisterous under the streetlight, gesturing the meaning of the poem's character and letting my total feeling for the poem hang out, as six or seven people stopped and turned to listen.

"Well, I don't give a good-Eagle-eyed-McFlegal-tripple-whammy damn! For I, Fearless Fos——"

"Wait! Hold it!" Some tall, bushy-headed white boy was saying, stepping toward me, wanting me to stand on the chair. "Here man," the white boy continued, "stand here so everyone sitting in the cafe can hear you."

"Uncle Sammy called me fulla Lucifer! Well, I don't give a good-Eagle-eyed-McFlegal-tripple-whammy damn! For I, Fearless Fosdick, will not serve!" A standing crowd of twenty or more were listening now. "Uncle Sammy. Don't shuck and jive me! Shiiit! I'm hip to the popcorn jazz changes you blow." I paused as if I were holding a special conversation with Uncle Sammy. "Huh? You know damn well what I mean! You schooled my naive heart to sing red, white, and blue stars and stripes songs and to pledge eternal allegiance to all things blue-true, blue-eyed, blond-blond-haired, white-chalk, white-skinned with USA tattooed *all over*!" Suddenly some white boy in a yellow T-shirt and jeans called to me from the back of the crowd, saying, "Hey, you!"

"Say it brother!" some black brothers from the audience spurted as the crowd smiled and I saw to my left a cop car drive up and stop in back of the crowd, and not giving it a second thought, I continued holding the pace of the poem.

"When my soul *trusted* Uncle Sammy, and *loved* Uncle Sammy and died in dreams for Uncle Sammy! You jammed your emasculate manhood symbol, puffed with gonorrhea, into my ungreased nigger ghetto black ass of my jewish, hindu, islamic, catholic nigger ghetto——"

"Hey you!" The yellow T-shirt spoke again, but I ignored him.

"Sure—free public health penicillin cured me. But Uncle Sammy, if you want to stay a freak-show, strong-man God!" As I saw a uniformed cop pushing his way into the left rear of the crowd, I concluded loudly, with hand gestures:

"Fuck your motherfucking self!" I stomped my foot in the chair. "I will *not* serve!!"

The crowd was raving as I stepped down off the chair to look at Weasel and Huey smiling along with me.

"See, Weasel, man, Bobby is the only brother off the block with trades and who can also communicate to people."

"More! More! More!" the crowd roared.

Suddenly, I was being pulled by my right arm by someone in the crowd. As I turned, I noticed the yellow-T-shirted white boy had me by the arm. He said, amidst the noise. "You're blocking the sidewalk."

"More! More! More!" The audience was still shouting for an encore.

Then someone else said, "You're under arrest!" I looked around to see the uniformed cop upon us, looking at me.

"Leave him alone! He's done nothing," someone from the audience sang out, with a couple more repeating the same thing as I snatched away again from the yellow-T-shirt's hand.

"You used profane language."

"Say, man, fuck you. Shit, I got a right to free speech."

"But you can't block the sidewalk."

"He wasn't blocking the sidewalk," Huey said. "The chair he was on is on the curb."

He grabbed my arm again. "You are under arrest."

I snatched away. "Let go of me, simple motherfucker!" And I stepped back. "Let's go, Huey."

But suddenly I was grabbed by both arms—one by Yellow-T-Shirt and the other by the uniformed cop—and I snatched and pulled as they held onto my jacket. I was being pulled and was also pulling myself out of my jacket, feeling it sliding off my arms. The crowd was shouting, "Leave him alone!" and "God damn cops!" and "He's done nothing."

I was spinning around, coming out of my jacket, falling against the crowd toward the curb of the intersection; tripping, and stumbling into the crowd, then seeing the uniformed cop grab Huey as Huey spun around, backing up toward me. The cop charged Huey as my ass hit the pavement. Huey sidestepped the angry, ruffled cop who had lost his hat, and *wham!*—Huey caught the cop right square in the mouth with a thundering blow that caused the two-hundred-pound cop to stagger. As I was on my back, being raised up by the arms, surrounded by spectators, I shouted, "Huey!"

Huey had tagged the cop again, and as for me—*wham*! I had the breath knocked out of me as Yellow-T-Shirt tackled me back to the ground. Yellow-T-Shirt and I were struggling now, on the ground, rolling and twisting as I finally got loose from his grip. I had to have my knife! From a sitting position under the feet of the jeering spectators, I spun and got up to my feet thinking to cut Yellow-T-Shirt's heart out jamming my hand into my pocket for my knife.

"Motherfucker! You better leave me alone!" And *wham*! I was tackled from my right rear. Someone else grabbed me around the neck; I was being choked, and suddenly I was tumbling and rolling on the ground.

Yellow-T-Shirt hollered, "You're under arrest!"

Glancing, I spotted Huey through an opening in the large crowd. He was still struggling with the uniformed cop, but it looked as though Huey was trying to hold the cop's gun in his holster and the cop was trying to pull it out. I struggled fiercely to be free. My head was being pulled to the ground. I got one of my legs free and started kicking. My face and eyes were now *on* the pavement. I was breathing hard, scared now. Was I being lynched?! Right here at the Cal campus?

A kick from a sharp shoe caught me in the forward shoulder. I saw nothing but feet coming at me, kicking. They were going to kill us. Suddenly, the arm around my neck loosened. Weasel and three other black dudes were kicking Yellow-T-Shirt off me

I moved rapidly as the grips on me were giving way. I kicked and moved myself free from them, scrambling to my feet, scared in a fearful daze, quickly running my hand into my pocket, getting my knife, my thumbnail was in the opening groove of the large blade. I had the knife open and swung around.

Where was Huey? I stepped toward an opening, the knife in my hand.

Now I was really wondering and worrying about Huey. I stepped out into the streets, going around parked cars and back toward the crowd, looking for Huey. As I got to the intersection, I saw Huey, handcuffed, being put into a police car by two cops. I confusedly wondered what the hell to do now. Then, as the cop slammed the door shut with Huey in the back seat, I said aloud, "Bail! I got to get to the Berkeley police station and bail Huey out."

I stepped off to the right, folding and putting my knife in my pocket, then, in a slow-running pace, headed for the car to go and bail Huey out of jail, remembering I had sixty-five dollars in my pocket that was left from my paycheck.

As I reached the parking lot, I heard a jingling of keys behind me. I turned around to see a uniformed cop running toward me, and then another, and someone said, "That's him—that's him!"

And they were upon me, as I backed against the wall with my hand jammed in my pocket. They grabbed me as I struggled, kicking and fighting only to be downed. Suddenly there was Yellow-T-Shirt again. I was slammed against the wall and Yellow-T-Shirt searched me, and quickly I was walked to one of the police cars across the street. I saw Weasel in the forward car and Huey in the rear car. I was stuck right in the middle one, in the back seat.

I was mentally and physically exhausted as the car sped down the road headed for the Berkeley police station.

They stuck me in a box-type room that had a big plate-glass window that looked out over the large police room. I did not see Huey and Weasel.

I sat awhile just thinking. I saw Yellow-T-Shirt, and the way he was walking around I figured then he must be a cop. He must be a God damn cop. With what now was happening, I figured I'd be charged with assault with a deadly weapon on a police officer; remembering what Huey had run down, that if convicted—shit! I could get one to ten years in prison. Damn!

I started wondering how in hell am I going to beat this shit. How in hell did it all happen? All we did was go up to check out some down-home folk record by street brothers, then, the poem——

I spoke aloud to myself in the soundproof room. I recited "Uncle Sammy," the whole poem, then sat back and resolved that I was a righteous, dedicated black revolutionary. At 3:00 A.M., I was bailed out of jail by my wife, Artie.

At 6:00 A.M., Huey was bailed out. But he was stopped at the door and locked up again. Huey's probation officer had a hold put on him. It was the next Monday morning before Huey was finally released.

Huey and I approached Virtual Murrel and told him of our weekend situation and explained to him to get us twenty-five dollars apiece to retain a lawyer Huey knew—a black lawyer named John George whom Huey would argue points of law with and directly and indirectly run down to John George how he should run our case.

But before our case could get to court, Huey and I one night after a meeting were about to get in our car when we saw the cops had stopped a black brother. Another brother was standing looking on as the brother standing with his hands against the wall was being searched.

We walked over. One cop said to the observing brother, "Ok, you—move on."

"Who me?" the brother asked, somewhat surprised.

"Yeah, you boy. Move on!" Putting his flashlight beam up in the brother's face. The other cop had put the first brother in the car and was on the radio.

"These cops are the shits, Huey," I said.

"Yeah. They fucking with this other brother for nothing."

"God damn. Can't a person look, man? I ain't done shit!" the brother said.

"Ok, you two, move on." The cop spoke to Huey and me, gesturing with his flashlight.

"According to——" Huey cited such and such ruling, "a citizen has a right to observe."

"Move on!"

"I'm sorry, officer, as a citizen, I retain the right to stand here. I'm not interfering. I'm observing. And any court of law distinguishes the difference between the two."

The cop walked over to the observing brother. "All right, up against the wall," he said.

"Hey, man!" The brother was now nervous and a little shook.

The first cop grabbed him by the arm and the brother snatched away and both cops were on him, hustling him, slamming him against the wall. One handcuffed him and in that moment another cop car swerved around the corner and two cops hopped out, drawing their guns and suddenly ordering Huey and me against the wall. The two cops came closer. They were the same two cops Huey and I had gotten into the scuffle with a couple of weeks before on Telegraph Avenue.

The two cops sarcastically said, "Huey Newton and Bobby Seale."

The first two cops, who now had handcuffed and arrested the brother who had been doing nothing, decided not to arrest us. To leave us alone. The hefty one Huey had slugged said, "Next time, Newton. You got it coming." and they got in their car.

With Huey saying, "You also remember what happened last time."

This scene was really too much! Huey and I decided to go down to the jail. We argued and requested at the desk the right of the brother to be bailed out on a jive charge of disturbing the peace. We waited two hours until the brother was booked while we talked to each other about how the Soul Students Advisory Council would further implement a community program of raising bail for black brothers and sisters. Bail and future legal aid.

When the brother was bailed out, we met him. He was surprised, shocked: "I ain't never got out of jail like—I mean—man, you-all really—shit, man, I'll pay you-all back."

"No, brother," Huey said. "You owe us nothing. Soul Students Advisory Council bailed you out."

"Yeah," I said. "We need brotherhood to begin to be *done* and not just talked about."

"Say, man, let me, ah, shake you-all's hands." Two big tears rolled down his face. I was filled with a staunch belief of the need for brotherhood and revolution and rebellion against the racist system.

I had my black trenchcoat on and I was pissed off at the bullshit talk that was going around, catapulted by Isaac Moore and Doug Allen. They were saying Huey and I had sold out the Council because we had taken money from a white man named Bob Scheer who was running for political office. They would not believe that we had not promised support, that we had only promised not to low-rate him in public. And a meeting was scheduled five days from that next Tuesday.

The shit was now out all over campus. Huey gave me a little insight when he told me that the whole shit was started by Isaac and Doug so they could take over the Council; then they would restructure Soul Students under RAM's control.

"See, Bobby," Huey would say, "we've put everything together. Now they want to take over. So from there, they'll turn it into an armchair cultural group. So, you know what?"

"Yeah?"

"When the meeting comes, we ought to resign."

"Resign?"

"Yeah. And from there we can organize a black community group of some kind and teach brothers like Malcolm X said: to righteously defend themselves from racists."

"Yeah, right."

"And create programs to help black people."

"Yeah, ok, Huey. I see. You're right. We resign and start an all new community-based group."

"There you go. Community-based instead of campus-based."

I needed a job by the time summer came. I dreaded working anymore in factories, where there were always a handful of overt racists and the bulk of other white workers kept their status over "niggers."

My previous job had me bored as well. The union wanted me to produce just so much, the number of parts per hour each work order dictated, when I wanted to see my own worth per hour. Then the times I did the work faster anyway, it further pissed me when the foreman would try and pat me on the back for being a company man. Then I would read the chicken-shit plastic-covered cost details of expensive machinery, it all made me know more how rich the capitalist owners really were. Shit! I quit; and I knew Artie was about to have a baby. So when summer came, I hooked up a gig at a local poverty program.

I created special black-history lectures for the young brothers and sisters who seemed bound, in the final analysis, to be one kind of "Stagolee" or another.

I got a young dude named Bobby Hutton a job there. Bobby Hutton readily became attracted to Huey and me. In fact, a crew of about twelve brothers ranging from fifteen to eighteen tried to hang around Huey and me constantly. Some would boast that they would be pimps and other underworld types. Huey would explain to the brothers that there were only about ten successful pimps throughout the whole San Francisco Bay area, so breaking into that "profession" would be damn near impossible for the naive young brothers. When Huey and I would catch them gambling, we would out-gamble them. We also began to blow to them the black struggle as we saw its developmental stages at that time. We would expound on the teachings of Malcolm X. And Huey would teach them how to know and understand law.

I was ecstatic! That summer on July 9 Artie birthed us a nine-pound baby boy. I named him Malik Nkrumah Stagolee Seale. Malik, after Malcolm X who had chosen the name El-Hajj Malik El-Shabazz. Nkrumah, an African statesman I greatly admired. Stagolee, which stemmed from those diligent years of studying black history and folklore. Stagolee was a bad nigger off the block. Artie didn't exactly agree with "Stagolee," stating, "What kind of name is that?" But I was determined. "Stagolee" it is and "Stagolee" it shall stay!

All in all I could feel myself developing to a great culmination point. Having birthed a son, and now being on the road to doing something about the situation of black people in society, bolstered my feelings of virility to an all-time high. Even the natural act of love-making became ecstasy, as though I had finally suppressed my latent beliefs of the act being sinful. This native began to know and love his oppressed class-brothers with an insight and a need to care and take on some responsibility in the struggle. "We" and "our" became a part of my everyday language; deep feelings of "share and share alike" enhanced my phrases, meanings, and goals.

Shit, yeah! I was searching to balance the scales of justice.

One day, Huey said to me, speaking slowly, as if he had hit on something really big, "If I can move one grain of sand from one spot to another, then the world will never be *exactly* the same. Can you get the scope of that?"

I went over exactly what he said in my mind, then answered, "Yeah!" I was awed at the possibilities. "Shit, yeah! One jive grain of sand. Huey, you a motherfucker!" I stopped, still thinking. "Where you learn that? God damn!"

We took off walking in our fast pace, headed toward Merritt College, down Grove Street, pouring out our understanding to each other; me listening to Huey's articulate philosophical-political-socioeconomic point of view, me answering with my own practical everyday words, with specific understanding of what we both had begun to realize about each other and our unity of goals. We were feeling that serious need to know, expounding on the urgency of organizing something. We were developing black revolutionaries who had become insightfully critical of our environment.

We would argue with and somewhat change our friends' Marxist views that the *lumpen* never did anything but pillage and/or ignore the revolutionary cause altogether. We downed that view when it came to applying it to the black American ghetto-dweller because we were off the block too, Stagolees.

"You brothers are jiving," Huey would argue at the cafeteria table.

"That's right. Still jiving." I'd break into the argument to back Huey's point. "You-all ain't moving no sand."

That night I sat on my bed listening to Malik's sleep-noises. God damn it. Fuck it, Bobby. I'm going to tell Huey we got to go ahead and start doing something for the black revolution in America and start moving some grains of sand.

Huey and I racked our brains as to how to get some community-based organization going, and especially how to properly deal directly with the police. We decided we would need to watch the police, patrol the police; black brothers were getting brutalized and arrested. Huey and I knew we could do it, but we'd have to do it armed.

"A law book, a tape recorder, and a gun," Huey said. "That's what we would need. It would let those brutalizing racist bastards know that we mean business."

At the poverty program office, Huey and I drew up a ten-point platform and program for our new organization, which we agreed to name the Black Panther Party for Self-Defense.

It definitely had to be an armed situation, patrolling the police. We discovered Richard Ioke had some guns. Huey discussed the situation very objectively with Richard, who finally gave us a shotgun and a forty-five pistol. I took the pistol and Huey took the shotgun. Huey had already checked with his probation officer who had said he could own a shotgun but not a handpiece.

But how, exactly, should we go about patrolling the police? For a few days after we got the guns we carried them around in my old car, going over the law, discussing taking arrests and keeping our guns in plain view so as not to break the law. We decided we would do battle only at the point when a fool policeman drew his gun unjustly. At that point of no return, and working within the fine framework of legality and illegality—boom!—we'd shoot it out and "let these jive simple-minded racist police know where it's at!"

We would carry on, enthusiastically building up self-confidence. We quelled talking of death, convincing ourselves that, as Huey said, "Once it starts, then we realize that we may wind up dead or in prison."

"Yeah. I'm with you, Huey. See, man, you the leader, the Minister of Defense of the new Black Panther Party for Self-Defense. I'm second to you, the Chairman. So we've started and that's it. I'm just glad, man, I found somebody. You, Huey, who's ready to really start doing something. Something to shock black people into getting organized against these racist dogs."

And for the first time I told Huey something about my past Nigger Tarzan experiences.

We were going to a party because Huey's girlfriend Laverne and my wife, Artie, wanted us to take them. But Huey said, just before we left my house, "We going to carry our guns and we're going to patrol these police on the way to the party."

We didn't see one police car on the way there.

We arrived at the party, guns in hand. Slowly, a few of the partyers were noticing, shocked, we had guns. The living room was full with dancing and music. We were introduced and we shook a few hands. One partially drunk brother stepped toward us, asking, "Say, what the——" Awkwardly, taken aback. "Hey, why you guys got those guns?"

The guns represent a new black organization, brother," Huey readily and enthusiastically spoke up.

"Say, wait a minute! Why are those guns here?" another exclaimed.

And some sister was stepping forward, saying, "Who got guns?!" She sounded questioningly angry, then she stopped in her tracks as she noticed. "Oh, my God!"

"No, ah, sister, our guns represent a new organization. The Black Panther Party for Self-Defense. Black people can now begin to organize in our community."

"We only brought them here with us to patrol the police who brutalize black people," I put in.

Huey said, "Ah, here, take a copy of our program, brother."

And another partyer said to Huey, "Say, man, let me see that shotgun." He reached out for it.

"No!" Huey raised his hand, turning away from the brother and stepping back into the kitchen. "No one touches a Black Panther's gun, brother. Furthermore, it's loaded. Someone could get hurt."

"Oh." The brother withdrew as other comments were heard, ranging from "come on, guns and shit?" to "later for this scene."

Then the host of the house came into the crowd, telling Huey and me she didn't want any guns in the house. Then someone suggested, "Say, you-all need to put the guns up, man." We readily agreed to do that, and put them in a closet, since it seemed to upset everyone.

Huey went back into the kitchen area to talk to a few interested brothers about our organization. Laverne had found a seat, and Artie and I danced once. Afterwards I got us all a drink and mingled with the crowd, talking.

We hadn't been there a good twenty minutes when I looked up to see a policeman. Someone pointed me out and I stood my ground as I expected the obvious question. The cop stopped right in front of me, asking, "You have a gun on you?"

"No, I don't have a gun on me." I spoke disdainfully. "But I have a gun with me. We checked our guns." The music suddenly stopped as silence hung over the once-swinging party.

"Well, the people who reside here don't want you here with guns."

"Well then, fuck it. And fuck them, too. Shit, I'll leave."

I headed across through the crowd, toward Huey, seeing and telling Artie, "Say, girl, get Laverne, let's go." Another cop was standing in the kitchen area. Huey and I quickly caught each others' eyes.

We headed toward the closet, got our guns, and Huey made a loud comment about the host being "a nigger bourgeoisie bitch" to call white swine racists on us. We escorted Artie and Laverne out the front door where a third cop was standing poised and ready. As we came out the door, there on the second floor, there were two more cops to the right of the door and another one to the left.

"Swine police everywhere," Huey said to me.

"Yep! Swine police every damn place." I suppressed my nervousness as we went down the stairs only to see even more police, some six or seven. But we coolly walked on.

"Say, Bobby, man, we checked our guns and that bootlicking bitch called these dogs on us." He and I both had our eyes on the police now behind us.

We crossed to Laverne's Volkswagen. Huey said to me, "Now look, if they're going to come up trying to harass us, don't say anything. I'll do the talking. We haven't broken any laws. Our weapons are not concealed."

"Right." I sat in the back seat with Artie.

Surer than shit one of an altogether different set of cops came up to the driver's window, just as Huey slammed the door shut.

"You have a driver's license?" the cop asked Huey. Huey went into his pocket, got his driver's license, and gave it to the policeman. Then the cop looked at the registration. He glanced up toward the rear of the car—I looked: two cops were standing at the rear of our car. Suddenly, I felt they would open up on us and riddle the car with bullets.

"You've got no business with those guns. You know that?"

"Say, look!" Huey spoke pointedly. "You want to give us a citation! Then do it, damn it! This gun is my private property. So don't stand there telling me I have no right to this particular property when it's clearly legal."

The cop then asked Huey, "You on probation?"

I was suddenly scared for Huey, knowing with one violation he could go to jail.

"Say, you." Huey reacted to the cop. "That's got nothing to do with it. Whether I am on probation or not, you have no reasonable cause to be here harassing us."

And the cop asked me was I on probation.

"No, I'm not! Now our guns are legal, so why——" I was hopped up, nervously looking back at the two cops in back of us.

"No, Bobby." Huey turned, looking at me. "I'll do the talking. You take the fifth, like I told you. Only one of us talks."

"Right, I'm sorry, Huey. But he's asking about probation and——"

"Don't worry!" Huey turned. "Say, officer! I'd appreciate it"—sarcastically direct—"if you'd give me my license and our identification so we can go; or cite us, to which I'll plead not guilty. Because the harassment is undue."

"Who do you think you are, some kind of lawyer or something?"

"That's irrelevant. Cite us or leave us alone!"

"What kind of shotgun is that?" The cop was stooping and looking.

"None of your business."

Then to me, the cop said, "Let me see your gun. You have a gun?"

"No!" I said. "You can't see——" I cut myself off, remembering what Huey said.

"Say look, swine! You think you can come on with this petty illegal search. Well, I'm not going for it because you have no reasonable cause to."

"You boys are going to get it, sooner or later."

"I'm not a boy and——"

"I'm not a swine." The cop stood with a half-assed smile.

I didn't like the scene at all. I saw us getting busted too soon in our new organizational operation. But I also knew Huey naturally was taking the cops seriously, because one had said, "You boys are going to get it." It was a threat.

Huey was talking on now, deliberately scornful: "And we're going to catch *you* wrong. With your brutalizing asses. So I'm letting you know we'll defend ourselves. Now go tell that to your swine chief and your swine mayor, and if you don't like it——"

"Say, Huey!" I felt the tension in Huey, ready now to explode.

Huey turned to me. "Huh?"

"Wait a minute, man, cool it. Ah, let's go." I said.

"You think we ought to? These swine are trying to harass us."

"We got a lot more work to do. Let's split. We surrounded."

"Yeah." Huey started up the engine. "We got a lot more of this to go through. You right."

From then on, almost every night for a month Huey and I patrolled the police in my car, hoping to see an arrest going on—so we could get out and observe and insure with our guns and lawbook there would be no police brutality.

We enlisted Bobby Hutton as our first member and named him treasurer of the Black Panther Party for Self-Defense.

During the day we carried around hundreds of copies of our ten-point platform and program, discussing and talking with people about it. I'd go to work at the poverty center with my gun.

One day Huey came up with an idea for a uniform for us. Black berets, creased black slacks, black leather jackets, starched powder-blue shirts, black ties or a black silk scarf tucked in around the neck, and shined black shoes. "You see, if we dress neatly like this, the people will see us with our guns in a better way."

And on January second, Bobby Hutton, Huey, and I chipped in our money and rented a storefront office a half block from Merritt College. It was the same place I had hurled the rock into during my one-man riot reaction to Malcolm's death.

I painted a neat professional sign in the bay window of our new empty office, signifying our headquarters. We acquired some twenty sturdy folding chairs, a desk, a long table, and a blackboard. At night, Bobby and

I would go to the North Oakland Service Center poverty office, where we both were still employed, and mimeograph off thousands of copies of the platform. At the college in the day Huey and I would leave our guns at my house but dress in our uniforms.

We picked up six more members, and we picked up four more guns.

Meetings at the office were every Saturday at 1:00 P.M. and Wednesday nights at 7:00 P.M. The police constantly had us pegged, black and white cops moving up and down the street as long as we were occupying the premises.

Our few members brought other dudes and one day, one sister came. Of course we had to make it clear, when asked, that sisters could join the Black Panther Party. We would welcome them.

We learned and taught all our new members how to break down and clean weapons. They'd participate also in our study groups and Wednesday nights we would read aloud the *Autobiography of Malcolm X*. We found this method was teaching Bobby Hutton, who we called Little Bobby, how to read. Huey would expound upon Frantz Fanon's *Wretched of the Earth* and discuss the ten-point program. Members read over the "legal first aid," how to take arrests, and so on. All had to understand when it was necessary to shoot back "at those racist swine who brutalize and harass our black community to death."

Our office really stood out on Grove Street. In a couple of weeks we wound up with about twenty consistent members who attended our Wednesday-night and Saturday-afternoon meetings. But most of the time we only had enough guns for about five of us to patrol the police. And most times it would be Huey, Little Bobby, and I who patrolled.

After the first three weeks of office operations in January 1967, Huey came up with a brilliant idea to get some money for our treasury: selling Mao Tse Tung's quotations, *The Little Red Book*, to students on the Cal University's campus. We peddled hundreds and hundreds of *Little Red Books* for one dollar apiece, and with the money we wound up buying six 18- and 20-inch-barrel riot shotguns. Some of the members got so bold as to wear bandoliers that they would crisscross across their chests, saying, "Yeah! Like *Viva Zapata!*"

With Huey leading and me backing him, we dared the police: from Huey's legal articulation to his outright stern reaction to a foolish cop here and there, telling police, "If you shoot at me, swine, I'm shooting back!" I could see amazement written all over the cops' faces, that we were some new kind of "nigger."

It always blew my mind to stand beside Huey and see, feel, and know the sight of it all. It was at the core of a known black social problem. It made me feel safe somehow from police brutality—something I hadn't experienced in its extreme but which I had read about and became angry about when hearing it happened to so many people.

I was really, at this stage of derring-do, beginning to know myself, but with a tinge of light and insight that was finally washing away the fear of the corrupt racist power structure's authority. I had always despised undue brutal punishment from my father.

Another day, Huey cussed out a fat-bellied, arrogant cop in front of our office while some thirty black community people watched, cheering—we knowing the law was clearly on our side, the people amazed at our daring moments of truth, the police shocked and afraid of these uppity gun-toting niggers.

Roy Ballard from San Francisco came to our office one February day following a Saturday meeting, asking us if we would join a few others and the Black Panther Party of Northern California in escorting sister Betty Shabazz, Malcolm's widow, from the San Francisco airport for her appearance at a Death Morning Rally for Malcolm.

Huey and I knew that the Black Panther Party of Northern California had been started by none other than Kenny Freeman, Isaac Moore, Ernie Allen—the old West Coast RAM group. Our analysis was that they had heard of us and that they—or at least Kenny Freeman, we believed—were out to capture the scene upon our probable death in the streets while patrolling the police. We resolved that we would help escort Betty Shabazz, but we asked Roy Ballard, his seemingly half-ass humble self, how many brothers they would have "with guns, too"?

"Ah, man," Roy Ballard said, "we got twenty, maybe twenty-five brothers with guns. They ready!"

"Ah, I don't believe you," Huey put to him, "because if you have twenty guns, then you are ready to get out there and deal with those cops. Bobby and I will get our brothers together and we'll join you. In fact, you don't need us to escort sister Betty Shabazz. But we are ready to work together with any black brothers who are willing to get on the same level we have started. We ought to always strive for unity in the black community."

I cooked our meals of piles of spaghetti or neckbones and greens, and while we ate, sucking and shining our neck bones, I raised jokes about the Muslim's organization not eating pork, with everybody sucking and cracking loose at Nipsy Russell's famous line of not having a grudge against the hamhock. Our grudge was against the racist white power-structure.

We would come in from patrol at night, unload our weapons at my house, and lay them all out across the long dining room table. My mother had no fear of guns, being off the farm. She would simply say, "You-all be careful out there with them white folks 'cause they might want to hurt you-all, Bobby."

We would discuss Fanon and Malcolm, and we even began to read quite a few quotes from Mao's *Little Red Book*, excerpting and expounding on thoughts of Mao that we felt were applicable to our black struggle. I relished the thought that some time back I would have refused to read any "Communist" ideas. But Huey pegged our philosophy as probably some future black cooperative socialism. And we scorned the backward black-cultural nationalists, who we saw as mainly "armchair revolutionaries."

Monday evening, Huey, Tucker, Little Bobby, the Forte brothers, and I dressed down in our uniforms, commenting to each other that we were "cleaner than a broke-dick dog." We angled our smooth felt black berets on our heads, almost covering our right eyes as we stood in the dining room of my house in front of the large, wide wall mirror. We got our weapons and headed to San Francisco to meet with the Black Panther Party of Northern California.

We followed Huey in as he stepped into the office. Some eight people were seated around in a semicircle including three smiling sisters. One heavy, tall, light-brown-skinned figure sat in a chair with his back to us as we approached the semicircle of chairs. We stood a moment, looking at everyone, them looking at us.

Roy Ballard said, "Ah, everybody, this is Huey Newton and Bobby Seale from across the bay in Oakland. They're going to be escorting sister Betty Shabazz."

The three sisters' faces were all aglow, obviously admiring us.

Roy Ballard introduced us around, then said, gesturing to the light-brown-skinned, big fellow in a lone chair, "This is Eldridge Cleaver."

We were discussing who would speak at the memorial rally.

"Ok," Roy broke in. "You brothers have the military, and we'll speak on the political aspects of the black liberation struggle in America."

"However we speak," Huey said, "political and military are one and the same. One is just an extension of the other."

"Oh, no," Roy Ballard countered. "They're two different things. See, Kenny and them here are more political than you brothers are. So we thought that you would handle the military. See, it's like this—"

"No!" Huey interrupted. "Politics is war without bloodshed and war is a continuation of politics with bloodshed. They are one and the same. So we won't separate the military from politics when we speak."

"But you have to speak on the military, Huey," Roy Ballard was saying, "Kenny is going to speak on the politics——"

"Look!" Huey was stern. "We are going to speak. Now, when I speak I will speak on politics as I've said it is. I'm not going to sit here and have an unnecessary armchair intellectualizing argument about it. That's the way we'll speak."

The room got very quiet. You could have heard a pin drop. I guess we were too much off-the-block niggers who could not be manipulated into being caught in a situation of being labeled by our inner black struggle with these jive intellectualizing black cultural nationalists as simply "military" who would appear less than a stern people's political party. I could see Eldridge Cleaver wanted to smile.

Huey said, "We came here to see all the guns Roy Ballard said you have. So if we are going to organize a plan of operation, let's get down to it."

"Oh, we got guns," Kenny said, half boasting. "We got guns!" As though he had to boast about it further.

The next Friday, the day of escorting sister Betty Shabazz, we arrived at Kenny Freeman's San Francisco Black Panther Party office, damn near late because they did not let us know what time soon enough. There were seven of us, and I also got my brother John to go along so we could use his brand new Chevrolet Malibu. We couldn't have a car breakdown in the middle of this operation. We all had guns. All of us were dressed in our uniforms except John, who was not a member of the Black Panther Party, but just my brother—a working city busdriver with a family by then. We met up with the San Francisco group. We all had to shake our heads in disgust at the fact that there were only four of them with guns—three had M-1s and Roy had only a jive twenty-five automatic pistol.

At the airport we piled out of our cars. We were jacking off rounds into the chambers of our shotguns, since we were well schooled by Huey on the law; that one could not have a round in the chamber of a rifle or a shotgun while riding in a car—it was really a hunting law.

Roy Ballard was moving around in a rush, roaring and ready to take charge, saying, "You sisters, stay here. You won't go in. It's too dangerous. This is for us black men."

"Wait, Roy," Huey said. "The sisters go too. I'll run the operation. You be quiet, brother."

"You sisters have guns?"

"Yeah," Roy's girlfriend said, smiling and opening her purse. "See, right here."

"Yeah, ok, that's good. You go with us just in case the sister has to use a restroom."

"Get everybody together, Bobby," Huey said. "Line everyone up in a column of twos."

Suddenly there were some ten security guards coming, spread out in a semicircle, making ready. Another one was speaking through a walkie-talkie. Other people now were standing off, looking at our scene, some behind the glass entrance doors. A few porters—black brothers—were looking with wonderment.

"You're not going inside the terminal!" A heavy-set, red-faced, plain-clothes cop said.

"Yes, we're going in," Huey shot out.

"Say, mister!" Roy Ballard broke in, having gotten out of line and run up to the plainclothes cop. "We're here to escort our sister Betty Shabazz." Roy was acting humble with his hands out in a pleading fashion.

"Get back in line, Roy, I'll do the talking!" Huey demanded.

Roy reluctantly went back to the rear of the line, mumbling.

And the white plainclothes said, "You can't come into the airport with those guns. This is private property.

"You're wrong!" Huey shot out sternly. "Any private property that accommodates over two hundred people dictates by law that we can exercise our constitutional rights there. We have the right to escort sister Betty and we're going in and that's *that*! This terminal accommodates thousands."

Isaac, Leo, and Kenny Freeman were hanging back.

I mumbled, "These sly chicken-shit son of a bitches!" I said aloud, "Let's get in line. Damn, you're holding up the show!"

"Ok, ok." I hollered to Huey, "Ok, we're ready."

"Let's move forward, follow me." Huey took off.

"Forward!" I said, from the rear of the double column.

We stepped off walking. The airport security guards were twenty and thirty feet distant, walking ahead and to the side of us. We passed six gates and Huey was halting us in front of an almost empty, red-carpeted waiting area.

Huey told the brothers, "Look, station yourselves along the aisle area but just inside the waiting area and keep your eyes on these dogs!"

Some fifty people had stopped and the security guards suddenly stationed themselves up and down the aisle.

Sister Betty Shabazz came off the plane with her cousin and we quickly surrounded them. Roy Ballard was busy greeting her as we escorted her out, guns in front, in back, and to the side, marching along, most of us in our blue-and-black uniforms. Outside, headed toward the car, I looked back and heard Sister Betty ask, "Who *are* these brothers?"

"Oh, they just some gun-carrying brothers," Roy said.

"Well, they are *beautiful*! I never expected all this. I mean *who* are they?"

And Roy's girlfriend said, "This is Huey Newton and Bobby Seale, Sister Betty. They something else. They run the Black Panther Party."

I looked at Huey and said, "You hear the difference between Roy and his girlfriend?"

"Yeah," Huey said.

Our three-car caravan headed to *Ramparts* magazine building, a twenty-minute drive. Huey, Orlando, Little Bobby, the rest of our Party group, and I went inside and we stationed two brothers on the front steps of the building. We stationed two more at a long hall entrance.

We entered the office to see this Eldridge Cleaver interviewing sister Betty in an admirable but casual way. He was all respect for the sister as we listened. I walked on to the front door and a plainclothes cop was standing at the bottom of the steps, arguing with Little Bobby, who was saying, "I don't care what kind of motherfucking lieutenant you are, you can't come in."

Two other uniformed San Francisco cops were standing out on the sidewalk. I stepped into the middle of them.

"What's going on?" I asked.

"Is that gun loaded?" the white lieutenant asked Little Bobby.

"That's my business. If I know it's loaded, then that's good enough." Repeating, but arrogantly, what Huey would tell a cop.

"I want to see that shotgun," the lieutenant said, stepping up the steps.

Little Bobby braced. "You don't touch this gun."

"Hold it!" I said. "Look!" I took two steps down. "Don't come here trying to intimidate nobody. That's his weapon. His private property. And you can't come in."

"Who are you?" the cop said to me. "You the leader or something?"

"I'm one of them—I'm Bobby Seale. But you better not try to come in here, unless you got a warrant or something." Suddenly a press car drove up; then another cop car, four deep with police.

I headed back to the office through a crowd of white *Ramparts* workers, who were all curious, and told two of our members to go to the front door with Little Bobby and Orlando. "And don't let anybody in, unless they work here or something."

I hopped down the hall and opened the door; Huey was right there.

"There are press outside with cameras," I whispered to him. "The sister said she didn't want any pictures and there are about seven police who want to get in. They're arguing with Little Bobby. I stopped that, but you better tell them about the cameras."

"Yeah, ok."

"I'm going back out front." I went to the front trying to get through the crowd of *Ramparts* workers.

"Let me through, damn it!" I demanded, as I could hear Little Bobby cussing out the police again. And I got through, stepping between our four gun-carrying brothers.

"Don't say nothing to these crazy cops, Little Bobby."

The cameras were rolling. I looked around to see two other cop cars drive up. Police were bunched together near the curb. The cameramen were on the steps, wanting to get in.

Huey came through the crowd. "No pictures!" he said to a cameraman. "Move back, please. Ah, Tucker, Orlando—you brothers come down here to the bottom of the steps. Ah, say! No pictures! Get back please."

"Let's get something to block the cameras from taking pictures," Huey said to me. "The sister doesn't want any pictures and no interviews."

We both got a *Ramparts* magazine from a pile stacked on a table and went outside, clearing the way.

"Guard the sister," Huey said to me. "Get the brothers outside to surround her and walk her away when she comes out. And we'll keep the magazines in front of the cameras, real close."

Huey came out in front of Betty Shabazz, Doug Allen, and Isaac Moore. M-1 rifles pointed up in the air on each side of her. She almost stumbled on the steps with Kenny, Roy, and the two sisters grabbing her as I stuck my magazine up in front of the camera that I was standing next to.

"Hey! What the fuck!" the cameraman yelled angrily.

"No pictures!" I said.

And Huey was on another camera with his magazine, saying, "No pictures! No pictures!"

"Get that out of the way!" the cameraman said to me.

About twenty uniformed and helmeted police were bunched together at the curb, more or less spectating. Some cars in the street had stopped, with drivers watching us.

As the cameraman would move, so would I, keeping up with his every step, holding my magazine in front of his camera. I looked around to see another camerman slap Huey's magazine down. Huey put the magazine right back up. A television mike man stepped forward and struck Huey, and as fast as he struck Huey, Huey popped him back in the mouth.

"Arrest that man, officer," Huey said, looking back at the large group of cops.

"Little Bobby!" I hollered, dropping my magazine. They were twenty-five feet up the hill, around Betty Shabazz. "Tucker, Reggie! Back here!"

"If anybody gets arrested it'll be you!" a cop said to Huey. And the tension was mounting.

The cameraman was coming back at Huey and Huey stopped as he shifted his shotgun to his right hand. I could feel it. Something was about to happen. The cops were bracing. I quickly ran up beside Huey, saying, "Let's go Huey.... It's tight!" I watched the more than twenty police seemingly all taking a step towards Huey's back. "Let's *go!*"

Huey spun around. Tucker, Orlando, and our crew were up on and around Huey and me, and we stepped back a little up the slope as the police were slowly moving in on us with short steps, all bunched in a crowd.

"Don't turn your backs on these backshooting motherfuckers!" Huey shouted.

We all turned to face the police, who slowly stepped toward us and Huey shouted, "*Spread!*" We readied ourselves, getting back.

I was ready to draw and Huey, I guess he noticed he didn't have a round in the chamber, because he jacked a round off into the chamber. The sound of it—*Clackup*—sort of gave the police a signal. They knew the sound well: a riot pump shotgun. I guess it made them feel we were going to open fire on them. The police bunched closer together and slowed their pace.

"You draw you gun on me, swine, I'll blow your motherfucking brains out!" Huey bellowed out in warning.

Clackup! Clackup! Clackup! Our brothers loaded up. Every cop stopped in his tracks and stepped back. It was like the proverbial Mexican stand-off.

Betty Shabazz, Roy Ballard, Kenny and their whole crew were gone. We found out that night that Isaac, Leo, Roy Ballard, Doug, all had had unloaded guns! Everyone pleaded with Huey and me to go over to San Francisco and "clean those jive stupid motherfuckers out!" We told them no, that there was other necessary organizing to do.

A San Francisco *Examiner* newspaperman came to our office, surprisingly to interview our organization for the first time. He had even brought cameras. The next day we hit the front pages. Our Oakland-based Black Panther Party was given the sole credit, in a negative way, for escorting sister Betty Shabazz.

Huey called me on the phone.

"Say, Bobby, ah, look, we've got to—better yet, come over here to my apartment. It's important. We got to make a special move."

"Right! On my way."

I hung up the phone, went out and hopped down the front steps into the Monday morning sun, got into the hog and drove up to Huey's apartment wondering what kind of special move we had to make, enthusiastically ready for the rundown.

I sat on the edge of the couch as Huey stood. He said, "Look, here in the papers. This guy, Mulford, assemblyman at the state capital, is trying to get a bill in against us carrying guns."

I tried to speed-read the article as Huey went on.

"They're after us. The police are behind it. They calling us gun-toting bandits and the real reason is because we've made them respect us because of, ah, the way we're using the law—blowing it in their faces when we patrol them. They're mad and probably scared we'll blow their cracker asses away." Huey chuckled a bit, which made me feel a certain light-heartedness about it all: the fact that we weren't dead yet. I felt that after we had escorted Betty Shabazz, stood off the San Francisco police, cordoned off a whole block out in North Richmond and dared the police to come up into that community after they had brutally murdered a brother named Denzil Dowell—because of this the Oakland police were venting their guilty racist asses to this jive assemblyman, Mulford.

I remembered how my Mama would say, "You always reap what you sow." And I looked at the brutalizing racist police as strictly being the cause of why we were revolutionaries—carrying guns, ready to blow their butts away at the slightest act of police brutality we may have caught them in.

"So look," Huey continued. "What we have to do is get ourselves, ah, more publicity explaining our political goals in the ten-point program."

"Yeah, ok."

"And what we have to do is go to the Capitol, armed, with all the brothers. Look, they're out to get a law on the books to stop us from carrying *loaded* guns! So they can shoot us on sight and cut our program; and the press distorting will tell the black community that to arm yourselves is futile, and no one will see the actual political goals. We show the essence of the political power structure's farce when we patrol the police, showing the people; and, therefore, we've begun to show black people about their oppressed conditions."

"Yeah, I can dig the set."

We decided to draw up a position paper, get Eldridge Cleaver to write a mandate we could read to the press in Sacramento.

We talked with some others, and Eldridge brought up the idea that Huey should not go to Sacramento, being that he was the main head leader of the Black Panther Party for Self-Defense, and that going would be likely to result in being busted for parole reasons. Huey insisted that he had to go, but we outvoted him and insisted that he should not. I would go and read the statement. Then Huey wanted it noted that the meeting was composed of the five of us who comprised a sort of Party central body, agreeing and deciding to make the move.

With that settled, Huey ran down specific instructions to me; about the possibility of a leak getting out that we were headed to Sacramento and the police and/or National Guard being there. I was to read the statement *for sure* and leave. He said, "Don't go inside the Capitol. Do it on the front steps, and if you are challenged by any police shooting at us, then you have no alternative but to shoot back. But outside of that, take any arrests. We'd rather get our political point across than have a number of brothers shot up and killed."

"Right. I got you."

"Little Bobby," Huey added. "You stay close to Bobby. He's our chairman."

"Right," Little Bobby enthusiastically put in in a youthful upright manner. "Huey, Bobby, man! You-all some of the baddest motherfuckers I ever seen!"

We all filled our gas tanks up when the caravan stopped at the nearest gas station. Twenty brothers and five sisters. I told each driver, "Sacramento, the state capital—ready!"

After we got out of our cars in Sacramento, I gestured to them all to gather around me on the sidewalk area as they held their rifles and shotguns upright in a safety position. I spotted Eldridge, in a Panther uniform, moving around and clicking pictures in a hurry at all angles. Little Bobby handed me a stack of the mimeographed statements, which I glanced at and rolled up in the thin black leather glove of my left hand.

"Ok, everybody just stay sort of loosely near me. I mean, don't crowd me. And where there's press, then that's who I have to read this message to." I held the roll up in the air. "So let's stay together, ok?"

"Yeah, oh yeah!" and "Let's do it!"

"And tell these murdering dogs about *us* shooting *them* for a change!" the older Dowell brother spouted loudly in anger.

I spotted a tall, heavyset white man and his wife. They were stopped in their tracks, standing, staring at us. I raised my black-gloved hand up in the air.

"Ok, you-all! Let's move on out!" Pointing out the direction.

I took off walking, looking into the faces of the white man and woman who had stepped completely off the sidewalk and onto the grass, looking with their mouths wide open with shock and fear at all these niggers with guns. I had to smile.

Little Bobby was to my left and Orlando to my right. I glanced all around in back of me. Eldridge was flicking pictures. There were no smiles on the hard mean black faces of our thirty men and women. Yet, I knew these brothers, all of them. And most were really easy-going dudes, unless riled. Shit, black dudes off the block just *looked* rough. Damn! Huey was always telling me I looked mean. And I knew God damn well I didn't even try to look mean. Maybe it came from trying to adopt the expressions I had seen in pictures of American Indians, I thought. Yeah, and it's their fight, too. They're on reservations: cooped up like black people in ghettos. I noticed white people passing and looking, most with awe on their faces.

I approached the first set of steps and saw the TV cameramen hustling toward us, and I stepped our crew to the top of the stairs and stopped as we met with the news.

An excited white reporter, microphone in hand, asked,"Black Panthers, right?" He gestured to the cameraman trying to situate his heavy camera.

"That's right." I spoke up sternly. "The Black Panther Party for Self-Defense." And I unrolled my stack of statements and handed him the mandate message and proceeded to read the message with force, right there in full view, glancing up from the page, noticing another camera had arrived. I felt the meaning behind the words, feeling myself reading a little too fast and slowing when I stumbled on a word or two.

"Bobby Seale, aren't you?" a reporter asked.

"Yeah, man." Five microphones were suddenly jammed up in my face and I unrolled the statements, kept four or five, and handed the rest to Little Bobby. "Tell Artie or somebody to pass these out to the reporters."

"Right!"

And I read the statement in full again.

"Are you going inside?" a reporter asked.

Then I remembered, from the movies I'd seen, that citizens had a spectators' section where they could watch the legislature in action. What are these cats called besides "assemblymen?" Are there two houses?

I was confused as a reporter said, "The assembly is in session. Bobby Seale, ah, is this a protest against Assemblyman Mulford's bill to stop this dangerous gun carrying by the Defense of the Black Panthers?"

The assembly was in session. I wanted to see——

Huey had told me don't go in, but everything had been so easy up to now.

"Ok, let's go!" I shouted out, looking to see if they all heard me. I was surrounded and I stepped toward an open door and walked inside about twenty steps. I didn't know whether to go to my left, my right, or straight ahead down the long hall.

I spotted more white people, with their mouths hanging open. Their frightened, still expressions said, in my interpretation, "Niggers with guns—niggers with guns!" I felt they were just where I wanted them. I stepped off, deciding to go down the long hall, as the reporters scooted and rushed and hustled and bustled all around us; then cameramen and more reporters with microphones walked backwards, asking questions, filming, as our band of gun-toting, bandoliered, shotgun-, rifle-, and pistol-packing, mean-faced Party members put on the air of force and vigilance. Tired, angry warriors, brave warriors. I could feel the back-down caused by our surprise presence.

"Say, look," I asked a reporter. "Where is the assembly spectators' area?"

"You have to go upstairs," he excitedly answered.

"Ok, everybody, second floor."

Reporters jammed into the elevator trying to film and ask questions, guns and rifles mixed with several cameras and microphones were everywhere.

We took off walking again.

"This way, Bobby!" A reporter pointed and I walked, turning to my right, with some of our crew getting ahead of me.

"You going in, Bobby?" An excited, big-eyed reporter pointed to the wide door to the right. "Let's find the spectators' section."

They followed as I turned and stepped out the tall open door.

Some speaker bellowed on the microphone about assembly rules being broken. I turned, telling the brothers behind me to hold it, holding up my leather-gloved hand. "Wait! We in the wrong place!" "Bobby! Bobby!" Who was calling me? Oh—I spotted Eldridge. "The message," he said, "Read it!"

"Yeah, Bobby, read it, read it again." The reporters were shouting for me to do so. "We didn't get it!"

"Ok, ok, everybody! Hold down!" I demanded loudly, as I noticed at least ten TV cameras and what looked like fifty microphones all around. It got very quiet as I prepared myself to read the message.

"The Black Panther Party for Self-Defense calls upon the American people in general and black people in particular to take careful note of the racist California legislature now considering legislation aimed at keeping black people disarmed and powerless while racist police agencies——" And I read the whole message; the crowded quietness of the area making every word felt.

"Say look," I said after I'd finished, "are we under arrest or not!" I spoke directly to one of the guards who had surrounded us.

"No," he answered calmly, "you're not under arrest."

I stepped back and turned. "Ok, everybody. We splitting." I led the way. And we headed out, the reporters following us out to the front steps. Another cameraman ran up to me and asked me to read the statement once again. I did. And as fast as I finished, we moved out, headed for Oakland.

The hot Sacramento sun had me wanting to take off my black leather jacket as we walked on the twenty-foot-wide walkway. I stopped by the rear car, the shade of the trees easing the heat some.

"Ok, now, we headed back home," I told everyone. "We got a big lunch. A couple a big boxes of fried chicken and sandwiches some of the sisters from North Richmond put together. We'll eat lunch somewhere back on the highway."

We piled into our automobiles.At my direction, everyone was to follow my car and meet up with the other two cars around the neatly manicured park that looked to be the equivalent of ten square blocks.

Everyone now was complaining about the heat. My black leather jacket was hot. I wanted to take it off. I was about to turn right to head back toward the freeway, but when the green light came on, I changed my mind in a flash, after seeing the service station across the street. I drove straight across instead of turning right, and up into the service station alongside a pump.

"You-all use the toilet if you got to," I said. "I got to come out of this jacket and Tucker got to get some water for my old car." Opening the door, getting out, watching the last car park, I felt I should have turned to leave Sacramento.

Somebody was asking the white attendant for the keys to the restroom. Bobby and Orlando were hungry. Mark Comfort and Dowell had made their way across the station yard to me, guns in their hands.

"Hey," Mark said calmly. "Here come a jive cop. He's stopping."

I looked around to see a motorcycle cop. He looked from one end of the service station back to us. He got off his traffic cycle, an older cop in a blue short-sleeve uniform shirt. He stood looking, confused, then started walking down the sidewalk. I noticed he was pulling out his revolver as he slowly walked on with a not-knowing-what-to-do awe on his face to see five or six rifles in the brothers' hands, and suddenly a few brothers were opening doors, getting more rifles and shotguns out.

"Hey, Dowell! Mark!" They came up behind me and walked with me. We were almost to the other cars. "Stay ready. Hey you-all, stay ready!"

I stepped toward the cop, dropping my hand down alongside the hand grip of my gun.

Clackup! I heard the sound of the brothers loading rounds into the chambers of a rifle and then a shotgun.

I raised my left black-gloved hand up, palm open, at the cop, who was not aiming his gun, but now casually holding it up at me. His eyes, however, were looking beyond me as I could see cold red fear in them that said, "All these niggers with these guns! Where did they come from?"

"Say!" I hollered out. "Put that gun back in your holster!" I let an angry tone prevail so the brothers behind me would also hear.

God damn, these brothers is ready! A few were behind the hoods of cars and others had taken open-standing positions. *Clackup! Clackup!* Shit! I turned to look in the cop's face, my right hand now resting on the hand butt of my own forty-five.

He slowly raised his arm, putting his revolver back into his holster, letting his eyes catch mine. I realized it was black niggers, block brothers, versus white fear.

"Now. If you want to make an arrest, make it! But don't draw no gun on us at all! You got that?"

He looked at me as though he couldn't believe I was there telling him what he better or better not do.

"You draw a gun or shoot at us, you subject to get killed. But if you want to make an arrest, then say so! And we'll take the arrest. But keep your gun in your holster. And don't make no mistake about it. The right to self-defense is here! Are we under arrest?"

The radio spurted with static. We could hear a sudden excitement in the voice over the radio though the words weren't clear.

"Say you-all! Look, they want to arrest us. Now everybody remember, we take the arrest. Remember, we *take* the *arrest!*"

Five minutes later the corner service station was surrounded with cop cars. Some traffic was being redirected. I walked around the service station area repeating to everyone to take the arrest, we've broken no laws.

I was handcuffed and put into the back of a car. I noticed over half my crew was still armed, holding their guns in a proper upright manner. I saw Eldridge on the scene taking pictures. And then I was whisked away to the Sacramento city jail.

Out on bail, all the brothers were black heroes to all the women. A few sisters almost snatched brothers they knew inside and into the bedrooms, loving them. We were put on a pedestal as bad tough black men. We were admired to the hilt—while on the other hand, in the press, the Black Panther Party was referred to as a bunch of hoodlums. "Hoodlums Invade Capitol!"

Huey and I read the papers every day for five days. To the press and white politicians, we were all full of Lucifer. We found out we had hit the front page of the London *Times*. We were asked to appear on every radio and TV show.

The Black Panther Party for Self-Defense was now a household word in the Bay area, and its leaders were Huey Newton and Bobby Seale.

Shit!—I worried in silence—four hundred miles from Oakland just ain't far enough away! Artie and I were in Los Angeles, eating in a greasy cafe. I had trouble trying to eat all of my food, as hungry as I was. Then I took solace in feeling good about my decision not to go to jail. Do I fear jail? So what! I'm still a revolutionary, I reminded myself.

This whole underground situation left me thinking I'd eventually have to rob a bank or something just to get money to survive. It would have to be done smoothly and right. I couldn't get caught. I looked at my disguised reflection in the large pane. The shadow of the building was getting wider because of the lowering afternoon sun.

Artie was finishing her food, saving her milk for last, I knew—her final eating rites. She picked up her large-size glass, looking down into the milk, and put the glass to her lips, turning the glass up farther than it should be, making the level of the milk rise above her upper lip as she blissfully gulped and swallowed the cool milk. An even, white film mustache covered her upper lip as she finished with a satisfying "Ahhhhh!" Setting the glass down and smiling at me, letting me know that she enjoyed the meal and especially the last finishing touch.

"How long we going to stay down here?" She licked her tongue out, wiping the milk moustache off her lip.

"I don't know, but I got to move. I'm going to have to leave California before the court appearance. Uh, that job you got. Do you think you can take care of you and Malik on fifty dollars a week?"

"Yeah, I guess so. But—can't we stay together? We can get Malik and go where you want to go."

"Naw, it wouldn't be cool, Artie. See, you still don't understand. I *told* you! I already made my decision not to go to jail. I'm gonna be *underground*! And in three days I'm gonna have to leave the state for *good*."

"I thought they was supposed to give all of you-all probation or something," she pouted.

"Probation! No. We was headed to jail! Especially me. See, I was the leader. So I sort of just figured I'd work on an underground basis. I told Huey I wasn't going to jail and he said, all right."

"Who cut you hair like that?" Artie said with a giggle.

"John."

Artie cracked up with laughter again like she did when I picked her up from the bus station earlier that day. "You look funny without your moustache. You look younger. And them sports clothes—and that tie! Ooowh, ugh! And all you hair cut off!"

"Yeah, but don't nobody recognize me either."

"Sure don't."

Outside in the hot sun, we stopped at the corner, waiting for the light to turn green. The heat was immense. I took off my sports coat, throwing it over my back. We headed for the rented room and Artie asked, "How come they ain't going to give you probation instead of jail?"

"Well, it's all fucked up. The D.A. up in Sacramento wants me and six others to plead guilty to disturbing the peace of the state assembly, and I ain't guilty. The press, the reporters, led us the wrong way. But the D.A. first said I'd have to serve six months and he'd drop the charges on everybody else but us six."

"Who?"

"Tucker, me, and four others who said they weren't showing up at all."

"Well, what's going to happen to everybody since you ain't going to show up?"

I stopped in my tracks, thinking now. What would happen? Shit! That means some twenty-four brothers would go to jail for sure. And John Sloan and Big Willie—their probation would be violated.

"What's the matter?" Artie asked.

"Oh, shit, ah, I'm just thinking. Let's go."

"Are we going to get Malik and stay together?" Artie asked.

"I don't know. I got to figure this. I can't let you and Malik run with me. I'd be on the move—on the run, backed in a corner, scared shit! Trying to beat a bat out of hell."

I took the key and opened the door to our second-floor room and stepped in, shutting the door. Artie flopped down in the old armchair.

"Artie, you know what?" I smiled a bit. "I just figured it out. I got to appear in court."

"I thought you didn't want to go to jail!" Artie said grumpily.

"I don't. But, see, I can do six months. But the other brothers, they'll all go to the joint if I don't show. And well, it's like Frantz Fanon said, we'd go to jail, those who are dedicated. All I'll need is for you to do everything to get me a lawyer. Get a better job. Leave Malik with my Mama or your Mama and try to make a hundred a week or something and pay fifty dollars a week for a good lawyer."

"Ah, I'm so full," Artie said with a yawn.

"Artie, you ain't listening, girl."

"Yes, I am."

"Well, I got to make sure you going to do what I say."

"I'll do it. I'm just sleepy from riding the bus all night. I didn't hardly sleep."

"Well, will you do it?"

"Yeah. But what about robbing a bank to buy a house?"

"Forget that. Not the house, but the robbing. Come here. Get undressed. I'm going to fuck you."

"Oh, no! That's twice today!"

"And one more time later on tonight before we leave. We'll get the midnight bus back to Oakland. Come on."

"Oh, Bobby, I'm tired. I'm going to be sore after this," Artie said disgustedly.

"Come on girl! Get up, get in bed. Let's screw, bust our nuts, and get some sleep in between."

"Ok, ok! But how can you fuck so much?"

"I don't know. I just do."

Greystone prison. It blew my mind to see all those guys banging their heads against bars. Guys would be in twenty-four-hour lockup sometimes nine, ten months, banging their heads.

There was a time of day that was silent, usually around one and two in the afternoon. People were sleeping. Then in the silence some dude would holler out, slow, "Up in here." It would echo off the high ceiling of this warehouse-prison. Then another prisoner, it might be in a cell a city blocklength away, would answer, "Up in here." Real slow. Other men would say it too, from one cell or another.

I was almost about to give up on this revolution thing—it wasn't but a year or so old. I would lie in my cell and trip two and three hours out of every day: I could see myself walking through the Village, see the red paint, see the clotheslines, the tree in the middle of the courtyard. I could hear what people said, in my mind. I knew and felt I was out of that jail scene.

I got even a better orientation and understanding of revolutionary living after Huey was shot and busted and in jail, and after the racist reaction to a cop being killed by a Panther. A pig was downed, another wounded with numerous shots. It was our signal that shot around the country: Oakland, California, was on the map for sure if there was some killing going on.

When I was out of jail, since I was Huey's survivor, his buddy and partner, I had to see about some defense, so off to San Francisco. Eldridge and I met the lawyer Charles Garry, with his superior mannerisms and nonchalance. I had thought that Huey should have some kind of black lawyer, up until I met Garry.

Going to the legislature in Sacramento had got us known worldwide, and when we started in organizing the Huey Newton Defense Fund the people righteously came in. Sacramento got us known: when we were there it seemed like cameras and microphones and newspaper reporters with their pads were everywhere. We were know r internationally after that—and after that they chased us—the press came to our homes, the college, our storefront office. We were on the AM show on TV and when we come out of there, there's five cameras, they got up and came over to see us.

UNCLE SAMMY CALLED ME FULL OF LUCIFER

When I got out of Greystone—December 8, 1967—I started in organizing and holding rallies around the subject of Huey Newton. Along with Eldridge Cleaver and David Hilliard and others, I was working to build the Huey Newton Defense Fund. Brothers and sisters would go out to street corners with tin cans, and the people filled up the cans with money, trying to set Huey free. Huey ran for Congress while he was in jail and got twenty-five thousand votes. The Oakland Auditorium was packed when we had a "Free Huey" rally there and we got ten thousand dollars for the defense fund from that rally. We gave speeches and held rallies all over the state. Of course, the cops started busting us on all the charges they could lie and dream up—from murder on down, busting us left and right.

I was sitting in our office—righteous energy was being used all over that office, people being busy with revolutionary tasks—when the phone rang and Hakim Jamal, Betty Shabazz's cousin, was telling me that Marlon Brando wanted to meet us.

Hey, this was "The Wild One," the man my friend Steve and I had admired and looked up to, even dressed like—— Wanted to meet us? *Whoooh!*

We rented a car so some of the brothers could go to the airport and pick him up, and they brought him to Eldridge's place. I was already there, and when he walked in the door and we were shaking hands, and saying the first words, I was telling myself in my mind that this was a real person, he wasn't on the waterfront, or Zapata—a real dude. He'd come to talk to us about a movie he hadn't started shooting yet, where he was going to be the white oppressor and in the end the black oppressed were going to shoot him. He wanted to get the feel of being with black revolutionaries, and he wanted to get our thoughts about the movie. We sat around until four o'clock in the morning, drinking wine and rapping. We told him about the Black Panther Party and our true principles. The next day I had to go to court to see about one of the bullshit lying charges the pigs had come up with against me, and Marlon Brando went with me. He stayed around several days, watching and talking to all of us.

Our Black Panther Party newspaper was selling all over the world. One issue would be selling twenty thousand copies in Chicago—at another time it hit over thirty thousand there. New York hit thirty-five thousand circulation—there were a number of Black Panther Party offices in New York—even though at the airport we would find twenty-five to thirty thousand papers soaked down in water—the pigs' attempt to keep our word from getting out. We had subscribers in Paris, Copenhagen, Sweden, England, Japan, Kenya.

*

They killed Bobby Hutton, who we called Little Bobby, on April 6, 1968. Two days before that they had killed Martin Luther King. Little Bobby was only sixteen years old.

Brando arranged for me to go to King's funeral. I had all kinds of conflicting feelings, and I just sat in a corner there. In our newspaper we had called Martin Luther King "bootlicker" and everything else—I hadn't written it but it had been sanctioned by me to be in the paper. Harry Belafonte, Sammy Davis, Jr., Sidney Poitier were all there—I just kept sitting in a corner. I saw on TV the wagon procession, and Rockefeller and Humphrey were there—wow, I thought, these cats are killing everybody. Maybe they want to kill me. At one point some people came rushing in and I got very nervous; I was nervously turned off. I didn't have my gun with me. I started walking. I said, "I'm going." I got on a plane and took my two shots of whiskey. I went home and got to sleep, then I got up next morning and did my Party work.

Three days later we had a funeral for Little Bobby. About three hundred Party members were there, in uniform, and Brando came, wearing a suit.

It seemed like there was a lot of death.

PART VII

They Tried to Kick Me
Out of Heaven

THE MAJORITY in the Party, sixty per cent, were sisters at this time. Some of the brothers would say, "Sister, you stay with me tonight. I'm the man, sister, I got the gun—I could get killed any minute." Sisters were saying ok, but not really wanting to—in effect, they didn't have a choice. Some of them came to me and described what was going on: "I stay with the brother if he wants me to, but I guess that means if I want to stay with another brother, I can't do it."

I told the brothers, No, this ain't right. "Oh," they said back, "it's easy for you to say that—there ain't a sister in here that can refuse you."

"No, you brothers is wrong. To some extent some sisters will want to get with me because I'm chairman, that's true, but a number of sisters have said they didn't want to, and I didn't get mad. And I rap with a sister, I don't make love unless we rap."

All over the country sisters wanted to stay with me. I know some of it was because I was chairman, but some was because I was standing up for them. I had a lot of sisters I was really close, tight friends with who were in back of this attitude. It was absurd, I found out, for a brother to be mad at a sister for not wanting him—though I had felt that rejection, those inner feelings of anger. Getting it on with a sister was more than busting my nuts; it was like fluid, like something going back and forth between us. I really got to know, get closer to sisters.

I was in Chicago at the Party office. You entered off a business street, went up a very high flight of stairs—it was a drab wooden place with three large rooms and a kitchen. There were posters all over: of Huey in the wicker chair, Emory Douglas posters, posters of Mao, Ho, Castro, Malcolm, Rap Brown. The Chicago members were so gung-ho they'd painted the walls blue and the trim black—the Party colors. There were about one hundred and fifty Chicago members—twenty or so dudes were there one night and we were sitting down to eat; ten or twelve sisters were laboring in the kitchen. Now a sister fills up a plate with the product of her labor and she brings it in, says, "Here you are, brother." Then the brother starts eating and he looks up and says, "Bring me the hot sauce."

"Hold it!" I said, loud, standing up. "Hold it right here!" The brothers looked up, with their forks full of food on the way to their mouths. "Call the sisters in, make room for them here at the table!"

"Chairman, they eat when we're finished," the brothers said, and, "Chairman, we're the men."

"You eat up all the choice pieces, and they get what you leave? Listen, brother—the worker deserves enjoying the product of the worker's labor. How you going to sit up here and talk about a person producing and not getting exploited? Don't nobody touch a thing." I stepped into the kitchen. "Come on out of there, sisters."

When the sisters were sitting down and eating the food along with the brothers, I said, "When everybody's finished eating, the brothers are going to clean up and wash the dishes."

"Oh, no, Chairman!" the brothers were complaining. "I don't know how you go about washing dishes, Chairman," and, "That's for sisters, Chairman!"

"Then tomorrow," I went on, "there's going to be crews, men and women, doing the cooking and the washing up. You brothers want to be revolutionaries, you got to be knowledgeable about how to take care of yourselves—and in the Party we don't have some people doing the work and other people having a good time off it. No one should be isolated doing a specific kind of work."

"But, Chairman," one of the dudes said, "we the men. The pigs come down on the Party, we the ones take the heat."

"No, brother." I shook my head. "That's wrong. When an office or an apartment is attacked, brothers and sisters both die."

Huey stood up for the sisters, too. He was in jail and I sent a message to him and he said, "You're right." David Hilliard, too. A sister sent in a report that she got kicked out of the party because she refused to relate to a particular brother. I had to write out a policy for the Party on that.

*

Chicago, in court, October 27, 1969. The marshal, directed by the judge, told me to sit down. I was thinking that I had to lower my voice, momentarily debating how I could sound more like a lawyer and not so furious.

"You know I am speaking out for the right to defend myself again, don't you, because I have that right as a defendant, don't I?"

Judge Hoffman: "You have a very competent lawyer of record here."

I found myself shouting, "He is not my lawyer. And you know I fired him before that jury was even picked and put together." Then I quickly remembered it was really before the jury had actually heard any evidence.

Judge Hoffman: "Will you ask him to sit down, Mr. Marshal?"

The marshal: "Sit down, Mr. Seale."

"What about my constitutional right to defend myself and have my lawyer?" To hell with sitting down. They got to gag me first. Denying me my rights? Who the hell he think he is?

I had a right to be my own counsel, especially since Hoffman had adamantly refused to put the trial date forward until my attorney, Charles Garry, recovered from his operation and could defend me.

"Your constitutional rights," Judge Hoffman started——

"You are denying them," I shouted loudly. "You have been denying them." Then, angrily, speaking fast: "Every other word you say is denied, denied, denied, denied." I banged my hand hard on the table with each repetition. "And you begin to oink in the faces of the masses of the people of this country. That is what you begin to represent, the corruptness of this rotten government for four hundred years."

"Mr. Seale, will you sit down," the marshal loudly demanded, standing up in my face, bits of spit spurting out of his mouth.

"Why don't you *knock* me in the mouth?" I looked him in the eyes. "Try that," I dared him, with a nervous anger. I stood waiting for him to do something in the silence of the tensed courtroom.

"Ladies and gentlemen of the jury," Judge Hoffman broke the silence, "I regret that I will have to excuse you."

I spoke to the jury, which was filing out of the courtroom, some glancing at me: "I hope you don't blame me for anything." Then I turned to Judge Hoffman. "And those false lying notes and letters that were sent that said the Black Panther Party threatened that jury—it's a lie, and you know it's a lie, and the government did it to taint the jury against me. You got that?" Something I kept telling myself not to do was to shout like a maniac, but I continued with: "This racist administrative government with its Superman notions and comic-book politics. We're hip to the fact that Superman never saved no black people. You got that?" I almost had to laugh at my own words as a few members of the audience quickly controlled their whispered chuckles. It helped me to lessen the rage that was swelling up within me. Yet, I was determined to defend myself. I had that right and I knew it. Hoffman didn't really understand all this, but he would actually have to gag and shackle me to my chair before I would willingly let him walk all over me, denying me my constitutional rights.

October 28, 1969.

"I have no further questions." William Kunstler, one of the lawyers for the seven other defendants on these "conspiracy to incite a riot" charges, which had been made up after the police had rioted in the streets around the Democratic Convention in Chicago, turned confidently from the lectern.

Judge Hoffman asked Leonard Weinglass, the Chicago Seven's other lawyer, "Do you want to cross-examine this witness?"

"I would like to request to cross-examine this witness," I interjected loudly, getting to my feet before Weinglass began his cross-examination. Across from me, prosecutors Richard Schultz and Thomas Foran flinched with a sigh of disgust at my bold gestures and mannerisms.

"You have a lawyer here." Judge Hoffman raised a little in his seat, showing a bit of disturbed anger after the past few weeks of my consistent interruptions of the regular procedures.

"That man is not my lawyer," I said, pointing at Kunstler. Then I pointed to the witness sitting in the box of the witness stand. "That man made statements against me. Furthermore, you are violating Title 42, United States Criminal Code. . . ."

"Sit down, Mr. Seale," a stocky white marshal stated angrily, raising his voice, and I noticed the three-hundred-pound black marshal, whom I privately referred to as Goliath, looking at me through threatening eyes. One mean look from this huge bastard would make anyone shut up, but I refused to let him intimidate my purpose.

"Hey," I said to the witness, ignoring the marshals. "Did you see me make a speech in Lincoln Park, William—Mr. William Frapolly?" And before he could answer, opening his mouth, I repeated in a demanding tone, "Did you see me make a speech in Lincoln Park?"

Schultz jumped to his feet, and all eyes were on me. I knew Julius Hoffman and Foran, who rested his head in the palms of his hands, would be perturbed at my new tactic of actually trying to cross-examine the witness. Hoffman said, "Mr. Marshal, will you ask that man to be quiet?" Hoffman's screwed-up old face peered down through his round metal-rim glasses. "And Mr. Seale——"

"Did you see me make a speech in Lincoln Park, supposedly on August 27, Tuesday?"

"Let the record show that the defendant Seale keeps on talking without the approval of the Court," Hoffman said, "and in spite of the admonition of the Court and in contempt of the Court."

I said, "Do you know a Robert Pierson?" Frapolly instinctively opened his mouth, looked at Schultz, then shut it. "A lying agent?" I angrily asked. Frapolly was now astounded a bit, and I could tell Foran and Schultz were taken aback by my new persistence. The jurors' eyes were on me as I glanced to them with a smile.

"You needn't answer any of those questions," Judge Hoffman said to Frapolly. "Let the record show that the defendant——"

"Let the record show," I loudly interrupted, "you violated that and a black man cannot be discriminated against in relation to his legal defense and that is exactly what you have done." I spoke to Judge Hoffman with vehemence. "You know you have. Let the record show that!" I deliberately emphasized this with even greater emotion.

"The record shows exactly to the contrary." Hoffman drew out his words.

"The record shows that you are violating, that you violated my constitutional rights. I want to cross-examine the witness. I want to cross-examine the witness!"

"I admonish you, sir, that you have a lot of contemptuous conduct against you," Hoffman said.

"I admonish you! You are in contempt of people's constitutional rights. You are in contempt of the constitutional rights of the mass of the people of the United States." I felt the need to give a stinging speech, to teach him, show him how wrong he has been. "You are the one in contempt of people's constitutional rights. I am not in contempt of nothing." I gestured outwardly with my arms. "You are the one who is in contempt. The people of America need to admonish you and the whole Nixon administration." I could see it was blowing his mind as he said nothing for a quick moment but smiled with amazement that I said that it was *he* who is in contempt.

Tom Hayden said, "Let the record show the judge was laughing."

"Yes, he is laughing," I said.

"Who made that remark?" Judge Hoffman shot out angrily, rising in his seat, looking out across the large defense table at the other seven defendants.

"The defendant Hayden, your Honor, made the remark," prosecutor Foran put in.

Judge Hoffman wrote something on a piece of paper.

"And me," I said.

Foran and Schultz sat down. I looked around and noticed Goliath had come up behind me. But I remained standing, wanting Hoffman to say something to me. The massive Goliath, I knew, was ready to pounce on me at the slightest indication of the word go.

Hoffman sent the jury and the witness out. "Do you want to listen to me for a moment?" he said.

"Why should I continue listening to you unless you are going to give me my constitutional rights? Let me defend myself."

Hoffman said, "I am warning you, sir, that the law——"

"Instead of warning, why don't you warn me I have got a right to defend myself, huh?"

"I am warning you that the Court has the right to *gag* you," Hoffman shot back. "I don't want to do that. Under the law you may be *gagged* and *chained* to your chair."

He'd said it! He'd said what I had been waiting for. But would he actually do it?

"Gagged? I am being railroaded already. I am being railroaded already." I gestured, my arms out.

"The Court has the right and I——"

"The Court has no right whatsoever. The Court has no right to stop me from speaking out in behalf of my constitutional rights."

"The Court will be in recess until tomorrow morning at ten o'clock," Hoffman declared.

"Everyone will please rise," the marshal intoned.

I sat down quickly. Everyone rose—the noise shuffling into silence. Then Judge Hoffman looked at me sitting. Would he chain and gag me for this? I could see his appalled face. I had him.

"I am not rising." I then wanted the whole standing courtroom and the press to note this. "I am not rising until he recognizes my constitutional rights. Why should I rise for him? He is not recognizing——"

Tom Hayden slowly descended toward his empty seat. I began putting on my thick winter coat, still seated in my chair. I had asked the Chicago Party members to buy it for me, thinking it would pad me from the blows that Goliath would be sure to get in on me sometime soon.

"I am not rising." Thinking to myself, if these marshals grab me, my coat would lessen any painful blows if a fight ensued.

"Mr. Marshal, see that he rises," Judge Hoffman angrily ordered.

"Mr. Seale——" the marshal began.

"And the other one, too," Hoffman put in.

Suddenly, Dave Dellinger sat down firmly in his chair, followed in a chain reaction by the other defendants—Rennie Davis, Abbie Hoffman, Jerry Rubin, Lee Weiner, and John R. Froines. Only William Kunstler and Leonard Weinglass remained standing at the defense table.

"Get all of the defendants to rise," Hoffman commanded.

"Mr. Hayden, will you please rise," the marshal asked.

"Let the record show that the defendant Mr. Hayden has not risen," Hoffman said.

"I would request counsel to tell their clients—Mr. Kunstler, will you advise your clients to rise?" asked the marshal.

Weinglass replied, "If the Court please, it is my understanding that there is no constitutional or legal obligation on the part of the defendants to rise so long as their failure to rise is not disruptive."

Beautifully put, I smiled in my thoughts. Right on!

"You advise your clients not to rise, do you?" Hoffman said.

"I have no obligation to advise my clients to rise. They are doing nothing disruptive in this courtroom."

"We will determine that later," Hoffman replied.

"I might add the clients are in protest of what you have done in their opinion to Bobby Seale's right to defend himself," Kunstler interjected.

"They are sitting silently," Weinglass added.

"Will you advise your clients to rise, Mr. Kunstler?" Hoffman continued.

"Your Honor," Kunstler said, "if you direct me to, I will advise them."

"I direct you to."

"Then I will pass on the direction," Kunstler declared. "You directed me to. I now pass on the direction to them. They have heard you direct me but I cannot in good conscience do more than that. They are free and independent and they have to do what they please. I have now passed on the direction."

"Let the record show that none of the defendants has risen," Hoffman stated. "The court will be in recess, Mr. Marshal."

Judge Julius Hoffman stood up—short, puny, black-robed—and eyed me again from out of his drawn, wrinkled face, then he turned and left the courtroom—which burst into excited voices, comments being stated by more than two hundred spectators, fifty or more press reporters, Schultz and Foran, and even those at the defense table. The background was filled with comments like "Right on, Chairman Bobby!" from Party members, and with pro and con statements made by other spectators as they began to file out of the courtroom.

The head marshal was coming toward me to take me to the lock-up.

"Out of sight!" Jerry Rubin said, as the defendants began to talk among themselves.

"Beautiful, Bobby, you're beautiful!" Dave Dellinger said, with his pleasant, almost ministerial, manner.

"Old Julie is going to have a heart attack yet, Bobby!" commented Abbie Hoffman, who was still seated and smiling with victory.

The marshals took me out. The huge Goliath was staring at me with disdain. Shit, I thought, these motherfuckers are trying to do everything to stop me. But Judge Julius Hoffman ain't no God damn God, although he acts like he thinks he is.

That evening in the top floor of the jail in the Federal Building I was chained and handcuffed along with eight other prisoners, leg irons on our right and left legs. We were then taken down forty flights in a secret elevator into the underground parking lot under the city-block-long Federal Building. As usual, when we arrived in the parking lot there was a group of spread-out marshals waiting to transport us back to Cook County Jail. And as usual there was "James Bond," as I called one of them, in a dark trench coat, with menacing face, standing ready with a machine gun in one hand, his coat pulled back ostentatiously showing his giant .357 magnum. He was ready to draw as we prisoners clumsily headed into the back of a panelled paddy wagon accompanied by federal and city police cars in front and back of the vehicle.

After a forty-five-minute ride across town, when we arrived at Cook County Jail, I spotted James Bond getting out of a car, stumbling over his pump shotgun and holding the machine gun in the other hand, carrying both while trying to coolly get out of the front seat of the federal car. He caught himself quickly and stood in a ready stance, both guns in his hands.

"God damn!" I said to Bob, one white federal prisoner chained next to me. He could also see out of the window. "You see that fool, man!"

"Oh, my God! Oh shit!" Bob laughingly said, with a note of seriousness. "We're dead! We're dead! Let's get out carefully, man."

"Maaaan," a black prisoner commented, dragging out the word. "What they let a crazy motherfucker like that—shiiit!"

"Just don't nobody stumble getting out," Bob warned.

"Yeah," I said. "That fool will think somebody is escaping."

"And open up on us," Bob said.

"And kill us all!" the black prisoner added.

James Bond I took very seriously. Three weeks prior, he had come out of the jail helping to cuff us with leg irons. When we were loaded and locked in the paddy wagon, still in the yard, through the wire mesh I saw him go to the little room where they all left their weapons when they entered the jail. He was handed what seemed like an arsenal of weapons. James Bond quickly strapped his two pistols on and then did something that blew my mind. He raised the cuffs of his pants and slipped a pointed six-inch dagger inside one boot, then did the same thing with the other boot. In addition to a machine gun in one hand and a shotgun in the other.

Being processed back into the jail each night was a double strip-search procedure. The first strip-search was near the holding cell at the rear entrance where we came in. We stripped only to our shorts there, and all clothing and personal effects were searched. Ten minutes later, we were all paraded through a short hall, past a large holding cell, past a dispensary where prisoners coming from court picked up nightly prescriptions that had been given to them, and out another door into a five-city-block-long, ten-foot-wide basement corridor.

As we entered the wide hall, we turned to our right, walking inside a three-foot-wide space to one side of a thick yellow line that was against the rules for any prisoner to cross.

We would then walk along very close to the wall until we came to our next stop, the second strip-search. We had to stand before a group of about ten Cook County Jail guards, whom we had to face buck naked, placing our clothes on the other side of the yellow line. Then proceeded to bend over so the guards could look up our asses to see if we were possibly hiding something, after which we would dress and go by ourselves to our respective tiers to be taken upstairs wherever our plastic-covered I.D. cards designated.

Behind the locked door of the hospital tier of Cook County Jail, the young white medic was smiling, with a hypodermic in his hand, ready to give me a shot. But I knew he was smiling because he already knew how I had upset the court again. He kept his small radio on a news station all day.

"You ain't going to let them gag you, eh, Bobby?"

"We'll see." I set my legal papers down on a desk and put my coat down. I dropped my pants just below my behind. The medic hit me with the huge hypodermic needle with 2,400,000 units of penicillin. Because of so many past experiences in and out of hospitals, I hardly felt the needle as he inserted it, then stung me again in the left cheek with another two million units. That process had gone on for a month every evening. The bed to the left of mine in the hospital ward had a middle-aged white prisoner in it whose hero in life was Howard Hughes. He was lying in his bed watching TV.

"Here it is, Bob! You're on the top!" he hollered out to me.

"Ok, ok, I'm coming." I buttoned my pants and took my pills quickly as I heard the newscaster running it down about Hoffman threatening to gag me. I went to my bed and the nurse and two medics followed behind me to watch as other prisoners there in the hospital, including the older black guard for the hospital ward, all gathered at the TV, looking at the news.

I was kind of surprised and elated that the news was actually making Hoffman look bad while also citing the fact that he would be justified by law to gag me. I had read the Allen court case, which set a certain precedent in terms of gagging defendants, but I knew that what Allen had done in outright disruption of his trial was totally different from my actions. The next day I would have to play it by ear. I had to beat Hoffman.

I ate my food, sloppily prepared black-eyed peas, pork chops, rice and gravy, and corn bread. I got undressed and into bed. The old black guard came in with leg irons in his hands to clamp me to my bed. I laid back, watching the TV. The medic came in a short while later and taped a needle in my left arm, attaching me to a tube that strung up to a quart bottle full of antibiotics. I pulled my shorts down with my right hand and the medic then placed the heat lamp over my testicles.

Feeling the soothing heat vibrations of the lamp conjured up feelings of how those bastards back at S. F. County Jail didn't have enough human sense to cure this thing before it got greatly infected, possibly doing irreparable damage to my reproductive organs. Even the God damn doctor didn't give a damn when I informed him that the dosage of penicillin he had given me wouldn't be enough to cure me. By the time I got to Chicago, and after a few days there in jail with the Cook County Jail guards not doing anything about my complaints about needing treatment, my right ball had swollen up to the size of an orange.

A guard passed my cell.

"Hey, man. I got to see a doctor."

He shrugged me off lightly and proceeded to walk away. I quickly pulled down my pants and held the swollen infected ball in my hand, gesturing to him with angry fury building up within me.

"Hey man. Look, God damn it!!"

"Oh, my God!" The guard said in horror and damn near ran down the hall.

My case of venereal disease infection was so bad, I was placed in the hospital immediately, and had been there during the entire duration of the trial.

Three nights before I was busted was probably when I got the VD. Always when I was in jail I would trip and spend time reliving past scenes—and this was one. I had wound up at an apartment that seemed to be full of Party members from both in and out of town, with people on mattresses in the kitchen and every other room. Two sisters from out of town had been after me all day. When I came into the house, they openly but very coolly walked up to me, whispered in my ear, and asked me to screw them. I responded with, "We'll see—maybe," as they followed me into the kitchen to get a beer. They began to hug and caress my body.

"Oh, please, Chairman, huh?"

"Not tonight."

"But we leaving tomorrow."

"Oh, Chairman Bobby, come on——"

The principle that backed up love relationships among Party members was simply that those who did not have an established one-to-one relationship with someone had the right, male or female, to make love with whomever they desired.

I had argued to help establish this practical principle. My wife and I had been somewhat separated because she did not like me working with the Party and the principles it stood for, so I really began to understand the need for such a principle in the Party—to ward off petty jealousies and unnecessary quarrels that might in the future ruin the real overall goal and purpose behind the struggle for freedom.

I had also witnessed before this principle was established that brothers were freer than sisters to make love with whom they chose. Brothers were sometimes ignorantly claiming or intimidating the sisters. "Whoremongering" would be the word used by Mama and Aunt Zelma to describe such activity, but I had long since buried those old-fashioned notions; there were freedoms that I felt every human being had the right to.

Even before this principle was mandated, however, I became a constant target or choice of the sisters, being one of the leaders of the Party. And they were such dedicated, truly fine, good-looking women that naturally I very rarely refused their irresistible body warmth and affection.

I went into Cheryl's room and laid with her. She had a full, honest-screwing way about her, like she really enjoyed the body touch, the feel and motion involved in making sweet love. She fell off to sleep telling me she loved me and I told her the same, feeling love in a very new and revolutionary sense.

I got up and took a shower. I thought of the other two sisters from out of town. The thought of making love to two women in the same bed intrigued me. I went to thei r room, opened the door, and turned the light on. They were awake, sitting up, looking susprised and smiling as I shut the door.

"Now, what's all this you sisters talking 'bout making sweet juicy love with me, both at the same time?" I said. "It can't be done at exactly the same time."

"Oh, Chairman," the fine dark-skinned one said, giggling.

"Come on, Chairman." The fine light-skinned Mildred smiled with delight, throwing the covers back for me to get in as my penis rose from looking at their soft, shapely bodies teasingly outlined in nightgowns.

"Yeah," the other sister said. "We'll make you feel good, Chairman."

I dropped my shorts to the floor, my penis beginning to stick straight out.

"Oh, shit, honey! The Chairman's bold, baby."

"Oh, my God," the dark-skinned one said, looking at my erect penis.

"Now, ain't this something." I smiled and turned off the lights and went and got into the bed with them as they enthusiastically began to take off their gowns and pull their panties off.

Mildred was all up next to me, holding my penis in her hand and kissing me as my right hand caressed the dark-skinned sister's vagina.

"Who's first?" I asked.

"I don't care, Mildred, honey. I just want to be with the chairman before we leave. All the other sisters can have him all the time." The slimmer, soft-butt, dark-skinned sister said.

"Chairman Bobby, you just do something to me just being next to you," Mildred said.

I situated myself on top of them as they lay side by side in the bed. I kissed one, then the other, as I caressed their bodies, placing my fingers in and around their vaginal areas. I got in between them again. I had one hand caressing each of their vaginas as they hugged and kissed me from each side; feeling their naked, soft, warm bodies, kissing one, then the other; all of us becoming highly aroused by the touch and feel of each others' sensitive bodies. They had their soft, full legs cocked wide open as we blissfully went off, and I was as erect as a steel pipe. The darker sister was fondling my penis and she mentioned that she wanted to suck my dick. I told her flatly, no—I had a thing against that because of the fact that the way I ran around I could have a venereal problem and not know it.

I started with Mildred, first softly and carefully loving her, fucking her so as not to hurt her.

"Oh, Chairman, all of it, Chairman!"

She wanted it hard, all the way in, the way I loved to screw, with feeling, impact, like wild young animals satisfying a necessary pleasurable need. She reached a tingling, mounting, shouting, erotic climax, while the other sister rubbed me and caressed my back.

I held back my ejaculation and rolled off Mildred and began to make love to the second sister, who, because of her shallower vagina, could not take the hard all-the-way-in screwing, so I gently made sweet love to her until I had the urge to come and started pressing it in much harder, feeling an ejaculation about to come. She complained that it hurt and I consciously held back so she could experience the gentle calm come that she liked.

Mildred, still caressing me, made bold gestures which meant to me that she wanted to screw me some more, so I started to make love with her again. We busted our nuts more passionately and violently this time, as I let loose, coming too. Totally exhausted, I fell asleep between the two of them.

A couple of hours later, I awoke, got up, and took another shower.

A sister named Carol suddenly came into the shower with me. After we were finished washing I laid her on her mattress in the dining room area and made love to her, and she reached her height of ecstasy, but I did not come.

I got up and went back into the bed with Cheryl and started dozing off to sleep. She awoke me, playing with my penis, and got me to screw her again. I couldn't come.

By eight o'clock in the morning, Cheryl had gone to do her daily political activities. I was awake again and through the door I spotted a fine Chinese sister in the living room. She must have come in very late, I thought. She came into Cheryl's room and I couldn't help but notice this pretty, fine, shapely, pleasingly good-looking woman in her ass-short see-through slip. She didn't know I was in the bed.

"When you come in? You weren't here last night."

"Oh!" She turned, a little startled. "Uh, I—I came in about two o'clock."

I talked to her for a quick moment about organizing the Red Guard, a revolutionary group in Chinatown that had a working coalition with the Party, as she started looking for something in the chest of drawers. My penis rose, getting hard as I looked at her bending over to look through the drawer.

She was getting ready to put on some clean panties. I lay back, checking her out, folding my arms in back of my head, which was resting on the pillow.

"Say."

"Huh, Chairman?" she said, turning around, pulling up her panties.

"Uh, I dare you," I said pleasantly, "to make *good*, sweet, love with me." I smiled at her, looking into her eyes to let her know I really wanted to screw her.

"Now?" she asked, looking at me with wide eyes, then at the slightly open door.

"Yeah, uh huh. Why not? Shut the door. Come on."

She said, "You think anybody will——"

"Come on. Ain't nobody going to say nothing. But then again, only if you *want* to."

"Oh, yeah." She smiled. "I want to, Chairman."

"Ok, then. Come on."

She got on the bed and I separated her legs, kneeling in between them and seeing the delight on her face as I looked at her, my eyes traveling from her face to her body. Her small, hand-sized breasts, her pretty fluffy vaginal area. My penis was throbbing hard as I rubbed her on her clitoris and around and between her full lips with one hand and carressing the top portion of her body with the other, flipping the hard nipples of her shapely little breasts. After a few moments we began kissing each other with full, open mouths, then suddenly the head of my penis was right there at the entrance to her vagina and I pushed easily and my penis started in an inch or so, while we were totally wrapped up in each others' arms.

I moved rhythmically, gently easing my erect penis into her tight, caressingly soft lips as we passionately kissed on. I slowly felt my whole long hard penis moving in and being accepted all the way into her vagina as I slowly moved into it. My passionately engulfed mind told me I was one with her, inside her purely nice, completely warm, juicy tightness. My mind was in the bliss of her soft smooth body and I was pleasingly surprised at how the Chinese sister took to me. We were in a whirlwind of delight. Very rarely did I experience this elevation in lovemaking. Grabbing and moaning to each other about how good it is. God damn, I thought, fucking this sister is a natural high. . . .

I believed I had contracted the VD that night. Since sisters could not tell they had the disease, I sent out messages from jail and made sure that they found out, so they could receive the proper medical care.

"Those chicken-shit bastards," I thought, coming to myself, "wouldn't even cure a man of a disease that may one day kill him. The inhuman motherfuckers." Garry eventually had to get a court order in San Francisco for them to even give me any dosage of medicine at all.

October 29, 1969.

The lights came on in the long, open-bay ward of the jail's hospital. The clanging of the leg irons being removed awakened me. I sat up quickly.

I've got to force Hoffman to gag me today, was my main thought. Quickly washing, dressing, and eating, I grabbed my legal papers after making my bed neatly. Thought, suddenly stopped at the medic's desk in the hall, saying aloud to myself, "Hold it, Bobby," and went back to get my thick winter coat. This might be the day for a knockdown-drag-out fight in the courtroom.

"Say, Bobby," the white nurse called out with a warm voice, "don't get yourself gagged."

She was smiling with a little worried look.

I said back to her, "I'm going to make Hoffman gag his own self in the eyes of the public."

I was ready, with a need to triumph. I would watch myself. I wouldn't threaten Judge Hoffman's life, nor the jury, like Allen had done. I will not tear up my legal papers. I can't verbally threaten to disrupt the trial. But Hoffman will either allow my right to defend myself or he will be forced to gag me. I doubted greatly that his racist superior attitude would allow him to let me exercise my constitutional right that was being denied.

All the defendants, Kunstler, and Weinglass greeted me. The courtroom was packed. Marshals were everywhere—shit! Dave Dellinger swiveled around facing me and said, "Bobby, they got more marshals than yesterday."

"Yeah. I see." To beat the hell out of me, I flashed. I could feel the tension in the air. Every door was doubly covered. A nervous, rebellious anger was swelling within me.

Judge Hoffman entered the room. The head marshal banged the gavel and gave the "All rise."

"Mr. Marshal, bring in the jury," Judge Hoffman said.

Weinglass stood and opened his mouth to say something, but Abbie Hoffman loudly bellowed out, "There are twenty-five marshals in here now, and they've all got guns."

"If the Court please," Weinglass interjected, "within observation of your Honor is a phalanx of marshals literally . . . Now, the jury is about to be brought in. They will enter from that door. The first thing that they will see as they walk into this room is a group of twenty marshals standing in very ominous posture, and I cannot begin my cross-examination of a witness. The jury cannot sit here unmoved by that."

"If you don't want to cross-examine that's up to you, sir," Hoffman replied. "Bring in the jury."

"Your Honor," Kunstler said, "we are objecting to this armed-camp aspect that is going on since the beginning of this trial."

"It is not an armed camp," Hoffman retorted.

Now, before the judge had come into the room, the marshals had told me that there were lots of Black Panther Party members in the audience, and the judge wanted me to tell them not to disrupt the courtroom. I agreed to do that, as I didn't want any of the brothers and sisters getting any trouble for themselves, and I told them, "Keep cool!" But now prosecutor Schultz started saying I had told them something very different, that if I was attacked they would know what to do.

I was on my feet, angry and pissed off that Schultz was distorting what I had said—and sure're than shit we were off and running again.

"He was talking to these people," Schultz said, "about an attack by them."

"You're lying," I shouted, stepping toward Schultz, trying to control the rage that was now boiling over within me. "Dirty liar," I thundered with the most boisterous anger I could muster and stepped back to my seat to avoid the temptation of knocking the shit out of his lying no-good ass. I kept my eye on Schultz, balled my fists, then took two steps toward him, shouting in my angered bass tone. "You are a rotten racist pig, fascist liar, that's what you are." I practically spit in Schultz's face. The marshals were now rushing at me.

The gigantic nigger Goliath was suddenly pushing me back with two crushing grips on my shoulders. Dave Dellinger stood, deliberately bumping his body into Goliath, who was throwing me into my chair, then bumping Dellinger back with his huge body. I grabbed for the table, tumbling over, trying to break a fall and stand back up at the same time. Goliath gave me a hard body blow to the chest that hurled me over backwards, sliding six feet, chair and all, into the press section, slamming into them as the reporters and artists scuffled out of the way, jumping out of their seats. "You are a fascist pig liar," I shouted from the floor on my back. The other marshals surrounded me, but, anger giving me strength, I said to the marshals, "Get my chair." I got up and walked through the marshals to the defense table.

When the jury came in, I stood up. "I would like to request the right again to cross-examine this witness because my lawyer, Charles R. Garry, is not here and because I have also been denied my rights to defend myself in this courtroom." Then I turned to Hoffman. "I am requesting and demanding, in fact, that I have a right to cross-examine this witness, sir, at this trial."

"Mr. Marshal, take the jury out," Judge Hoffman said in reply.

"And all the defendants support Bobby Seale's right to have a counsel of his choice here and affirm that he has been denied that right," Dellinger put in.

"Why don't you recognize my constitutional rights?" I asked.

Hoffman wouldn't answer. "All I want to tell you is this: if you speak once again while the jury is in the box and I have to send them out, we will take such steps as are indicated in the circumstances.

"Bring in the jury, Mr. Marshal."

"If a witness is on the stand and testifies against me," I said, "and I stand up and speak out in behalf of my right to have my lawyer and to defend myself and you deny me that—I have a right to make those requests. I have a constitutional right to speak, and if you try to suppress my constitutional right to speak out in behalf of my constitutional rights, then I can only see you as a bigot, a racist, and a fascist, as I have said before and clearly indicated on the record."

The jury filed in and took their seats.

Later on, Weinglass had finished with the witness and I stood up.

"I would like to request again—" I paused, knowing the word was too weak, "demand—" I raised my voice, quickly glancing around at the marshals, "that I be able to cross-examine the witness." I looked directly at Judge Hoffman, not wanting him to speak over me, speaking faster. "My lawyer is not here." Judge Hoffman looked back at the jury marshal. "I think I have a right to defend myself in this courtroom," I said, wanting the jury to hear each word.

"Take the jury out," Hoffman said in his high-pitched, squeaky voice.

I stood for a moment thinking somehow I had to get to him.

"Mr. Seale, I have admonished you previously——"

"I have a right to cross-examine the witness."

"——what might happen to you if you keep on talking. We are going to recess now, young man. If you keep this up——"

"Look, old man," I snarled the term angrily. "If you keep up denying me my constitutional rights, you are being exposed to the public and the world that you do not care about people's constitutional rights to defend themselves."

"I will tell you that what I indicated yesterday might happen to you ——" Hoffman began.

"Happen to me?" I cut in. "What can happen to me more than what Benjamin Franklin and George Washington did to black people in slavery? What can happen to me more than that?" I pointed and gestured, with a vengeful tone.

"And I might add," Hoffman continued, "since it has been said here that all of the defendants support you in your position, that I might conclude that they are bad risks for bail and I say that to you, Mr. Kunstler, that if you can't control your client——"

But I would not be shut up. "I still demand my constitutional rights as a defendant in this case to defend myself. I demand the right to be able to cross-examine this witness. He has made statements against me and I want my right to——"

Hoffman cut me off. "Have him sit down, Mr. Marshal."

"I want my constitutional rights," I shouted, noticing Goliath walking fast, coming around the front of the table as I continued speaking, spotting the anger in Goliath's face and that of another marshal who followed him. "I want to have my constitutional rights."

Goliath was upon me. David Dellinger stood up in front of me, and I gestured and waved my hands and leaned a little to look around Dellinger's back at the judge. "How come you don't recognize it?" *Wham*— Goliath bumped Dellinger out of his way and hit my shoulders with the palms of his two big hands, throwing me into my seat with all his weight, and my chair was rolling again, sailing straight back with the marshal upon me and the chair turned over backwards again with me in it, right on top of the front row of press people. I tried to scramble up. The marshals had all rushed me as I looked up, enraged. I was grabbed and snatched up off the floor by two marshals and my arm was pushed up my back in a hammerlock as pain shot through my arm.

"How come you won't recognize my constitutional rights? I want to cross-examine that witness." With my free arm I pointed, somewhat bent over, at Frapolly sitting in the witness box. Then I said, in a whisper, to Slim, the marshal holding me, "Hey man, damn it! You hurting me." Slim eased off, letting my arm back down but still holding it, saying, "Hey, man, be cool."

There were some more exchanges—the judge was indignant that I called George Washington a slaveowner; the judge told us that Kunstler was my lawyer while Kunstler kept saying that he had told the judge that he was not my lawyer; the judge told the others that they had better rise out of respect to him and they had better stop supporting my cause or their bail would be revoked and they'd be sleeping in jail. They said that if that's the price, they would have to pay it, because they were behind me. Altogether we got to the point where Judge Hoffman said—when the jury was outside the room—that the marshals should take me "and deal with [me] as [I] should be dealt with in this circumstance."

When they'd done, Slim and Goliath picked up the chair and me and we entered into the courtroom, me being carried, chained in a metal chair and gagged.

The courtroom filled with "ooowwss" and "ahhhss" as they placed me at the defense table. I could even hear a few mumbled "Pigs!" in the packed audience.

I was placed on the opposite side of the defense table from where I had been sitting. Press people were writing frantically and artists' pencils were streaking across their pads.

October 30, 1969.

They had four large, thick belts which were bolted with special key-and-lock attachments at the buckles. My legs were both strapped tightly by Goliath. Nummy, another marshal, was securing my wrists and forearms to the chair, as another one, Arizona, who was wearing doctor's rubber gloves, gagged me. Arizona then took a stretch-type cloth bandage wrapping and wound it around and around my head, over my mouth, the back of my neck, my ears, and under my chin; it gripped my vocal cords like a vice.

God damn these motherfuckers. My breath was short and faint, and I couldn't even gesture to tell these bastards. Goliath began double-checking the straps on my arms, finding them, in his opinion, too loose, so he began to redo them, tightening them. I could feel the loss of blood circulation in my hands. I shook my head vigorously indicating that they were too tight, but Goliath smiled and paid no attention to me. As I wiggled my head, the stretch wrapping got tighter and tighter—my whole face felt trapped. This son of a bitch—I cursed him in my mind.

Goliath proceeded to retighten the belts around my legs, squeezing the life out of me, then started tightening again the knot at the top of my head. I started shaking my head, but the stretch bandage got tighter and tighter. Slim and Goliath picked up the chair, carrying me into the courtroom.

I had lost all blood circulation in my left hand and both legs. I slowly looked around, searching for Marie Learner, one of the lawyers, then trying to signal to her to come to me, moving my head. She was talking to Kunstler, looking at me. I started gesturing with quick, hard motions. The wrapping around my head was killing me. Fear was suddenly with me as I began to imagine that I might pass out and die before anyone even noticed. I had a flashing memory of Malcolm X saying, "Your heaven and hell are right here on this earth." Marie got a pencil and put it between my fingers and put a pad under my strapped-down right hand. I tried to write but dropped the pencil. She picked it back up, placed it between my numbed fingers, and sort of guided it to help me spell straggly words, so I could tell someone.

Weinglass was looking back at me writing as he stood at the lectern, having stopped his cross-examination. When I finished the note, it was brought to him. He then addressed the Court. "If your Honor please, the buckles on the leather strap holding Mr. Seale's hand are digging into his hand and he appears to be trying to free his hand from that pressure. Could he be assisted?"

"If the marshal has concluded that he needs assistance, of course," Hoffman answered, then turned to the jury. "I will excuse you, ladies and gentlemen of the jury, with my usual orders."

But Goliath had lunged upon me by then as I was struggling to move my head forward to the tips of the turned-up fingers of my right hand, straining, only a couple of inches away from the portion of the gag below my nose. I was just about to snatch the gag down off my mouth and—

Wham!—Goliath elbowed me hard in my gagged mouth, knocking my head back as he grabbed and attempted to retighten the strap. Suddenly Nummy was there, too, trying to pick up the side of the chair.

"Your Honor," Kunstler said, "are we going to stop this medieval torture that is going on in this courtroom? I think this is a disgrace."

"This guy is putting his elbow in Bobby's mouth and it wasn't necessary at all," Jerry Rubin yelled.

All this was happening in seconds.

Nummy began picking the chair up from one side, tilting it, as Goliath pushed the chair back down while elbowing me hard again. Two other marshals proceeded to pick up the chair again. There also seemed to be some struggle going on at the defense table.

"This is no longer a court of order, your Honor," Kunstler cried, "this is a medieval torture chamber. It is a disgrace. They are assaulting the other defendants also."

Goliath with a blow slapped my turned-up hand down and two more marshals were around me; they began to pick up the chair, too.

Suddenly, I was being lifted up into the air a couple of feet. Another white marshal rushed in. A stray elbow struck me right in my testicles. That hurt like hell. In those seconds of stumbling, balancing, bumping confusion Goliath suddenly got the bright idea of helping to pick up the chair which was then raised more than five feet in the air. I could damn near look directly into Judge Hoffman's eyes, when Goliath suddenly lost his balance, sending the whole team of marshals out of control and heading straight for the floor.

Their weight carried me with them, sitting high in the air strapped to the God damn chair looking down on their heads, then sailing through the air, thudding into the metal-folding-chair press section. Press people scrambled frantically to get out of the way of this oncoming disaster. And me, I was right in the middle of all that shit, hitting the floor fast and hard as I struggled, trying to grab the gag with one sort-of-loosened hand. With a surge of strength, I got the gag and snatched my head up and back.

"Don't hit me in my balls, motherfucker," I shouted, in anger and pain. "This motherfucker is tight and it is stopping my blood."

"Your Honor, this is an unholy disgrace to the law that is going on in this courtroom and I as an American lawyer feel a disgrace," Kunstler said.

"Created by Mr. Kunstler," interjected prosecutor Foran.

The marshals struggled to get me strapped securely in the chair while others began to carry me out of the courtroom.

"Created by nothing other than what you have done to this man," Kunstler shot back.

"You come down here and watch it, Judge," Abbie Hoffman warned.

"You fascist dogs," I cried, "you rotten, low-life son of a bitch. I am glad I said it about Washington used to have slaves, the first president——"

I was being carried away amidst a heated exchange among lawyers, defendants, and Judge Hoffman.

"Somebody go to protect him," Dellinger said.

Then Foran jumped in: "Your Honor, may the record show that that is Mr. Dellinger saying someone go to protect him, and the other comment is by Mr. Rubin."

"Everything you say will be taken down," Judge Hoffman told the defense table.

"Your Honor," Kunstler said, "we would like the names of the marshals. We are going to ask for a judicial investigation of the entire condition and the entire treatment of Bobby Seale."

"Don't point at me in that manner," Hoffman admonished.

"I just feel so utterly ashamed to be an American lawyer at this time."

"You should be ashamed of your conduct in this case, sir."

"What conduct, when a client is treated in this manner?"

"We will take a brief recess."

"Can we have somebody with Mr. Seale? We don't trust——"

"He is not your client, you said."

"We are speaking for the other seven."

"The marshals will take care of him."

"Take care of him?" Jerry Rubin cut in.

"Take that down," the judge said. "The court will be in recess."

Eventually, Hoffman declared a mistrial had taken place about me, that the other seven would continue to be tried but my trial would take place next year. In the meantime, he said I was guilty of sixteen contempt-of-court actions, and I would be putting in three months in jail on each one of them, consecutively. But Francis J. McTiernan from Charles Garry's office came in, and I wound up back in California for a while.

PART VIII

All the Sins That Ain't

IT WAS ON A WEDNESDAY, I remember—I was in jail in California, fighting extradition, and some guard spotted a *Jet* magazine in my cell.

"Ok, Seale," he said smugly. "Just for having this contraband, you lose visiting for two weeks."

"What?" That pissed me off.

"No visiting for your ass."

"Man, fuck a visit. You simple pig motherfuckers think you can threaten me with a visit?" His face registered instant anger. "I say you are a low-lifed pig for taking my visit."

"I'm no pig!" He angrily shouted at me, turning red in the face.

"Yes, you are." I could see he actually hated the thought of being called that. "A rotten low-lifed racist, two-bit pig!"

"Ok," he said nervously. "Now you lose three weeks visit for saying that."

"Three weeks! Pig! Pig! Pig! Cruel and unusual punishment. You violate my rights and at that point, as far as I'm concerned you are a *sloppy, scurvy,* foul traducer, masquerading as a victim of an unprovoked attack, because I'm the one who is really attacked by you—your kind, your ignorance. You got that, huh? You are a pig, motherfucker! Pig! Pig! Pig!"

"I'm not a pig!" He was angry, but with fear all over his face. As though the very word would strike him dead. "I'm no motherfucker! I have nothing to do with my mother! Take it back!" His expression really shocked me. "Take it back, Seale!" He pleaded and ordered in one heaved-up breath of hate and fear all mixed together. He almost made me feel sorry for him. I had never seen anything like it.

"Then you drop that shit about the *Jet* magazine. Call me Mister and I'll call you Mister. Take my rights and you are a pig!"

"Ok, ah, that's, that's six weeks no visiting!"

"What? You stupid son of a bitch. Look at yourself. Think about what you do to prisoners. Pig! Pig! Pig! A thousand times! Now take visiting away for a thousand weeks. What you are doing, pig, is the very thing you couldn't take if you was locked up. So, you are a pig! Now, get the fuck away from my cell, pig! And take visiting hours and ram them up your ass! You got that. And as long as I'm here and everytime I see you or think about you, you are a pig!" He disappeared.

The reaction that guard had really blew my mind. I just couldn't get over it. He was, deep down inside, actually hurt. And the word mother-fucker—I couldn't even smile, although I wanted to. Actually, this par-ticular guard had been sort of easygoing. He wasn't even as bad as the one black guard who had been asked by an inmate for a match as he passed the inmate's cell.

"Say, brother," said the inmate, "got a match?"

"Who the fuck you calling brother!" the black guard stated indignantly.

I could hear the whole conversation from my cell, which was about ten cells down the block.

"Say, man. I just asked for a match."

"Well, I ain't your God damn brother!"

"Well, fuck it!" the inmate said. "I don't want to be your God damn brother, either. You chicken-shit son of a bitch!"

"You think you tough, with your punk ass."

"I'm tough enough for you, so, fuck you. Keep your God damn match."

I heard nothing for a few moments. The guard must have left. Sudden-ly, about five minutes later, that guard and about five others opened the inmate's cell. The inmate started cussing and shouting and the next thing I knew, the inmate was being beaten, brutalized, as the whacks of the guards' clubs got louder and louder amidst the silence of the other shocked and frightened inmates.

"I want this punk in the hole," the black guard breathed heavily, tired by his bloody workout.

The next morning after I insulted the guard I had sort of forgotten about the fray.

"Guard! Guard!" I yelled out for ten minutes, to complain about not having been allowed to take a shower for over two weeks.

Five guards showed up.

"Ok, Seale, let's go. You're being moved."

"Oh, yeah? Right on," I said, stooping to the floor to pick up my stack of legal tablets and other copies of motions and notices that Garry had filed in court for hearings to try and prevent my extradition.

"Leave that there. We'll get that," the guard I had called a pig said with a nervous tone in his voice.

"No! I keep my legal papers with me at all times," I said, picking them up. "Where am I being moved to?"

"Don't worry about it," a blond guard said in an angry tone.

I looked at the faces of all five guards, including the one I had called a pig a thousand times. Suddenly he had a half smirk on his face. They were going to beat me—yeah, that's it—I'm being moved to be beaten.

"Let's go!" the blond one shouted.

"First, where am I being moved to? And, I want my commissary first," I angrily shot out.

"You won't need that where you're going."

I stepped out of my cell, walking, then thought and worried about would these motherfuckers kill me or beat me so bad I would have to be put into the hospital. There ain't even no hospital in this fucked up-jail. The hole? But that was illegal—I remembered the local San Francisco courts had ruled that it was not to be used. But I knew it had been used, they would just move quickly and take out whatever prisoners were in there when the local congressmen or whoever would inspect the jail.

"So, you're taking me to the hole, ok." I stepped up my pace a little. "Come on. I'm not scared of your God damn hole. But you sons of bitches are scurvy low-lifed pigs! You and every last one of you who condone this shit. Your minds are mired with filth and fear."

"You're going to get enough of calling us pigs! You're a punk! A nigger punk!" Two more guards were there.

"You see, pigs!" I spoke with a sarcastically laughing tone. "You are angry because you know what you are doing is wrong. Ha! Now you can call me all the niggers and nigras you want and you can call me all the punks you want, but I'll stay in your damn hole and you'll still be scurvy pigs. So it won't work with me. The only way you will ever change my mind, my thoughts and feelings about you, is when you stop violating my rights and all the other prisoners' rights in this jail."

I was quickly and furiously snatched around my throat from behind. I instinctively grabbed at the gripping arm, causing my papers to spew all over the floor. In a flash my legs were grabbed by two guards and the blond guard began to strike me repeatedly—rapid hard blows to my stomach. I loosened my grip on the tightening arm and was now not able to breathe as I began striking out. The guards had me pinned on the floor; my breath was going quickly, my eyes were about to pop out of my head from the pressure of the gripping arm. I knew they were definitely going to kill me. The guard was savagely striking me, devastating blows in my balls, again, again, again. I was passing out, dying, being murdered. I slumped aimlessly. My mind blanked out completely—with one lasting image of the blond guard grinning with a knowledge of brutal sadistic victory.

I don't know how long it was—I was coming to. Where was I? I was trying to cough a breath, cough a word. Then I could make out some light. Then I saw a hazy image of standing guards shadowed against the light in the hall. The windows. My testes began to pain. The windows to the aisle. One guard appeared, then another. They were laughing, standing in the aisle. Their images became clearer outside the entrance door of the hole.

I scanned the cell with blurred vision. There seemed to be nothing in it. Rubber floors, sealed rubber walls, my hands told me. It was frigid cold to my body, to my butt, back, and legs. I looked down at the lower portion of my body. My legs had no clothes on them, nor did my whole body. I was buck naked. I was totally stripped.

I tried to cough again.

A guard threw some blue-colored jail clothes at me that landed on my naked legs. They had choked me, I remembered. I felt weak but alive as I tried to talk, heaving in a breath, then looking at their devious grinning faces.

"P—p—pig, motherfuc—fu—cker!" They slammed the solid door to the hole with a muffled *wham* and locked it.

The light to the hole came on. It was a small box. A blindingly bright light shined from the ceiling. A very high ceiling. No window. I stood up, shaky, having a hard time breathing, and put on the ragged pants, which had a more than forty-inch waist size that overwhelmed my thirty-inch waist. I ripped out a strip of the shirt and made a makeshift string belt to keep my pants up.

So this was the hole. I had never before been in the hole in any jail in my life. It was named appropriately, I thought, for this was a hellhole if I ever imagined one.

Four straight-up walls covered with some rubber-type material everywhere. The corners were a continuous rubber coating. No bed or bunk. Not even a toilet, as I suddenly noticed a drain in the center of the floor. This is where they expected you to relieve yourself. The pig bastards.

I heard a flushing sound in the room, a gargling. Water was steadily rising up the five-inch diameter of the drain hole. It rose quickly, flushing out over the floor. It was filling the whole floor from wall to wall. The smell of crap and piss filled the damn-near airtight box as I noticed pieces of shit, defecation. More turds appeared, bubbling out of the flowing water, touching my feet as I backed into the corner near the door. The flushing sounded, resounded as the water rose higher, covering my feet. I looked around in fear now. There was no place to go! A seven-foot-deep, six-foot-wide room, filling up rapidly with filthy toilet water.

I saw that the bottom of the thick door was airtight. Frantically, I looked all around the cell as the polluted, shit-infested water quickly rose to my ankles.

These sons of bitches! Pig motherfuckers! "Pig!" I shouted, with pain in my throat. "Pig motherfuckers!" I imagined myself swimming, having to wade through this shit, literal shit! Scared and wondering would the water keep rising until this hole filled, as it kept rising higher and higher.

No! They won't kill me—they can't! I'm too well known——I was groping for hope, trying to believe my scattered thoughts.

No! They are not going to make me afraid. I'll die first. I'll hold my breath until I pass out before I knowingly suck in one breath of this polluted murk.

The water was now above my ankles. The spirit of the people is greater than the man's technology, I began to say over and over, building my faith. How did Nat Turner die! He took it! They hanged him. They'll drown me if this damn thing fills up to the top. The God damn door is airtight—I'll swim—I'll swim. The next time they open this door, I'll fight, I'll kill the motherfuckers—I'll kill them!

The water was now about eight inches deep. Suddenly it stopped, then started to recede, getting lower and lower as I watched.

These pig motherfuckers! They're trying to torture me . . . They must be trying to *make* me suddenly confess to a crime I didn't commit. I'll die before I do that! I'll die with the world knowing that I stood up, that I'm a revolutionary. I won't give in—I won't——

The third day in the hole, I was tripping, half asleep, controlling myself through my escape dreams. The water would still rise, but I had long since realized that it would have to drain before it rose high enough to be fatal. I had resolved to do my fifteen days in the hole, having mastered the torment of the shit, waste, and suffocating odor.

I braced myself, subconsciously tensing my muscles, ready to strike as the door suddenly began to open. A different, middle-aged guard stood looking at me. He was shaking his head in disgust, looking at the shit- and piss-covered floor and room.

"Son of a bitch!" he exclaimed as he looked around. His manner took away the filled-up hatred I had for him as a pig guard. "Step out here, Seale."

I walked slowly, cautious, wondering what surprises lay in wait outside the door, with my hands balled in a fist behind my back.

"What's happening?" I asked.

"Stand right there. These sons of bitches!"

I stood with my back against the wall. He's talking about this filthy hole. Why? I wondered. The guard yelled for someone, "Get over here!"

Then he said, in a disgusted tone, "These day-shift bastards let this place go to the dogs."

"Why do people think they should treat people like this?" I asked.

"I don't know, Seale." He shook his head. "This fucking jail. Shit! They know that piss hole is plugged-up in this one. How long you been in there?"

"This is the third day."

A trustee came around the corner, pushing a wheel bucket with a mop in it. He began to swab the floor of the cell as the guard walked off.

The prisoners to my right, in regular cells—small overcrowded tank cells, were looking at me from behind the bars. One said, "Say, Bobby, man. We saw them pigs put you in there the other day. What they do, knock you out man?" They spoke very quietly.

"They choked the shit out of me, man."

"Pig motherfuckers."

"Say, look," I whispered to them. "Ah, is somebody got a lawyer who can contact my lawyer, Charles Garry."

"Oh, yeah, ah, I'll pass the word for somebody to tell they lawyer. What to tell him? You in the hole?"

"Yeah, tell everybody to pass the word to get in touch with Charles Garry."

The guard was back at the cell-block door, unlocking it.

"Cool it. The guard's coming," I whispered.

"We'll get the word—cool it, everybody, the guard's coming."

I was locked back in the hole, now with the cleaner smell of pine oil mixed with the odor of shit and piss.

The next morning, way past the five o'clock feeding, the hole door was opened.

It was the blond-headed guard who had beaten me in the hall. I stood back against the wall, balled my fists, looking at him, ready to try and kill him if he even looked like he was going to attack me.

"Your lawyer's here, Seale," he said, with a snarling hateful grin.

I stepped slowly, walking on ahead of the guard. I walked down the long aisle and saw Garry standing with his hands folded. He spotted me walking toward him.

"What the fuck these sons of bitches do to you!" Charles was bellowing, angry with a certain authority, looking around with his ability to maintain a threatening stare. "Where are your shoes? Where's the God damn hole they put you in?!" He got closer to me. "Phew! What kind of shit!" The stench of my body almost made Charles puke. "What the hell's going on!" Charles bellowed to the guard, who just nervously looked on. "Well, look, come on, I got the press in the interview room. Come on, tell them."

Garry opened the door and we went into the interview room. Lights flashed. Cameras everywhere started to roll, following us as I sat down.

"What they do to you, Bobby!" a reporter asked. "Whew!" the reporter reacted to the stench of my body as he stepped back, sitting down.

I spoke hoarsely, "Ok, look——" I began to explain the whole three-and-a-half-day ordeal.

New Haven.

The guard I called World War Two unlocked the cell and I went to the dayroom, passing by prisoners engaged in various games. I took the razor with the locked-in blade he handed to me and lathered soap on my goatee and whacked it off. World War Two was smiling as though he thought the captain had won out over me—the captain had not allowed me to mix with other prisoners without being clean-shaven—but he did not know what I had planned.

I immediately went to one of the long tables where prisoners sat with card games going on, and I sat right in the middle. A whist game was to my left and a poker game to my right. The prisoners watching the games quickly made room for me to sit.

"Everybody! Look!" I said and gestured for all of them at the table to gather closer, and they readily responded. The noise of the TV and other card games and conversations drowned out my voice beyond the range of the prisoners who were gathered around me. They listened to me with that certain respect accorded me since I was who I was. Bobby Seale, the known Black Panther; with a murder beef—which I knew overshadowed any other beef in any prison or jail.

"Now, I don't feel it's right for us to be locked down just because a prisoner's got a beard or long hair. There are four prisoners locked down now because of their hair. I've shaven my goatee off," I looked from face to attentive face with stern seriousness. "And I only shaved it off so I could get out here in the dayroom with all of you and hip you-all to the fact that the protest and issues I'm going to raise have got to be respected by the captain and the Connecticut State Jail Commission."

"What we going to do?" two of them asked.

"Now, I run the whole operation. I'll tell you every day the step-by-step procedure."

"We going to fuck up the place?" one brother asked, smiling.

Shit. They were associating automatic violence with me. I'm a celebrity to them. A notorious, dangerous character. I could tell a few wanted to impress me with being bad and tough.

"Now look. Wait! Don't do anything. Just go along normal, playing cards, watching TV every day. I'll do all the initial protesting first. I'm professional at this. Now, I'll list the other grievances, uh, my lawyers will get it in——"

"Say, Bobby, man, can't we get some commissary, like other dudes. The commissioner, he got so much money, man, and when commissary time come, ah, like they ought to give us dudes some commissary too. You know, man?"

"How you mean, brother?"

"I ain't, ah, me and Skip here ain't got no money on the books."

"Oh, yeah. We can include that, too."

"Yeah, good, 'cause it's——"

"I want to fuck it up, Bobby," Skip said.

"Don't talk so loud, brother," I warned. "Be cool. We all in this shit together. Let me do everything. The guards will look and wonder what I'm doing. And I don't want nobody jumping the gun, ok?"

"Ok, Bobby."

"Right!"

"Yeah, he told you man, he professional," a prisoner said.

"Say, man, you really ice that agent cat, uh, what's his name?" a white prisoner asked.

"Say, man, look, don't ask me nothing about my beef and keep yours to yourself." I shook my head as though I was perturbed by him. "You and everybody else come out better that way, ok?"

"Ok. I'm cool!"

"Nobody," I looked around at their faces, "don't ask me 'cause I'm not telling you or nobody but my lawyer. You got that?" I said, pointing at the white prisoner with the authority of being knowledgeable.

"Now, let's get back to why I want to talk to you, 'cause we got to cool it. So look, every prisoner—white, black, Puerto Rican, or whoever—we have to be organized together as one unit and I'll hip all of you how. We got to get the four locked-up cats out! Because they are prisoners just like us and they're being subjected to cruel and unusual punishment, being locked down all the time, only because of long hair. It's a violation of the Eighth Amendment of the Constitution of the United States. I'll break it down later because it'll all have to go to court for us to win. The captain and the mail commissioner are violating the law. We can protest to the highest court in the land."

"Court? Aw, man," another white prisoner said disgustedly.

"Say, wait, man. I got one of the top law firms in the country behind me.

They fight, so don't be discouraged, ok? Now, let's, ah, play cards and act normal, just be everyday prisoners. Oh—don't say nothing to the guards at all about what I'm planning. Just observe me. I'll talk to all of you more. And when the time comes, I'll let each and every one of you know what to do. Everybody got that?"

"Yeah."

"Right on!"

"We with you, Bobby."

"Don't nobody get into nothing out the ordinary, 'cause I don't want no pig goon squad coming in on us too soon, ok? Now, let's play cards and remember what I said. Come on. Relax. The guards are looking."

They all went back to their seating positions around the table.

"Ah, you guys playing whist?" I asked, looking around. The guards were looking at me intently.

"You play?" Boston asked.

"Shit! Baby, I'm a whistologist!" I spoke a little loud.

"A what?" the brothers cracked up laughing at how I came off.

"I'll be your partner," Boston said.

"Right! What you playing, rise-and-shine?"

"Yeah, five-card kitty," Skip's partner said.

When my down came, I played whist skillfully and professionally, like I had learned. I had to let them know and make them feel I was not just Bobby Seale, but I was also a prisoner like them. Ultimately, they had to identify with the issues. Also, I could tell these dudes got a real hang out of playing and winning at cards—and I had to righteously, skillfully, win a few of these card games, indulging in their daily jail interests, so that when some necessary action had to come about, they would move and do as I instructed.

I flipped and shuffled twelve cards in my hand, like a professional gambler, and smoothly spread and held my cards with one hand, then grouped them, tapping on the table, waiting for Skip's partner to bid.

"Study long, you study wrong," I said. "Come on, say it, so we can set your asses good! If you take my partner out, we going to set you so far back down south, back yonder in the sticks, that they going to have to pump sunshine to your ass all the way from California." I had the whist table jived down, smiling as my whist-table psych-you-out lingo prevailed. "I mean, we going to set you so far back in the sticks, they going to have to use jackrabbits to bring your mail to you, and that'll be two weeks late. 'Cause I'm going to make you come by the church house for prayer meeting."

"God damn, partner!" Skip said. "Bid! Fuck them! Take them out!"

"And get se-e-et!" Boston said.

"Yeah," I added. "And go down in the hole so far, you find yourself setting way back down in Tallahassee-cut-shoot-when-come-from-ten miles north-of-Mule-Creek-junction."

The whole crowd of prisoners cracked up laughing at my whist-table shit talking and Skip's partner had to laugh as he said, "Ok, ok, ah, pass."

"Aw, naw!" Skip hollered. "Why you let them talk you out of it!" Skip argued. "I got the hand, partner!"

I laughed myself. I would slap a card on the table, my knuckles and fingers never touching the surface, making the card spin where it hit, hoping that my partner was hip that a card spinning meant to come back in that suit on his next play, and a card not spinning meant I didn't have the suit. And the consistent slapping of cards on the table confused our opponents, since most whist players know slapping a card means come back in that suit.

My partner and I won five hands in a row. I played whist for the next two hours, and when my partner and I were set, I went and stood around the table where six white prisoners and one black one were playing poker.

When chow came, the prisoners lined up to the barred gate of the dayroom. But I sat and waited. As the prisoners filed out across the hall into the chow hall, I finally stepped up and said to World War Two, "Lock me up." And I turned left, walking toward the barred gate that led to the lower block, where my cell was.

"Oh, it's chow time, Bob," he said.

"I know. Lock me up!"

That was my first move, not eating, not a bit. I figured World War Two would report it—if not today, then tomorrow.

After chow there was the normal one-hour lock-up, then the prisoners were allowed back in the dayroom. When we were let back in, I played poker. That same basic respect for me was there, something I knew well, in that prisoners with felony beefs outranked the other prisoners.

I had even a higher status in their eyes for being one of the leaders in the Party, second in command under Huey Newton. I had the reputation in their minds of standing up to defend myself against racist pigs, cops. And we, the Party, were known to shoot it out in numerous battles with both cops and Panthers killed and wounded in action. But more than that—I had famous legal representation and a community organization backing me up, and, of course, I was in the news media and I was charged with "icing," as the prisoners say, a suspected agent of the CIA or FBI. That was the ultimate jail status, because it appeared to other prisoners that I had certain power—gun power, people power, and guts. And they knew that ultimately the establishment would love to lock me up and throw away the key until that fatal day of execution. Many prisoners put their hopes in the Panthers. Hope that we could do something about them getting fucked over.

I reemphasized my profession—that I was a community organizer, organizing against what I called the professional racist, fascist, power structure and all the corrupt officials and lesser flunkies of the Establishment from cops to snitches, from the filthy rich to the local bankers. I stood up for the uneducated and the misguided who found themselves in jails, prisons, and the wretched condition of all oppressed people in their ghettos.

Again, I, with my progressive ideas, played poker as well as they did, losing some and winning some as they did, but rapidly reading all stud card-hands and calculating odds and betting properly against the bluffers and the slick poker faces that didn't trick me. I knew some crazy wild-card poker hands, too, that had some laughing when I said: "Ok, whores, fours, one-eyed jacks and king with the axe."

It reinforced my opinion that when a revolutionary goes to jail, staying one with the basic lifestyles of prison activity, there develops a certain status he can hold, as long as he doesn't go overboard intellectualizing theories, but holds to his principal point of view.

When that evening chow came, I stepped out the gate. The guard shifts had changed—Ernie was there, smiling and bullshitting as usual.

"Ok, Ernie, lock me up."

"Ok, lock me up," Ernie joked. "You don't want to eat, eh, Bobby?" He was more serious now. "What's the problem?"

"Aw, just a little protest. Just lock me up."

I walked behind Ernie, who was not doing such a good job at exaggerating his Italian-American accent: "Oh, yeah, he's a gonna protest. Okay, kid-a, right on!" Ernie held up a clenched fist and smiled as I watched the cell door close.

By the fourth day of not having eaten at all, drinking only coffee, tea, and water, the guards were used to locking me up at each meal.

In the dayroom, I asked Ernie to get me a list of the prisoners who had no money for commissary. I had won quite a bit at cards: cigarettes, candy, coffee, chocolate, and tea.

"Say, Skip." I handed him the small slip of paper. "Get these cats and tell them to come over here. I got some commissary for them."

"Huh?" Skip raised up from his seat, looking over to see. I had quite a stash out there on the table. "Say! Jack, you going to give all that?"

Skip went around the dayroom to get everybody—but only reluctantly telling the white prisoners. "Say Bobby, man, these *white* dudes, man, don't you think you ought to cool it on them?"

"Say look, Skip, didn't I tell you I was the professional organizer?"

"Oh, yeah, I see. Thanks, I'll pay you back."

"You don't owe me nothing," I said to everybody. "That stuff is yours. What you owe is something to yourself. Your right to fight for your rights—the consciousness, and the right to stand up. So don't even think in terms of paying me back."

"Yeah, man, I got you, but I still say giving all that stuff away, God damn—and the white dudes——"

"Look it's a Free Commissary Program. Like, did you ever hear about our Party creating a free breakfast program for hungry school children in the black community?"

"Yeah, I remember hearing, yeah."

"Well, that way, we wanted people to see the good intentions of our protest. I mean, people had to see that we were honestly *for* them. Like out in the community, we are battling, getting shot at, being put in jails and getting killed, all to protest and organize the people around programs, issues—to ultimately change the way the Establishment, the way shit is run. I mean, revolution, man, means change, but it must be changed to where the *people* have more power, Power to the People, *all* the people, white, black, green, red, brown, yellow. I don't care what color or ethnic group, even polka dot."

"Guard!" I hollered out. I knew World War Two was on duty; it was the eighth morning of my fast, strike, and protest. I decided I now had to demonstrate to the prisoners the need for them to stick together. They were in the chow hall for breakfast and by this time they should all be sitting at their tables, eating—just time enough, I had calculated. "Say, ah, I'd like to go to the chow hall."

"Sure Bob," World War Two said.

I walked down to the chow hall, stepped readily across to where no tables were, and hopped up to stand on a chair, speaking loudly and quickly, grabbing their attention.

"Hold up, everybody! Say, brothers, everybody! As you know, I'm on a strike, a fast, in protest of the fact that the administration of this jail, from the commissioner on down to the captain and others are violating the Constitution by subjecting prisoners to cruel and unusual punishment, being locked up around the clock in cramped cells. I came here to let you know that I am continuing my protest. So at one point, you will have to move, brothers. But only when I say, to let them know that we all stand together against any pig operations of cruel and unusual punishment."

"Go head and tell it!" Boston shouted.

"So I'm sticking to this strike until our other four brothers are allowed in the dayroom just like us." I paused, then went on, knowing I must conclude. "When we move next, we move together, in unity! In unity against all pig operations of oppression in this jail system. Power to the People!" I raised a clenched fist. "Power to the Prisoners! Thanks, brothers, for your undivided attention. Finish your breakfast." I hopped down off the chair as they applauded enthusiastically.

"Right on, Bobby!"

"We with you!"

"Tell it some more!"

And I said, loudly, "Lock me up!" I looked at World War Two, knowing he had thought at first I was going to the chow hall to eat. He acted as though he felt stupid, from the nervous way he was gesturing and looking at me as though he were very unsure about me.

I stood in my cell a moment. Then I heard a voice from the chow hall.

"Lock me up!" Was that Heavy?"

"Me, too. Lock me up!" I heard Boston's voice.

"Yeah, lock me up, too!" came another.

Then I could hear the other protesting prisoners saying, "We with you, Bobby."

Not now, I thought. They can't do it now. I ain't gave them the word.

"Look, don't go on a strike. Not till I say so."

"But I'm with you."

"I know. That's good. But we only got a few. Everybody has to start at one time."

In a while, a guard came and took me to the captain's office. I ran down the Eighth Amendment to him, but of course it didn't get through. "Power to the People, you little lightweight fascist," I ended the argument. I snatched the door open. "You guys got problems when it come to respecting other human beings in this jail. Why? Because you are more scared to be locked up than we are—later!"

The captain was up on his feet. "Just get on back in that cell!"

"Lock me up!" I said, walking past the guard, headed down the hall. The captain was mad and pissed at me, but I knew why. I was blasting him.

When we got to the aisle alongside the dayroom, I said loudly, "Say, you guys! The captain is locking me up in my cell because he says I'm inciting you. He's so ignorant. He can't understand people's rights or why I protest. Now I have *no* beard and I'm being locked up anyway.

"Let's go! Get down there in the cell!"

I stopped. "Look, we stick together. We move when I say. All right!" I walked on down the aisle.

"Right on!" The prisoners' voices roared.

"Don't do anything until I give the word!" I tried to say amidst their noise.

"Right on!" Boston said, gesturing with a clenched fist.

"Power to the People! Power to the Prisoners!" I shouted, walking off toward my cell. And from the dayroom came a continuous stream of slogans.

"Right on!"

"Right on, Bobby!"

"We with you."

"You got problems, captain!" I said, looking at him, stepping in my cell. The captain followed me into my cell.

"Your ass will be locked up for good!" the captain shouted, angrily stepping up in my face. I sidestepped him and moved out of the cell. "Get back in here!" the captain ordered. The prisoners in the dayroom were quiet.

"Fuck you! When you come out!" I shouted, but I was nervous.

"You just get your ass back in here!" the captain angrily ordered, pointing to the floor.

My thoughts rambled around the fact that I just knew they were going to move on me hard and brutalize me—choke me—but I held my ground against the captain.

"Now, if you want to fight, motherfucker." I backed up against the wall readying myself with balled fists, thinking and knowing that I'd kick these motherfuckers in the balls if they tried to grab me or beat me. I controlled my fear as I stood my ground, determined to defend myself. There would be no more scenes of brutality without a fight. In the middle of all this shit I was remembering the recent scenes in the California jail—in the hole.

The captain stepped closer and said, "You're not so tough, Seale."

I replied calmly, looking him dead in the eye. "Captain, I'm about the toughest revolutionary you'll ever run into in your whole life. So, mother-fucker,"—I was cool—"get your fat pig ass, out of my *cell*!" I shouted the last word and I braced up, looking at World War Two and back at the angry captain. "You got that! I'm tougher than your kind will ever be. Don't fuck with me. Like the Anglos fucked over the Irish and Italians, and the way Irish did your people, because black people and the Black Panther Party are the last ones to be fucked over by *all* of you! You got that! Yeah, I'm tough, motherfucker. Tough! But not the way you know, not the way you know."

He stepped out the door of my cell, puffed-up red and mad. And I walked into my cell and said to the Polish World War Two, "Now lock me up!"

Shortly after that, I passed the word that the prisoners were to strike. The strike went off beautifully. All the prisoners, just leaving all that delicious food on the table without touching a bit, shouting, "Lock me up!" and "Cruel and unusual punishment!" Protesting in support of the four dudes and myself who were locked down. Spirits were high as all of us locked-up prisoners chanted and recited, "Power to the People!" and "Stop cruel and unusual punishment of prisoners!" while rattling the doors of our cells.

The strike lasted for two days. I gave the word that the men could go back to eating, since the point was more than made. Plus I knew that hunger might cause someone to forget the issue and either riot or give in to the captain, and that would make the whole strike a worthless effort. I later met with the captain to make sure there would be no reprisals toward the prisoners. Months later, with Charles Garry, I took the jail authorities to Federal court and we won a ruling that it was cruel and unusual punishment to keep prisoners from wearing beards and long hair in the day room.

As for me? I was shortly afterward placed in a different location in the jail, after another very heated argument with the captain about him letting me take my legal information and papers with me. I had two isolation cells. One where I slept and the other, which was directly adjacent, as a sort of a personal exercise area.

I didn't even worry about the trial, with its murder charges and threat of the electric chair. In fact, I had developed an unusual calmness about myself, conversing here and there with Ernie and even old World War Two when he would approach and ask me different questions about the struggle for certain rights and freedoms.

New Haven, May 22.... Last week the jury began its deliberations in the trial of Bobby Seale, chairman and co-founder of the Black Panther Party.

Now as the end nears, it seems more than ever a trial filled with curiosities. Not Chicago . . . in some ways not even the New Haven trial of Bobby Seale. He was something of an invisible defendant, in part because he was on trial with Mrs. Ericka Huggins, and most of the prosecution's witnesses had a lot more to say about her than about him.

But his invisibility was also part of defense strategy. . . .

And the defendant's own demeanor. He leaned back in his chair, his eyes half-cocked, his eyebrows raised, watching the witness chair with a look of a man who has resigned himself to the prospect of being bored for a week or two.

Mr. Garry adopted the same pose . . . after Mrs. Huggins' attorney had spoken, he'd say simply, "I join in whatever she says."

Sometimes, too, he and Mr. Seale would both close their eyes completely and the jurors would gaze at what appeared to be two sleeping men.

Added to that picture was the defense decision not to put Mr. Seale on the stand in his own defense. And added to that, the description Mr. Garry gave outside the courtroom of Mr. Seale, two of whose alleged crimes are punishable by death. "I can't get him to talk about the case," the lawyer would say, reporting that the Panther Chairman preferred to stay in his cell and design housing projects. . . .

When it came time for summations, Mr. Garry told the jury, "Frankly, I don't see the need to say anything," but knowing quite well that juries are unpredictable, spoke none the less.

——*New York Times*,
May 23, 1971

New Haven, May 25. The judge in the murder-kidnapping case of Bobby G. Seale and Mrs. Ericka Huggins dismissed all charges against them today, saying that "massive publicity" about their aborted trial had made it too difficult to try them again.

The trial ended yesterday in a hung jury.

"I find it impossible to believe," said Superior Court Judge Harold M. Mulvey, "that an unbiased jury could be selected without superhuman efforts . . . efforts which this court, the state and these defendants should not be called upon either to make or to endure."

It took four months to select the first jury. Mr. Seale, who will be held until bail is set in Chicago for his appeal of a four-year contempt sentence meted out by Federal Judge Julius Hoffman in the 1969 Chicago Conspiracy Trial, sagged low in his seat and looked numb.

Judge Mulvey noted today that both defendants had been held in jail for more than two years, awaiting trial.

The judge's decision was read from handwritten notes at about 2:40 P.M. and it stunned those in the crowded courtroom.

The judge said he had "gained a rather wide knowledge" of the defendants. "I have observed a rather remarkable change in [their] attitude," he asserted, "and I don't think it is feigned."

In agreeing with the defense, Judge Mulvey avoided the necessity of dealing with another of Mr. Garry's motions: an application to dismiss on the grounds that the jury had decided to acquit Mr. Seale on the first day of its deliberations, but had been stymied by one juror who insisted on getting an agreement on the charges against Mrs. Huggins.

——*New York Times,*
May 26, 1971

Judge Mulvey blew my mind, leaving me dumbfounded as he read from notes on his bench. I had gone to the courtroom sort of nonchalantly disgusted, figuring I'd have to go through a whole second trial.

After two years of caravans of police escorts, handcuffs, leg irons, epitaphic descriptions that berated my character—me, I, Bobby Seale, self-professed revolutionary, was actually cut loose.

I said nothing to the three state troopers in the car as they talked among themselves.

——The Party—its goals and philosophical and revolutionary development—and I, by some curious development, had something to do with all of this phenomenal change occurring in my country. Can't wait to see and bring about the housing development projects I've designed. The security of the home—God, how important that is——

——The Lord God—Mama was going to be happy for me. That girl really stood her ground. A few months back I read a newspaper clipping with a picture of Mama boldly imprinted on the paper—Mama, in her Sunday hat and fancy church dress, at Glide Memorial Church, standing there at the pulpit, telling everyone how she prayed for me to be set free. Mama—I bet she prayed to the Lord God every night that I not be sent to the electric chair. That woman's too much.

"Feels good, eh, Bob?" I vaguely heard a state trooper say, then I noticed the news of my release was being announced on the car radio.

I gave him an agreeing nod as he smiled at me from the front seat.

——George, telling tall tales, talking about me with a certain pride in a chip off the old block: "I taught him to obey and do right. Ah, shit, them people ain't had no business with him on trial no way!" I suddenly realized how I missed him and Mama.

It sure has been a helluva God damn road I've traveled. How I used to rage with fear; but, for what purpose? What had happened to cause me to be that way?

Damn, I got to see my son, Malik. Let's see, two years in jail, he's almost five! Yeah, in two months—damn, I sure hope he don't have to go through fear-based rages. Wish I could make him a brother or a sister. Them pig motherfuckers really fucked me around in that damn San Francisco Jail. I got to see him, raise him, hip him to this world and all the sins that ain't—people say he looks just like me, too—and I suppose he does. You finally made a baby, Bobby . . .

215

Hey—damn, how wrong I was about Mrs. Jesilovich, it was kind of silly on my part to get up and say those things about her, protesting to the judge that she not be admitted on the jury. But her face seemed so staunch. Ha, ha—she had kind of reminded me of Aunt Zelma, stern, with strong Christian beliefs embedded in her thinking, prejudging people on the basis of those misunderstood teachings. God damn, Mrs. Jesilovich had actually *cried* when the foreman of the jury announced that they were hung—*cried*, because Ericka and I had not been acquitted. Looking over at us with the most sorrowful expression. Shit, I guess everybody gets everybody wrong somehow, until they see——

The state trooper wheeled the car up along the wide driveway toward the front of the jail. I picked up my briefcase of legal papers, turning to the edge of the seat toward the door. I stopped momentarily, hearing a distant chanting noise—"Power to the People! Bobby's Free! Power to the People! Bobby's Free!"

"They like you, Bob," the state trooper said. I looked around at the state troopers waiting for me to get out of the car. They had half-smiles on their faces.

Suddenly, the chanting turned into a roar of ravings and whistling.

"Bobby's free"—that sounded kind of foreign after the previous consistent two-year-long cries of "Free Bobby!"

I stepped up to the front door of the jail. The desk sergeant reached to push the button that unlocked the front door to the jail and I stepped through the barred gate. The desk sergeant was smiling, looking at me. "Power to the People. Bobby's Free." I resented him saying that, as I figured he was just trying to be funny.

"Say," the captain was walking to the door of his office. "You made it. I'm glad for you."

"What the fuck you mean? Shit. You thought I was going to go down."

"Yeah, but——" He gestured his head, shrugging his shoulders. "I'm glad you're free. They say you'll be bailed out in a couple of days. It's good you made it."

"Yeah." I paused, wondering. "Ok, ah, thanks," I said, trying to figure the honesty in his words and manner.

"Hey, Bobby! Oh, man! Oh, shit!" Ernie was saying, pushing back the barred intersection gate, opening it for me as I approached. "You kicked they fucking asses!" He was really jubilant. "Oh, my God, shit!"

I stepped inside the barred intersection as Ernie carried on in some wild victorious enthusiasm that made me realize he must have deeply hoped for it all along. Something more than just friendly words as Ernie locked the first gate.

"Hey, Bob!" World War Two was walking up fast, joining me and

Ernie. "I just want to say, I learned a hell of a lot from you and I'm glad they cut you loose." His words sounded geniune—honest sincerity that I never expected from him. Not being able to hold back my oncoming smile, I stepped up to him and shook his hand.

"Yeah, sure, thanks, man."

"Oh, shit!" Ernie said. "You should of been here! Fuck, twenty minutes ago when the news announced you were cut loose. The fucking inmates were in an uproar. They started shouting, 'Power to the People, Bobby's free!' over and over. Then after about five minutes, the captain and all of them went in the dayroom with the prisoners and everybody! We were shouting, 'Power to the people, Bobby's free!'"

PART IX

A Grain of Sand

I WAS REMEMBERING that upstate New York was said to be loaded with conservative types—KKKs and Minutemen. We were on our way to Attica prison.

We piled in the car. "Ok," I said to the lawyer, "let me have a rundown."

"Well, the Negotiating Committee is at a stalemate. Everything seems to be just waiting for you, Bobby. Tom Wicker of the *New York Times* and William Kunstler are here."

"What's that warden's name? He's sort of fat, I saw him on the TV news—Oslow?"

"Oswald."

"Sounds like some comic-book character. What's he like? A hard-nosed fascist?"

"They have a lot of people telling him what to do."

"Is he ignoring the Negotiating Committee?"

"Well, we can't say. We'll be there in twenty minutes."

After fifteen minutes we turned off the main highway to the town of Attica, population 1001. As we approached the two-block business district, I got a feeling of tension around the town. It was an afternoon before a Saturday-night lynching.

Then we were following a two-lane road not two miles from the town of Attica, moving back and forth in traffic, nearing the outside area of the prison with its great long high wall, a gun tower projecting above its top, and a parking lot loaded with sitting helicopters and armed state troopers galore.

I was attuned in my own mind to feel and think that whatever the problem, if I was called on I could go out and deal with it. I found out that in this situation—where the Attica prisoners had rebelled and were holding guards hostage, and although they had taken over the prison because conditions were so wrong in there, they were surrounded by every kind of trooper-held gun—they were waiting on me, having asked me to come and help them out. Things were at a standstill, waiting for me. Kunstler, particularly, stressed that to me.

But when we were out there sitting in the car, Kunstler came out and had to say, "Oswald doesn't want you in there."

Well, shit. I held a press conference, saying our intention and purpose was to save lives, of both the prisoners and the captured guards. Then we split, wondering what else we could do.

Halfway back to Buffalo, here come the state troopers. We're getting uptight at first when we hear the siren, but: "There's only one car, cool it, cool it, let's see what he wants."

The trooper drew up alongside and said, "The warden says you can be let in." Another state car came up, and they turned their red lights on and escorted us, one in front and one in back, to the prison.

Now, I knew that the prisoners were waiting on what I would say, that the Black Panther Party was crucial here. I knew I could not compromise the prisoners' demands, but I had to talk to the prisoners themselves—their demands had been reported on TV, but not clearly.

Warden Oswald met with me and said, "I hope you straighten this out."

I went into the prison yard and sat with some of the inmates at a big long table in the yard. Three different dudes gave me three different lists of demands; I had no idea who they were, and couldn't recognize them today—it was nighttime, and we were sitting in the dark. One of them said the prisoners wanted a helicopter to get them out of the yard, and then they wanted transportation to certain foreign countries. They didn't want anybody to know about this plan. Wow—how could this be pulled off? This was outside the public demands. I said I'd be back the next day.

The following morning, Oswald insisted I tell them that certain of the demands—the public demands—were disallowed. I said I wouldn't tell them that, but I wanted to just rap with them. Oswald wouldn't let me go in. I got on a plane and went across the country to Oakland.

I had to talk to Huey about this situation—Huey was out of jail at this point—and I couldn't do it on the phone, because then the whole Central Committee of the Panthers would get busted for conspiracy. How could we get these brothers out to foreign countries?

Huey and I sat down in Oakland with the record player blasting to drown out what we were saying, in case the apartment was bugged, and we leaned close and talked low. I ran down to him what was happening and the brothers' wish to leave the country.

"We can't do it," Huey said. "We can't get a pilot who will risk his life. Let's get onto Charles Garry—he's going to be getting in more lawyers, up in Attica, from the Lawyers' Guild."

We phoned Oswald and we said that I was coming to help with the situation, and Garry and I got on a plane right back to Buffalo. We then drove to Attica, and at nine in the morning we heard on the car radio, live, the guns shooting at the Attica prisoners. They were shooting them, just shooting them down.

CBS correspondent Dan Rather reported that the prisoners were cutting throats, and that was why the troopers started shooting. A couple of days later he took it back—the prisoners hadn't cut any throats, he had been misled and misinformed.

I was not an astute negotiator. I was a good organizer, I could get people to see through bullshit and discern ideas, and I could help people to get together behind an issue. But when it came down to the fine politics behind negotiation, I don't think I was all that good. I could get people up and energized behind an idea, but it would take somebody else to do the negotiating. I feel like some of the death and brutality at Attica happened because I failed.

One of the early days of the campaign for Bobby Seale for Mayor of Oakland, before I officially declared myself a candidate, I was wide awake listening to birds chirping in a musical symphony, thinking, suddenly, "The only solution to pollution is a people's humane revolution." Remembering the applause to that statement when I first said it that November election night in Wisconsin—or was it New York?—or was it Boston?—a month following Nixon's and Dellums' reelection. Shit, I couldn't pinpoint the time of the occasion.

I lay in the bed, reached to the nightstand, lit a cigarette and rolled back toward Leslie, who was fast asleep, her warm naked body lying against mine. I put my hands under the cover, feeling the extreme softness of her body, then looked at her as she rolled over. I had really fallen in love with Leslie's warm kindness and the articulate perceptions that she held—I had learned to develop, with her, true, deep feelings. What was it about her that seemed to capture me? Was it her good, straight, black hair that she seemed to have a problem keeping nappy in a natural, as it would tend to fall back to being straight all the time? No, it was more: Leslie's personality was the real essence of her continued attraction. I'd learned to like that so much.

Shit, I was remembering a year back—her easy acceptance of me, but very philosophically, as just "Bobby" and not "Chairman." I remembered liking that most even though I also felt a sort of long-desired physical attraction.

One sister who said she was in love with me would never say anything else. I'd ask her did you do this or did you do that, she didn't say nothing, and I was the only one talking. I finally figured out I might as well be talking to myself. Initially I had enjoyed making love with her, but——

One thing I got around to learning was that making love was what I wanted, not just busting my nuts. The times I was in prison I would bust my nuts whenever possible, when I could get the situation set up so there was a fine woman with me for a while alone, but it was usually not much satisfaction, it was a defiance thing inside the prison walls.

Outside of prison, it was a developing thing—and it developed to where making love wasn't defiance of the church and all that; it got beyond just an everyday need for sex and it got firmly attached to the need for love, which had always been there. I had learned that real love for a person could ease a lot of inner loneliness.

But, beyond that, I thought, this is a revolutionary love affair. The struggle for liberation better be first and foremost with any woman I screw, especially one I might team up with. Yeah, I'd better face it, like I'm feeling. A need for it to be permanent. No wait! Just long-lasting, "permanent" is too absolute a word. But, even so, principally, if I want to feel love for Leslie, I'll do that, too, regardless of how many other sisters I want to screw and who want to screw me.

A soft three-rap knock came at the door, followed by, "Chairman?" It was Carl, speaking in a low tone of voice.

"Yeah." I spoke up to make my voice carry in the large bedroom. "What time is it?" I asked, knowing my digital clock had the wrong time—maybe two hours off.

"It's five o'clock, Chairman." And that was Herman.

"Ok! Right on! Thanks!" I said, throwing the covers back.

I hollered out to Carl and Herman to get everybody in the house up, that we needed a morning meeting.

"Ok, energy, energy! We got to move and make it all pop if we going to win. We're going to put this mayor's campaign on the power structure's mind."

I started getting dressed—a four-hundred-dollar suit—and woke Leslie up, telling her, "Get ready to type the itinerary—come on, baby, it's campaign time."

Leslie stepped to the dresser, picking up my watch.

"Say, Les, look here." I put my shirt on, looking at her. "You know what?"

"Huh?"

"I'm going to let you know that I got a strange feeling in my head that I, ah, let's say it this way—I dig you. Remember care, respect, responsibility, and knowledge?"

"Yeah." Leslie stopped, looking at me, as I buttoned my shirt.

"Well, it means my understanding of love. It's a thing I'm trying to figure out. Why your quiet, easygoing personality, mixed with a special kind of physical makeup, attracts me—like even the way you, yourself, can expound and also understand the philosophy of a revolutionary way of life. That sheer sense you have of what it's all about. You know. Anyway, ah——" I tucked in my shirt, zipping and snapping my pants. "Just remember that I love you."

"Oh, Bobby. I love you, too."

"Ok, wait, honey. Let's not kiss now. Set the clock. Then go get the itinerary and type copies, five-six copies, file one, and I just wanted to say that—well, it's just that I've been believing in one way I couldn't ever love anybody. Like the old way—like a girl I remember, Carol Atkins, mixed with an idea in my life of wanting to marry a dream, an Indian girl."

"What?" Leslie was smiling.

"Nothing, girl. I'll tell you someday." I stood in front of the dresser mirror, finishing the knot in my tie, straightening it. "Say, Les?" I looked at her setting the digital clock. "Have you ever wanted a house—I mean a home of your own?"

"I don't know. I suppose so. Why?"

"Nothing. I was just wondering if you'd like to be with me in a nice-sized home, like if I become mayor, I'd see to it or try to convince the Party to let me live in another house."

"Oh, that would be nice."

"Yeah, but it might be a little selfish. Then again, it would also help me to function better." It was 5:15. We went out of the bedroom and met with June, Francis, Adrianne, Herman, Audrea, John, and Joan.

The incumbent mayor and the big money behind the power structure now had to watch and try and discover the seriousness of my opting for the mayor's job, organized and backed by none other than my own Party, with its track record of not taking any shit from nobody—not only in Oakland but across the country, from armed police confrontations to judges in courtrooms.

Huey and I having walked through a first-degree murder trial each, there were now no legal holds on us, as all felony charges against us had been dropped. We were trying to expound on and build the concept of community control! Community control of the police department and all the city agencies and functions—to transform them so that they would serve the people. Also to make the Port of Oakland the economic base of the city, yielding more in annual funds; for construction of decent cooperative housing; to build up further all the Party's program of free health clinics, mobile units taking medicine and aid to the people in a cheaper way than building clinics for every one hundred square blocks of residence. And ultimately increase the aid programs of free food and clothing to the point of balancing the degree of unemployment affecting families with the need to create more jobs.

Our research team came up with so many facts, from the near one hundred-million-dollar gross income of the port and the low ratio there of minority workers to an additional three million dollars the city should have each year but didn't seem able to account for, including the slick ninety-nine-year leasing of the port land actually owned by the city. Some of the leases were as old as 1932, with the same low annual payments. This was a fact that was crucial to our effort to get the people to start understanding Oakland's economic base. "The Port of Oakland is the second largest containerized port in the world—not just in America," I said over the radio in the fifteen- and thirty-second spots we had bought for the last three weeks of our voter registration drive.

Actually becoming Mayor was not the major point—most of the time we told each other that the point was an educational campaign, getting the issues stated and known. We hoped that this would put pressure on whoever ended up mayor to do things right, to do what the people needed and wanted and felt. Sometimes, though, for a few minutes here and there, I did find myself believing and dreaming I would be mayor. Then I'd tell myself, no that is not realistic, don't be a fool—stick to the issues.

We gathered together and handed out ten thousand bags of groceries, then came back at another Black Community Survival Conference in the heart of West Oakland a month later with five thousand more bags. I could see the empty lot where my father's shop had been as I looked out from my high platform under the warm Saturday morning sun.

And come June, the whole organizing process for another ten thousand bags was under way. For this third Conference the Oakland Auditorium was packed to the brim, and outside of the six thousand seats, black people were sitting everywhere in the aisles. The free entertainment was provided by the Sister's Love, The Tower of Power, and John Lee Hooker, who all racked and blew the blues to contemporary rhythms and songs that seemingly took the whole audience on a fantastic, exuberant trip, from youths eight years old and up to older poor sisters still in their everyday clothing. But while dancing in the aisles, I also remembered times of gaiety and happy moments in the past. John Lee Hooker laid it down: "I don't want you to be no slave. I don't want you to be no fool. I don't want you to, aw, baby, I just want to make love to you—love to you——"

Five hundred or more people were out front on the lawn getting sickle-cell anemia tests.

Percy Steele of the Urban League was entering the rear door. Then behind him came Ronald Dellums in a neat denim suit. Dellums was to speak before I did and Percy was to present the Party with a plaque, which would be received by me and one of the sisters. Percy was commenting, "Chairman, you dressed to kill."

"Aw, naw, it's all in the image that black folks see."

"Oh! Now he's politicizing," Percy Steele said.

"And this hat here!" Elaine Brown exclaimed. "I'm trying to keep myself together for it." She picked it up, looking at it.

"Put that hat on, Chairman," Audrea said. "You the toughest candidate I ever seen. Put it on, please." Leslie and Percy smiled at each other and at me.

"Yeah, ok." I took the black, wide-brim, flat-top, smooth-felt hat, which matched my black, conservative-cut suit. The front creases of the suit fell over newly shined black shoes. It was the first suit I'd worn since my early days as a black nationalist. And now, the Party had me decked down, looking clean and sharp like a righteous people's political candidate.

Herman was straightening out my clothing in his concerned campaign-manager style.

"I mean, this nigger is sharp!" Elaine said, as I placed the hat on my medium-length, soft natural, then cocked it to the right just a little, being coached by Herman.

"No, wait, you-all. You got to see more than that. See, Ron. What Huey and I've done is try to symbolically relate the ghetto lumpen to the political scene; but at the same time, the suits with conservative cuts and colors Herman and I have chosen for the campaign are exceptionally—well, not unique, but part and parcel of the way that people identify with, that they see and want. At the same time, we want everybody to be able to accept a merged revolutionary-political-cultural style. Mixing the extreme lumpen-style dress with the conservative cut and color—a special sharpness!

"Now, this hat, well, I ain't going to wear hats in the campaign—it's just symbolic of what I'm going to do."

As we stepped out the door, I stood back and aside for Ron and Percy to step out through the Party members, and I extended my arm up and out toward the stage full of groceries. The loud music of John Lee Hooker drowned out the exclamations of Percy and Ron, who took a second look of surprise at the double level of full grocery bags on the forty-foot-deep and eighty-foot-wide stage—groceries on the floor under the tables and crammed on top of the tables the entire length and breadth of the stage behind the curtains.

"God damn!" Ron exclaimed. I'd never heard Ron cuss before. "Say man! Wow! How'd you and Huey put that together?"

Ron gave his usual powerful, uplifting, enthusiastic speech in his resounding, dramatic way, reflecting upon the oppression and the present problems of human liberation for all the poor. The audience would listen, then applaud loudly, then fall silent as he spoke on. His speech made me feel good, and when he ended with that last abrupt powerful phrasing he did so well, the audience rose in a standing ovation.

Emory opened the door hurriedly. The loud applause burst through the open door.

"You're on, Chairman!"

"Yeah, that's cool. Let's go out. We'll stay behind the curtain, down off the stage, so we can go out on cue."

We opened the door and went out to hear Elaine speaking and introducing, until she said, loud, "——Bobby Seale!"

The audience jumped into a loud, raving, whistling, foot-stomping, enthusiastic hand-clapping.

We moved from behind the curtain onto the stage, one bodyguard and June in front and Emory behind me, as I appeared, looking out from under the wide brim of my hat. The loud applauding continued and continued as we slowly walked toward center stage where Elaine Brown and Percy Steele stood.

All of us were taking in the fantastic uproar. Elaine stepped toward me as we slowed at the center-stage mike.

"Bobby Seale!" She stretched her hand out toward me as I stepped away from June and Emory, who stood back.

The audience hit their feet, standing, applauding, whistling, stomping, hollering; and it went on and on as I realized that up until Elaine pointed me out, the audience had not recognized me in my new garb. The press began flashing their cameras, taking pictures, and the cameraman Huey had arranged to come moved up near the stage, filming the long line of uniformed Party members in their black berets, powder-blue shirts and blouses, clean black skirts, and creased black trousers. The entire Oakland, California, base we had developed was there in all the overt exuberant enthusiasm of the raving and thundering audience.

"I hope everyone has registered to vote, because the power structure in this country and in Oakland is about to feel a new kind of people's politics that just won't quit!"

Applause made me pause for a moment.

"So let's let them know that I ain't and the Black Panther Party ain't and the whole community from North, East, and West Oakland ain't about to just sit aside and let them continue their jive crap, talking that mess whenever an election comes up about. . . . They going to do this and my position is that. . . . They are jiving and making promises that they ain't got no intention of keeping at all.

"That is, when we say that we going to give away ten thousand full bags of groceries, we mean exactly that, fulfilling promises and doing what we say. And I for one want this Black Community Survival Conference Day to be remembered as a day when I came out in front of all you brothers and sisters to say that to cast a vote is something you do when you know its time to change the political power; to put it back into the hands of the people and elect representatives who intend to do what the people say. *That's* why I want to let you see—I mean know that there exist without a doubt ten thousand bags of groceries!"

I turned as the eighty-foot-long curtains behind me shot up in the air revealing the bags of groceries, and as I looked back at the silent, awed audience, a lone voice said, "God damn!" The audience was ready to go into a delayed applause, but I held up my hand.

"We ain't jiving. Hold it—hold on, brothers and sisters." They stopped their applause at my serious tone of voice. "I want everyone here, right on, to know that I, Bobby Seale—just as we promised these ten thousand bags of groceries—that I, as you may have heard, am running for mayor of Oakland—I"—I took off my hat and made a swirling motion—"I'm throwing my hat into the political arena!" I stepped back a little. "Today!" And I let go of the hat, which went sailing out above the heads of the audience, who ahhed as they watched the hat sail out fifty feet into the crowd.

A sister screamed and, standing to her feet, snatched the hat in motion and put it on her head, cocking it to the side, as the audience went into resounding applause.

"All right! All right! I applaud for *you*." She spoke loudly, the hat firmly on her head. "Bobby Seale! The next mayor of Oakland! Right on, Bobby Seale!"

Oakland, Cal. April 18. . . . Black Panther founder Bobby Seale with an extraordinary display of political organizing edged into a runoff Tuesday with Oakland incumbent Republican Mayor John Reading. . . .

He now faces a head-to-head contest May 15 with the 35-year-old Seale. . . .

Despite the narrowness of the results, the vote was a major achievement for Seale and the Panthers, who put together an effective precinct organization and get-out-the-vote effort. . . .

Although political observers predicted a Reading victory in the runoff, no one was underestimating the potential of the organization Seale had fashioned in little more than a year. . . .

Charles Garry . . . watched the returns come in with something close to incredulity.

"And just two years ago," he marveled, "I was defending Bobby against murder charges in New Haven. . . ."

Seale was second with 21,000 votes. Behind him were Otho Green, whose middle of the road thrust for black and white Democrat votes failed, and John Sutter, who obviously drew from the same constituency as Green.

Mal Malnick, co-director of Reading's campaign, observed that, "The difference was that Seale delivered his 20 percent as he said he would. He proved to be more competent than Green or Sutter. . . ."

——*Washington Post*,
April 19, 1973

Oakland, Cal. May 16. . . . Reading, 55, won a third four-year term. . . . when 70 percent of the voters went to the polls to cast 77,476 votes for him and 43,719 for Seale, 36, a co-founder of the Black Panthers.

The Republican mayor said he would seek out Seale "very soon to see if we can find common ground on which to work together in solving community problems."

——*Washington Post*
May 17, 1973

Our organization now had a new and better image and character, but where once across the country we had ten thousand members, we had dwindled down to a few hundred. It left me feeling the whole organization had to be rebuilt nationally.

Our meetings were geared more toward the business ideas we couldn't get off the ground and which we needed to keep funds flowing in to support the Survival Programs, especially the new school; we were trying to get donations to purchase the school under its own nonprofit-corporation status.

My input was habitually and enthusiastically there, but without any real belief that there would ultimately be a thriving, effective national organization. As the Vietnam War's end was slowly sneaking up on us, I did not feel or believe our Black Panther Party would ever reach that point where we were there, out front, as the righteous spokesmen for black folks and united with other organizations.

Then the beginning exposure of the Watergate mess suddenly burst onto the scene. To read the accounts of Watergate was to see a new version of the verbal-critical-radical-revolutionary line that now berated the fascist Nixon into the corner where we all knew and had said he should have been in the first place.

I found myself again an international nominee to run for mayor.

"Would I?" was the next question.

My answer was, "No, I have no desire to run for mayor of Oakland again." I knew we now had the political voting base in Oakland to state categorically opinions and positions for or against the city government's rights or wrongs. Yet, with all of that, I personally did not want to run again for mayor of Oakland. Why I felt that way was a subconscious mystery to me.

Sitting in a cafe, my bodyguards and I ordered our food, as I sat looking off into space feeling ripped off. I had just learned that a plan of mine for an international trade center was being put to the drafting board—but the people who were doing it had slanted it from a center for the wholesome good of all the people into a profit-making thing that would benefit only, as usual, the few. Once again profit was going to be the only standard, the only deciding factor. A good idea from the black revolutionary camp became co-opted—no, fucked up. Little children need decent homes; old people have lost their dreams and live totally in fear without a place to run to.

We ate and split, and as we rode, I sat quietly thinking and wondering could I work myself up to wanting to run for mayor of Oakland, and it came to me as my bodyguard-driver asked, "What's the matter, Chairman?"

"Oh, nothing. I was just thinking how those bastards are going to make a personal selfish profit venture of our idea for the Trade Center."

"Well, we'll just have to run again and take over."

"Yeah, I know. I remember how for years in our family my sister, my brother, and I struggled with our father to build a house and he wouldn't. He used all his money for his own selfish needs, doling out crumbs like the government does when we start talking about killing their asses. You know—the past riots, the shootouts. But my sister, mother, and I shrewdly outmaneuvered my father, making sure the house he bought wasn't in his name. We had unified family control over it. You know, like I blew all the time about the people controlling the Trade Center's profit and the cooperative housing we'd build from the profit. The housing would also be controlled out of the reach of a selfish fatherlike government. Remember when I ran down about how even a person who, for whatever reason, decided to leave the cooperative housing would be forced to automatically sell it back to the others who stayed, trying to make a home?"

"Yeah, kind of."

"Well, I knew that the only way *for me* to talk about being mayor—had to be that personal, deep-seated need that had been instilled in me, the need to outdo, outmaneuver, and topple the selfish authority and then unify the natural, unified, and cooperative selfish right of the people to have decent homes to live in."

"Cooperative selfishness? How can you be cooperating and also be selfish?"

"Well, it's simple. If all the so-called bums in the world suddenly began organizing, saying they wanted a more decent life, then they would have to pool all their tactics together—their bumming tactics, getting forty-five cents here and a dime here and a quarter for a short neck—but then they would have to be educated into a consciousness of giving up half to their hierarchy, which also must have a total understanding of the objective of said decent place to live, stay, and run to. I mean build and institutionalize a righteous bum's pad. You know, some place to run to. With its intricate rules that they, the bums, would deal with to counter their quasi-given-up behavior, countering the need for alcohol."

"Yeah, but bums? Ha!"

"Say, 'ha'? You dudes got it wrong. If you can check where I'm coming from. I'm talking about the class struggle. Bums in society are the epitome of the bottom of the lower class. You got bums who are black, white, green, red, yellow, and polka dot. So I use them as an example of the bottom of the cruddy barrels of the ghettos of America and the world! In other words, I learned the degree of selfishness in myself, but somewhere along the way I wanted to get all black people to cooperate with all poor people. Now I want to even get a bum program going—you know."

We all cracked up.

"Look, wait a minute. See, I mean—don't you remember when we had the free food, the grocery bags? We were boycotting Bill Boyett's liquor store because he refused to donate ten dollars of his profits a week to the Free Breakfast Program. Now, you remember that along with the winos most black people bought liquor there? So in a way they—the ones who were poor—were just higher-class bums."

"Ha, ha, ha!"

"No, wait. 'Bum' is just a term. No home, twenty-five cents a night in a flophouse—the only place to run to from the death that bad weather can bestow. Aw, some die because they freeze to death or catch sickness from being drunk so long that they don't wake up and run to the flophouse. But, see, I'm not calling poor people who bought wine bums. It's just a word I use to denote the class level of those totally down and out. Anyway, remember out in front of Bill Boyett's store, the hope-to-die winos would cross through twenty or thirty people picketing the store? Why? Well, because they were down and out, and selfish! Talking about 'I got to get me some more of that wine.'

"So what we did to keep the winos from buying in Boyett's store and to get the bums—no, winos—to cooperate was organizing their selfish need with ours by giving them free bottles of wine. Then they united and drunkenly spouted our boycott rhetoric."

More laughter.

"Yeah, really. We had free food, and the winos really without knowing it, were in fact practicing cooperative selfishness."

"So you saying the lower class has to have something to struggle for."

"To *fight* for. I mean, China is ready to *fight* for the right to keep their land and their rights on the earth. Everybody around the world will fight for something, down to the bum who will fight for his wine. I mean, he may not—oh, no, I done seen some niggers fight over some wine, but when it comes down to organizing, people have to have something tangible to fight for. Something that gives them individually a selfish satisfaction. I mean, selfish satisfactions are always changing and developing. And all the off-beat and even the more human philosophies are pointing to the necessary and varied tangible things people need. Everybody in the world has to have three basic things, outside of water and air, to live. They got to have food, the most important; clothing, to some extent, depending on the weather and environment; and housing, shelter. You know those tangible things. But to me body and soul is best kept together with a piece of earth and shelter where each family of human beings can develop and function. I mean, that's why I really wanted to see the Trade Center idea become a means by which more poor people could get decent housing. They'll fight better for a home. Without that house or even the prospect of ever getting it, a person like me has no desire to continue fighting."

I stopped, thinking of what I was saying.

"Yeah, Chairman, you can sure break it down."

I sat there feeling I had made a Freudian slip. Now I knew why I did not want to run for mayor again. Yeah, I didn't have that house I always wanted. But I had told myself that to want a house of my own that I built myself was selfish. And there I was, realizing that if I had become mayor I'd have probably fooled around and while fighting for everybody else's house, I'd have built one for myself. And now I was being honest with myself. I still selfishly want me a house. My house.

Fuck it, that's what I ought to do. Get me a house built. Just building it. Damn, I ain't never really built a whole house—me.

But if the Party says I'm building a house for me to live in with their money—no, I won't do that, never, even with the Party actually owning the house. Then it really wouldn't be my house. Now, why does it have to be mine? Shit, because—no, wait—it's my retreat, my solace. Like every living soul on earth and I ain't no different. So ain't no rich exploiting government going to give it to you unless you sell out and I sure ain't about to do that. I never sold out to George's shit. But I *can* build it myself, with my own hands.

I woke up.

——Am I dreaming again? No—I don't want to. I opened my eyes. I felt I suddenly had to awaken. Ever since the campaign, all the time, I dream all kinds of crazy shit.

The room was dark. What time is it? I rolled groggily over with a bad taste in my mouth and raised a bit to get a look at the digital clock beyond the foot of the bed, thinking, "A strong leader makes a weak people." Was I dreaming that? It was two o'clock in the morning. Shit! Why was I dreaming that? Oh, yeah, that came from *Viva Zapata*. What kind of dream was that? What was it about? I can't seem to remember. I can't hardly ever remember dreams anymore.

But, yeah, I was telling somebody—I was trying to tell Huey that—no, wait, I was telling Mama that Jesus Christ was a revolutionary. Oh, shit, and George was dying, and I was scared. George was begging forgiveness. He wanted to go to heaven. Damn, and there was something else, where were we—— What was it? I can't remember. I lay a moment, trying——

——Was Malcolm X a strong leader? Yeah, he was. I'm a—a—I guess I've always wanted to be a strong leader. But is it true that a strong leader makes a weak people? No, probably a *dead* leader makes a strong people. Confusion makes a weak people. And too many people have left the Party. I guess because they got confused—or just did what they wanted——

I lay there wide awake. Leslie was asleep. I had a notion to wake her and screw her and then talk—tell her that we made a mistake breaking down the organization like we did—tell somebody. Leslie and I had been together, true revolutionary partners, for three years.

If it's true that what Huey and I organized was sort of a social accident, like he said then, it probably can't ever happen again. At least, not exactly like it went down then. Really, we, the Party, are going to go downhill from here or just stay at the level we are now, with only a hundred members, and that's that. Shit—fuck this shit——

I was rambling, feeling totally discouraged about any future moves that could be significant. Then thinking, we ain't had no new significant moves since the campaign. That was it—for over a year now. Just speaking engagements, the school, the sickle-cell program. From ten thousand members and forty or more branches and chapters to only an Oakland headquarters and a North Carolina chapter. Too much! How in the fuck did we live through all this shit. And this bodyguard shit. It's really fucking with me. A sort of ritualized effort, distorting my views unnecessarily, to believe some pigs and fools want to kill me. But shit, I still need my gun.

I rested the back of my head in my hands, looking up at the dark ceiling, listening to the faint sounds of the digital clock, flashing in my thoughts that humankind's clocks and watches measured life and living—of four billion, four *billion* human beings in the world, needing and struggling for food, shelter and clothing.

If that racist Cecil Rhodes were living, like he said, if he could he'd annex the stars of the universe. And then again, the universe has been annexed in the minds of humanity. If man can't see the natural inner-connected function of the world, then it ain't my fault and it ain't Malcolm's or Martin Luther King's fault. Fuck it, we all contributed—Huey, me, Che Guevera and a whole lot of other dead and living revolutionary people.

Wait, everybody did something while they lived—they moved one grain of sand, even if they only shat as a baby, or cried, or even if they just turned over inside a womb. Why have I been thinking like this over and over for the last month or so? And I know why, if I simply let myself accept the fact that I ain't got no right to try and fool myself.

I got out of the bed and turned on the lamp, then got up, looking for a cigarette. I smoked, pacing around the floor, noting the dream, trying to remember the whole of its parts, searching myself for a reason for such a dream. But I couldn't for the life of me remember. Then I thought, Maybe I don't want to remember it. Maybe I'm refusing to remember it, 'cause at this time I want to make a decision.

I stopped and I spoke to myself, softly, aloud: "If I should move one grain of sand from one spot to another, then the world will never be the same." Huey, Jack, that was one of the heaviest statements you ever made, and brother, as far as I'm concerned, we done moved our grains and a few tons to boot. Wait! That's it—yeah, I was dreaming I was on a beach, a sloping beach and then there was a house, a white house, an old wood-frame house and its yard was beach sand. There was no water around, just beach sand, and suddenly Mama was leading me up a hillside and the street was sand and then there was George on my other side, and they were leading me away from the house. I was stumbling almost and Mama was saying, "Come on, Bobby," holding me by the arm, and George was holding the other arm. He was old and poor, with gray hair, and he was going to die in the dream. Why were we walking up the sidewalk to — yeah—heaven? I told Mama and George we had to take an airplane, but George had never flown; and then I was telling Huey that a strong leader makes a weak people. Oh, yeah, now I know, yeah. I smiled, knowing that I didn't have to tell him why. We were a team, friends who dug on moving our grains, fascinated with each others' methods of getting on out there and doing it. And I needed Huey, a psychological dependence, a friend. Now, a lot of racists and pigs hated us for our sand shoveling—for our contribution to——

I walked to the bed and began to softly shake Leslie, wondering should I wake her and tell her what I suddenly was going to do. I can write something out for everybody else, to explain. But, shit, no—no, I don't need to write nothing. I'll just do it.

"Say, Les." I shook her, speaking softly. "Les, wake up, Les." She wouldn't wake. "Leslieee." I shook her harder. "Leslie, wake up."

"Huh? Oh, Bobby."

"Say, get up! Come on, girl. Hey, come on, wake, girl."

"Oh, what is it?" Leslie began to awaken, looking at me, smiling.

"Just ah, ah, get up. Come on. Put on your clothes. We going somewhere. I want to——" I cut myself off.

"Huh?" Leslie was trying to understand. She had a tired, worn-out, sleepy expression as she sat up and put her feet to the floor. I began to put on my clothes, telling her to get her clothes on, quietly asking her to hurry. Then I thought, Shit, I hope ain't nobody awake downstairs, 'cause they will definitely try and stop me.

I figured I'd have to sneak downstairs quietly and find the car keys.

"Bobby, what are we doing?" Leslie asked, trying to get into her clothes.

"Just get dressed and get your coat—oh, here. Bring your purse. This big bag of yours. Say, how much money you got?"

"I don't know—a hundred—ah, well, it's all in my purse."

I checked. I had ninety dollars. Then I figured, hell, I'll just ask Mama and Betty to let me have some money. If we got two hundred and they give me five——

"Say, now quietly go in the kids' room, get them a couple of changes of clothes."

"What?"

"Keep your voice low—don't wake anybody, Les! Oh, let me get the Python." I stepped to the closet and reached up on the shelf and got the six-inch-barrel .357 magnum, stuck it in my belt under my coat, and got some ammo.

Leslie, now hurriedly dressing, looked at me with a worried expression. "What's the matter, why we getting up like this?"

"Look." I was stern in the face. "Just get dressed, get the kids' clothes, and don't do nothing or say anything to wake anybody. Do what I say now, you hear?"

"Ok," Leslie whimpered, shaking her head, wearing a rather frightened look.

I opened the door to our room and eased down the carpeted hall into the kids' room. Romaine, Leslie's son, was on his bed, sleeping. I rolled his limp body over and up into my arms, blanket and all, carrying him down the stairs to the big car. I went back to get Malik and took him to the car.

"Now look, let me say one thing," I told Leslie. "Do you want to be with me—whatever happens?"

"Yeah, but what——"

"Don't worry. Come on." We made our way out the back door, around the house, and to the car.

We went to Mama's house and got the kids out, leaving them in Mama's good care for the time being.

"Mama, I'll phone you tomorrow. See you. Let's go, Les." And I quickly went out the door.

"You-all be careful out late at night like this," Mama said. And I pulled the door shut and we hopped into our car, headed for the San Francisco airport.

I left the parking ticket in the car and the keys under the floor mat. I would tell John to get word to the Party to come get it. Leslie and I made our way to an open ticket counter as I randomly chose the closest and next flight leaving the Bay area, and I bought two one-way tickets.

"We ain't got no clothes," Leslie said.

"Yeah—we'll get some shit. I can move too many grains of sand."

"What sand—what you mean?"

"Ah, nothing. I just want to build a house."

"Why?"

"To live in. I want to build a house, grow a garden, do some canning and barbecue some meat. Raise our children. I just got to build me a pad from the ground. Everybody can dig on some decent shelter and food and clothing. You know. So we can be together and—well, it's just something I want to do. All my life since I was a little boy, when George built our first house. And I'll protect it. If anybody tries to break in it——"

I was suddenly thinking of the gun on me and I stopped because I saw the airport security check. Leslie suddenly remembered, too.

"Oooh! Bobby, we can't get on the plane with the gun."

"Yeah, shit." I'd be in jail so fast with a jive chicken-shit federal beef like that. We turned around, walking.

Somebody passed, looking at me as if he was trying to recognize me, and I thought, shit! This airport's almost empty, anybody'll see me, and without bodyguards. If the police see me—shit, them two white boys there might be police.

"Say, Les. Let's go up there to the newsstand, uh, get something to read and get us some dark shades."

"What are we going to do to live?"

"Get a job, like regular workers."

"Oh. Well, if we, ah—I don't know, Bobby. I guess I don't think we should leave like this, and——"

"It's the best way, Leslie. Say, look. *Do you* or *do you not* want to be with me? I mean, see, I couldn't probably get along with anybody else—you know me. Now, if you want to stay, stay—ok?" My expression was firm, but I hoped Les understood.

"No, uh, uh, no, Bobby! I *want* to stay with you, but—it's just that—what are we going to do? I mean, well—it's all so sudden."

"Ok, look. We ain't married, but then again over the last three years or so—we *are* married. See—later for the system! We know it ain't shit. Girl, I'll work somewhere."

Leslie put her arm through mine and I took off, walking, headed down the stairs to go through the luggage room. I spotted some baggage lockers.

"Wait, Les." We stopped. I looked to the left and right and saw no one, then checked my watch to see what time it was. We had ten minutes to catch the scheduled plane.

"Look, you know what——" Les was looking around, confused and seemingly a little frightened. "Les, look at me!"

"Huh!" Les started.

"Look, I don't need this gun—I don't need it at all. Not no more."

"But, you ain't got no bodyguards—and—oh, hell, Bobby!"

"Yeah, and I'm glad I *ain't*! They reminded me of getting killed and dying too much, anyway, God damn it. Like I'd get killed, which meant they'd get killed—so they overexaggerate the scene, and—I had a weird dream about Mama and George." I surprised myself with my next words. "Yeah, it was like they were bodyguarding me up the hill."

"What, Bobby?"

"Aw, it ain't nothing. See, look, you see those lockers?"

I had Leslie take the magnum into the women's restroom, wipe our fingerprints off—she had never been busted and her prints might not be on file.

Les walked twenty steps to the women's restroom and went in. I stood waiting impatiently, then looked up to see a white janitor coming down the long aisle, pushing a broom down the edge of the wall, coming my way. I stood back against the opposite wall, listening to the jibberish of the foreign cats and noticing their short stature.

Finally, the short, stocky white janitor got near me, looking at me with my shades on, and passed me. When he got to the other end, he turned around to start a new line of sweeping headed back my way. When he got to me, he stopped.

"Hi!" He hit at the trash with the front of the broom.

"Hi," I said, looking away down the hall, seeing a black porter pushing a dolly for carrying bags coming my way.

The white janitor smiled. "Say."

"Yeah." I casually looked at him.

"Ain't I seen you somewhere before?"

"Naw, I don't think so."

"You sure? You sure look familiar. Like I seen you—guess not." He took off, pushing the broom, and he passed the black porter, still coming.

As I watched the black porter I thought about having a job somewhere like his, then I knew that I didn't *want* that kind of job. I looked back at the restroom door, hoping Les didn't come out right at this moment.

"Say, Bobby!"

I jerked around.

"How you doing, man?" the black porter asked, with admiration.

He recognizes me—just like that. I eased myself.

"It's cool, brother!" I hollered to him as he rolled the dolly up and stopped at the door, ready to go out.

"Flying out, huh?" he asked.

"Yeah, you know—I'm always on the move."

"Yeah, you got it! Man, if we had a million cats like you, man, instead of all these churchgoing Christians, we'd really have a righteous revolution!" He smiled.

"Yeah, I know what you mean. But they have to organize."

"Yeah. You take it easy—hear, man?" He pushed off, opening the door.

"Right on. You, too." And to myself I said, If we had a million, they'd have to be a million *un*baptized Nigger Tarzans—sinners, like me.

I glanced and saw Leslie coming out. The janitor was gone. The two Orientals kept on talking. I stepped toward Leslie and we went over to the lockers. I struggled to get the key out.

"I can't get the God damn key out, Les. Fucking machine. Fuck it, leave it inside there. Let's go."

"But Bobby, don't you think we should give it another try?"

"Fuck it. Let's go catch the plane before it takes off."

We cut out, back up the stairs, running, went through security check. I felt we were somehow being allowed by society to escape, as I kept my eyes on the police, who looked at me while I wondered if they recognized me. We hustled down the long hall to our gate and were the last ones to board the plane.

Three empty seats near the rear of the coach section, and we buckled our seat belts, relaxed.

My resignation was a reality as the plane rolled out and taxied down the runway.

Leslie looked at me with a sad, confused face, as I smiled at her.

"Say, girl. Ain't nothing wrong." I smiled and brushed her hair. "Ain't no way, through all our transgressions, you know, we know we was right, like I was telling you."

The plane's power pulled me with it as I looked out over Oakland and watched it recede to the horizon. I turned to Leslie.

"Say, is this Monday?"

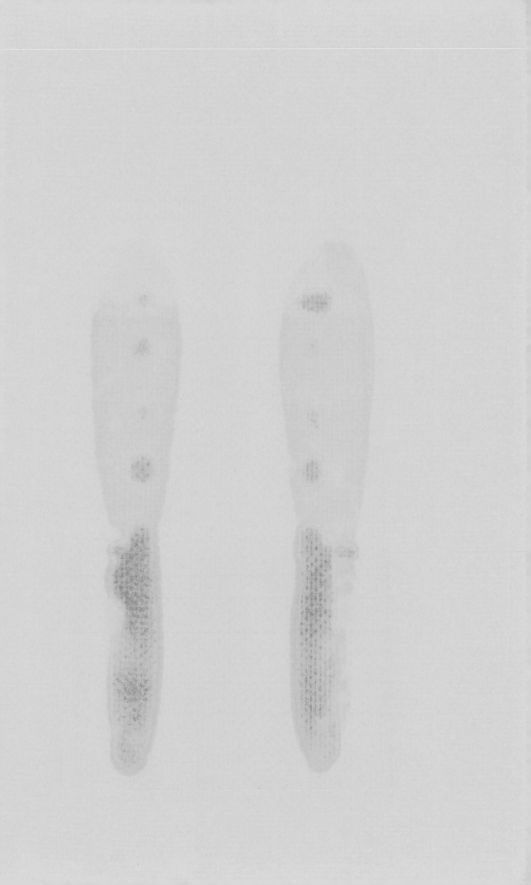

DATE DUE	
APR 2 9 1998	
MAR 2 2 1998	
APR 2 7 1999	
MAR 1 5 2004	
DEC 2 0 2004	

GAYLORD   PRINTED IN U.S.A.